THE WRITER'S PORTABLE MENTOR

A Guide to Art, Craft, and the

Writing Life Priscilla Long

WALLINGFORD
PRESS

The Writer's Portable Mentor
A Guide to Art, Craft, and the Writing Life
By Priscilla Long

Editing and proofreading by Geri Gale
Design by Nancy Kinnear
Cover design by Tracy Wong (WONGDOODY)

ISBN: 978-0-9842421-0-8
Library of Congress Control Number: 2009939474

WALLINGFORD
PRESS

Wallingford Press
P.O. Box 95145-2145
Seattle, WA 98145-2145

The Writer's Portable Mentor

A GUIDE TO ART, CRAFT,
AND THE WRITING LIFE

Also by Priscilla Long

*Where the Sun Never Shines: A History of America's
Bloody Coal Industry*

Writing is a labor, shot through with delight.
—Scott Russell Sanders

CONTENTS

INTRODUCTION

A Writer's Practice

FOR WRITERS DEDICATED TO THEIR CRAFT, learning the craft never ends. Yet the pleasure in it deepens as we achieve, upon occasion, a virtuoso sentence, a virtuoso page of writing. This book is for writers who strive for virtuosity. It is designed to mentor you, first, in practices that catalyze productivity — for basic productivity underlies everything else. And second, in craft techniques and strategies that will aid you in your quest to deepen the work and carry it forward.

I wrote and rewrote *The Writer's Portable Mentor* during years of teaching both apprentice writers and writers who are seasoned and quite well published but who want to deepen their skills and extend their range. It is for you if your goal as a writer is to develop faster, become more skilled, or go in new directions. My goal is to help you realize beautiful and accomplished works on a regular basis and to get them out into the world. *The Writer's Portable Mentor* is particularly oriented toward writers of creative nonfictions (or, as some prefer, literary nonfictions) and short stories. But poets, novelists, and magazine writers may profitably thumb it for the reason that a well-stocked toolbox of craft strategies and creative approaches can be taken into any genre or form.

And we writers do proliferate forms. Some of our best essayists are poets; our best poets write novels upon occasion. Creative nonfictions use the techniques of fiction and in the world of literary culture, hybrid forms are rampant. The best magazine writers play words as if they were notes, just as poets do. The best essayists can out-jumpcut the best short-story writers: Film has entranced us all. And so it goes.

I am a writer in several of these genres, with creative nonfictions, fictions, poems, and essays in print, as well as a scholarly book on the history of coal mining. My own history has been to cross genres: My poet's ear gets into my prose, and subject matters mutate from poem to paragraph.

The Writer's Portable Mentor is here to guide you through six areas of vital concern to the practicing writer:

basic productivity
language work
training in observation
grasping and employing deep story structures
developing sophisticated (rather than habitual) sentencing skills
the regular practice of completing works and publishing them

Here's what you can expect from each of these areas.

Basic Productivity. Creative work is, first of all, work. The artist, wrote Katherine Anne Porter, "must roll up his sleeves and get to work like a bricklayer."* We writers commit to a work process — a daily work process — without any guarantee of artistic or commercial success

---

* Quoted in Virginia Tufte and Garrett Stewart, *Grammar as Style*, vii.

(except of course we expect to be paid for commissioned work). Creativity studies have shown that high-achieving creators produce not only more masterworks than do average creators, but also more duds.[*] Even Picasso produced duds. In other words, high-achieving creators produce more. They have learned how to work. This interesting fact should encourage us to give first priority to the daily work habit and to push away anxieties about whether or not this piece will be good.

But the more skilled we become at our craft, the better we get at realizing works — completing them and making them good. "Nothing we create," writes the novelist Walter Mosley, "is art at first. It is simply a collection of notions that may never be understood. Returning every day thickens the atmosphere. Images appear. Connections are made."[**]

The Writer's Portable Mentor utilizes timed writing in a notebook — called writing practice — to guarantee productivity. In writing practice, developed by Natalie Goldberg in *Writing Down the Bones* and by Peter Elbow (in a form called "freewriting") in *Writing Without Teachers*, the writer writes continuously without stopping for a period of time (five minutes, ten minutes, a half-hour) set on a kitchen timer. Writing practice can be used to observe, to question a character ("What do you want?"), to write a scene, to conceptualize the next step or the next work, to write a character's backstory, to write from the point of view of a non-point-of-view character (to discover how this character actually views the situation rather than just faking his or her dialogue lines), to uncover memories, to write the entire draft of a book review, essay, or chapter.

Language Work. If you love literature, if you aspire to art, then the clay you work is language. *The Writer's Portable Mentor* contains practices that will get you nearer to language and help you gather more language to work with. This is not about strutting big words, but about working with clicks and knocks (sound), pewter and copper (color), the vowel

---

* D. K. Simonton, "Creativity from a Historiometric Perspective," 122.
** Walter Mosley, "For Authors, Fragile Ideas Need Loving Every Day," 163–164.

scale. To work with language is to make like Adam and put a name on a thing. Is that a tree or is it a black walnut tree? To work with language is to reach back in time to get a word root, to thus deepen the felt layers of meaning. A *flagrant* violation (from Latin *flagrare*, to burn) has fire in it. It is a conspicuous violation, that is, it burns brightly. Feeling the heat of the old fire burning inside *flagrant*, we can then start to play with the word. Something flagrant is neither subtle nor hidden nor moderate. It may be hot; surely it is not frozen. We might speak of flagrant red hair or a flagrant display of hubris in launching a rogue war, but flagrant ice cream is oxymoronic and a flagrant bonfire is redundant. Just so, *mellifluous* (L. *mell*, honey; flowing) has honey in it. We writers collect words. We work with sound. We repeat words as if they were notes. We look up the root, and then, given the word's ancient meaning, we play.

Training in Observation. Visual artists train themselves to see by drawing whatever is in front of their eyes. Some visual artists, including abstract painters not particularly known for drawing, draw for years and years. As writers we can likewise train ourselves to see by writing whatever is in front of our eyes. The Here and Now assignment, in which you sit and write what your sense organs receive, without opinion or comment, comes to us from the visual arts. It can be used to observe a street, a person, a river, a jazz band. Other observation exercises in *The Writer's Portable Mentor,* such as Observing Gesture, are variations of the Here and Now exercise.

Good writing incorporates acute observation. It renders concrete detail in place of received opinion and general language. Good writers can become better writers by training themselves in observation as visual artists do.

Deep Story Structure. There's a dynamic — a dialectic if you will — between writing freely and continuously in your writing-practice notebook to discover what it is you have to say and writing into a specific structure (a dramatic narrative structure, say, or a twenty-part collage) to create a finished piece. You want that structure, even though you may be clueless as to what it will be when you begin. (Alternatively, you can assign yourself a given structure, much as a poet assigns himself to write a sonnet. Prose can be as formal as poetry. If you begin with a given form, then the job is to find among your own concerns the content that feels right for that form.)

But let's say you know what you want to write, but you don't know how to shape it. To write without a structure is to be lost in the woods. It's okay to be lost, but not for too long. The skilled, prolific, professional writers amongst us are writing into structures. That is the way to save yourself from years of frustration.

The Writer's Portable Mentor explores four different "story structures" (applicable to short fictions and nonfictions) including the dramatic story structure. This dramatic structure is still extremely common and many professional writers spend their careers exploring its protean possibilities. But in our postmodern era, other structures are also proliferating. Here we take a look at three other structures: the theme structure, the collage structure, and the braid (two- or three-strand) structure. Beyond these specific forms, we strategize on how to go about structuring anything you might be writing, from essay to cookbook to memoir to novel.

I myself love to work on assignment. I complete the assignments I give to my classes (which comprise adult writers), and hand in my homework to class members as they hand in their homework to me. Often, in the Advanced Short Forms Seminar, these are structure assignments: Write a collage; write a story using the dramatic structure employed by Tim Gautreaux in his short story "Welding with Children"; write a one-sentence story that is 1,000 words long. One way to advance the project of creating a body of work is to take each suggested structure as an assignment, perhaps even putting each form to use two or three times. But note this: The word *assignment* does not mean doing a piece for practice. We do our assignment (and *do* get our practice). Then we go on to revise the piece, send it out, and ultimately see it published.

Sentencing Skills. Consciously shaping sentences to reflect and intensify their meanings is a high skill that most of us could stand to further hone. The great writers have mastered the sentence forms — simple, compound, compound-complex — and use them fluidly, even if these old-fashioned categories are no longer considered current linguistic terms. I am thinking of William Gass and Joan Didion. I am thinking of Ernest Hemingway. I am thinking of Mary Oliver and John Berger. I am thinking of Louis Menand.

This work is about manipulating the form of the sentence so that it both says what it means and performs, embodies, or enacts its meaning. A shattering experience might be rendered in a shattered sentence, that is, in fragments:

> The burst door. Wood ripped from hinges, cracking like ice
> under the shouts.
> (Anne Michaels, *Fugitive Pieces*, 7)

What difference does syntax make? Who cares whether you use a fragment or a compound sentence or a simple sentence? The answer is that a sentence emits a feel that derives in part from its structure. Consider this compound sentence from the Book of Job:

> His breath kindles coals and a flame goes out of his mouth.
> (Job 41:21)

To my ear the biblical sentence (like those found in the sacred writings of many faiths) carries a kind of solemn authority. What is the craft technique behind this solemn authority? It is, I believe, the form of the compound sentence.

The process of composing sentences consciously tends to begin slowly, involve a few frustrating moments, and become increasingly pleasurable — even gratifying — as you see your work gain in muscle and clarity.

Completing Works and Publishing Them. At a certain point, beginning to publish is an essential component of doing creative work. And that means sending it out, exposing it. We all get rejections. But work never sent out is never finished. Hidden from the world, it remains safely (and sadly) on the writer's shelf. There are strategies, techniques, and values that inform the process of putting work into the world. The last section of *The Writer's Portable Mentor* considers the issues and practices of becoming a published, visible writer, a writer whose work takes its place in the world.

THROUGHOUT ALL THIS WORK, our core strategy, our quintessential tool, is to learn craft from models of virtuoso writing. We read because we are readers, but we reread because we are writers. We scrutinize sentences, beginnings, deep structures, ways of bringing characters onstage. Robert Louis Stevenson said, "I have played the sedulous ape to Hazlitt, to Lamb, to Wordsworth, to Sir Thomas Browne, to Defoe, to Baudelaire, and to Obermann.... That, like it or not, is the way to learn to write."* In this way we keep learning, down through all our years of writing. Our best teachers are the masterworks we scrutinize.

But what, you may ask, is the difference between this and plagiarism? Particularly because we are looking so closely at models, it's important to be excruciatingly conscious of acquiring technique while leaving alone image, word, and idea. I may write using a compound sentence (a form, a deep structure), but I may not use *your* compound sentence. I may read Tom Andrews's masterpiece seventy-six-part collage titled "Codeine Diary," and thus inspired, set out to write one myself. I will look closely at how he carries forward in chronological order a single childhood story, intermixed with hospital and dirt-bike experiences and

---

* Stevenson quoted in Robert Hendrickson, *The Literary Life and Other Curiosities*, 3.

so on. But in my writing, I will not use any word or phrase or idea appearing in his work. His work is my teacher for the moment, but the subject matter I choose to do my work in will be worlds away. And in the end, my collage may well end up with forty parts or with eighty-three parts because it will begin to exert its own demands.

Will constant close reading weaken or sabotage your own voice? Only if you read one or two writers exclusively and try to write like them all the time. "Raymond Carver" voices were common during the 1980s. But these Carver imitators did not love Colette (an opposite sort of voice). They were reading Carver and avoiding Barry Lopez and Annie Proulx. Not to mention Alice Adams, Tobias Wolff, or Jean Rhys. No matter what your own aesthetic, whether minimal or maximal, whether spare or lush, or some of each, it helps to read beyond it into other aesthetics and even to dabble in other aesthetics in your own writing.

To develop our own voice, we write truthfully, and in detail. We strive for extreme accuracy. We use our own material, whatever we discover that to be. We write about whatever is central to who we are in this world. We work out our own thoughts in our own words, not to please, not to impress, but to discover what it is that we have to say.

From models we take strategy, structure, and technique. The fact that we are working our own most urgent material acts as counterweight to the model and ultimately allows us to pull it away altogether, with only scents or hints of the model extant in the new work.

WRITING IS HARD WORK, but the more you sink into it, the more pleasurable it becomes. The more absorbing it becomes. Yes, there are times of frustration. Perhaps the essay you are working on refuses to lie down. Perhaps twenty publishers have rejected your memoir. Perhaps your novel has bogged down and you're clueless how to finish it. Ambition is always fraught with anxiety. But the more you work along, steady as a gardener or a baker or a cake decorator, the more writing repays you. It takes on its own life. It's a way of looking at the world, a way of living in the world. On some days — despite all the talk of sweating bullets and opening veins — it becomes its own kind of happiness.

HOW TO USE THIS BOOK

If you are like me, you will read the last chapter first. Then you will read the acknowledgments, then maybe Chapter 3. This is the way to begin. But after reading *The Writer's Portable Mentor* in whatever order suits you, you may feel a bit overwhelmed. There's a lot here.

I suggest first rereading Chapter 1 and taking it to heart: Basic productivity underlies everything else. Then take the chapters one by one. *Actually do the exercises!* Actually begin doing the Here and Now practice. Actually begin your Lexicon. Actually write that list of ten compound sentences.

But — and this is crucial — do every exercise in relation to some piece you are working on. Don't just make up sentences on the fly, out of your head. Instead, in your writer's notebook, write out a paragraph from the piece you are working on as it currently exists. This is your "before" paragraph. Then work the paragraph, using whatever craft technique you are currently deepening (as well as any others). When you get an "after" paragraph you like, type it back into the piece.

Work on sentences the same way. Compose your list of ten sentences using, say, the adverbial clause of manner. Shape every one from the material in your piece. Make your sentences, not just formally correct, as if you were taking some sort of remedial English class, but as dazzling as the model sentences you are looking at. Then fit some of these recast sentences back into the piece you are working on.

Actually doing the exercises is what will move your craft skill up to the next level. Keep in mind that it will take time to develop your ear to make a move new to you sound right. Read your new passages out loud and work on them until they sound good to your ear. No matter what level you are working at now, you will start to see your writing get better. And what a pleasure that is.

Note: For the most part, I've drawn the model sentences and paragraphs in *The Writer's Portable Mentor* from the works of other writers. Upon occasion, I use a passage of my own, and any model sentence with no author ascribed came from my own hand. Sources for all passages quoted, chapter epigraphs, and footnotes may be found in the bibliography.

PART

I

Your Move

Care of the cow brings good fortune.
—I Ching (30. Li)

I.

Daily Writing

Practice is something done under all circumstances, whether you're happy or sad. You don't become tossed away by a high weekend or a blue Monday. It is something close to you, not dependent on high-tech gyrations or smooth workshop leader talk. Writing is something you do quietly, regularly, and in doing it, you face your life....
—Natalie Goldberg

WRITING EVERY DAY IS THE KEY TO BECOMING A WRITER. Writing every day is the key to remaining a writer. It is the only secret, the only trick. Don't despise the fifteen-minute write. Don't despise writing in your journal. Don't despise writing down your complaints for fifteen minutes before going to work. Any writing counts.

Keep a timed-writing (or writing-practice) notebook. In it, write for fifteen minutes every day. Of course on some days you will write for longer than fifteen minutes. But — and this is important — a long session one day does not apply to the next. The day after a long session, sit down once again to your fifteen minutes. Decide the night before when that fifteen minutes will be. The next day, when the time arrives, say at four o'clock in the afternoon during your coffee break, stop whatever you are doing and write. This advice does not originate with me — I got it from Dorothea Brande's *Becoming a Writer*. Ever since I read that marvelous book some twenty-five years ago, I have written every day (excepting one or two migrainous days per year). I write early in the morning, in the silence of dawn, soon after pouring that indispensable mug of strong hot coffee.

Write without stopping. Do not be concerned about being good, interesting, or correct. Writing is a discovery tool that belongs to you. If you can't think of the next thing to say, write your hesitations, write "Okay, let's see, what else, well, maybe..." Do not lift your pen into the air. (What would happen to a bird in flight it if stopped flapping its wings?) Do not rush, do not stop. Write continuously for fifteen minutes. You can continue if you want, or you can stop. It is not better to continue. It is not better to stop.

Writing in your notebook for fifteen minutes a day is a practice that continues no matter what article or book you are working on, no matter where you are with that poem or novel. In other words, the timed writing in the notebook is not superseded by work undergoing revision on the computer.

Writing practice in your notebook underlies all your other writing. It keeps you connected to your writing no matter what else is going on in your life. It keeps you connected to the external world and to your interior life. It provides you with a resource base, ever expanding, out of which you produce finished pieces.

It keeps you generating new writing. It forever eliminates the sporadic work habit. It recognizes that generating new work is qualitatively different from that of rewriting, and that both need consistent attention. The fifteen-minute write makes the difference between being a writer and wishing to be a writer. It makes the difference between being an author who no longer writes and a writer who may also be an author but who still takes up the pen every day, for better or for worse. Writing practice moots the concept "writer's block."

I have found that fifteen minutes is not a token span of time. I once had a client who wrote for two hours every day for about five years. She was really making progress! But then she underwent a major, exciting career change and took on massive new professional responsibilities. There was no way she could get to her two hours. Sadly, she stopped writing for a decade. Fifteen minutes is obtainable. It's obtainable whether you are a physician with a grueling schedule or a working mom with three toddlers (or both).

The fifteen minutes is not token, I've found, because it keeps you connected to what you are working on, no matter what your current circumstances. In a busy life, a week and then two weeks can go by in no time at all, with little or no writing done. The practice of writing for fifteen minutes per day simply deletes this problem.

Why a notebook? Why not a computer? There is something about the connection of hand to page, body to page, breath to page that is different from typing on a keyboard. Norman Mailer said, "It's hard to explain how agreeable it is to do one's writing in longhand. You feel that all of your body and some of your spirit has come down to your fingertips."* It's also easier to carry a notebook than a laptop (though you may carry a laptop too) and it's easier to take out a notebook and write for fifteen minutes and then put it away. I encourage you to purchase a notebook, a nice notebook, not too heavy, one that opens flat and has pages you like. Write in that notebook every day.

The writing done in writing practice can be about anything. It can be a journal-write (here I differ with one of the originators, Natalie Goldberg). It can be an observation exercise. It can be work on an essay,

---

* Norman Mailer, "Generations," in *The Big Empty*, 5.

story, article, or scene. It can be used to conceptualize new work. ("The story I want to write next is…" Set your timer and write.)

Often I hear, "I'm sick of moaning and complaining in my journal." There is no need to moan and complain (I enjoy doing so once in a while) and there is no need "to journal" at all if you are sick of it. Writing in your journal can involve describing what is in front of you. Describe the gooseneck lamp, the pile of books, the mahogany mug bristling with pens. Do a recapitulation in which you detail the previous day from beginning to end (an exercise from Ira Progoff's *The Journal Workshop*). Or set the timer, begin a short essay, and write it straight to the end for a fast first draft. Or write for fifteen minutes a single unpunctuated sentence that begins, "What I want to do with my life is…" That's what Buckminster Fuller did before going on to become Buckminster Fuller.

There are ways to shape your writing practice so that it advances your own goals more efficaciously.

∼ In your notebook, begin each practice session on a new page. (Do not run the sessions into one another.) Date each session and when you're finished, if obvious, give the writing a descriptive title or label (Thoughts on Cloning, Remembering Susanne). These labels become clarifying when you are looking back through your notebooks for themes, concerns, bits of writing.

∼ If you are working on a story, essay, review, or other piece in your writing-practice notebook, type what you've written as soon as you can, the same day if possible. Soon after you've handwritten a scene, type that scene. Then draw a line through the handwritten version. You can still read it but you know it's typed — superseded.

∿ Observation exercises should be part of every writer's practice. Every time you go to a new city or a new country, do the Here and Now exercise. Spend fifteen minutes describing your teenager. If you are a teenager, spend fifteen minutes describing your parent. Go to a coffeehouse and do the Observing Gesture exercise, an exercise that trains you to observe and describe body language.

∿ Plan. Conceptualize new work. Organize your day. Where would you like to be as a writer a year from now? What pieces or chapters do you plan to complete this month?

∿ Join or start a writing-practice group, which is entirely different from a critique group.

The Writing-Practice Group. Every Tuesday and Friday at Louisa's Café & Bakery on Eastlake Avenue East in Seattle, just before 2:30 p.m., the writers gather. Everyone is welcome. (We buy coffee, or have lunch beforehand. We want this coffeehouse to stay in business.) Seattle authors and master-teachers Jack Remick and Robert J. Ray, friends of Natalie Goldberg, established this writing practice fifteen years ago.

Each arriving writer writes a start line on a piece of paper and puts it on the table. For example: "Her lips were blue" or "He slammed the door" or "I lied." Then the writers begin writing, all using the same start line. (You soon discover that you can quickly go from any start line to any piece you want to work on.) When the timer goes off, each writer reads, in turn. There are no comments and there is no feedback. (This is different from a critique group.) After the writers read exactly what they have written, in all its roughness, the timer is reset and the writers resume writing. There are several cycles of this, and then everyone goes home or back to work.

Writing-practice groups vary start lines and vary the segments of writing time. One way is to write for five minutes, ten minutes, twenty minutes, and then five minutes. In another way, the writers begin, "Today I am writing about..." and proceed. Everyone writes for a half-hour, reads, then writes for another half-hour. One of my writing buddies and I used to meet at a café to write. We alternated making up assignments for ourselves. One time we decided to describe for one hour without stopping a philodendron that sat between us. We did so, and we were astonished at how much there was to see in this common household plant.

The above-mentioned Jack Remick and Robert J. Ray have written several entire books during writing practice, scene by scene, chapter by chapter. After writing practice they go home and type up what they have written, and work on it further. I think I should repeat that. After writing practice *they go home and type up what they have written* because they are using writing practice to produce completed, polished, and ultimately published work.

Use your writing-practice group to further your own purposes. Don't write passively, don't write to please others at the table. Write to play or explore when that's what you want to do. Other times, work on your story, novel, essay, or review. Then go home and type.

HANDS ON: JUMP-STARTING AN ESSAY OR STORY

Do this exercise today. Do not put it off. Do it to give yourself the next thing to work on as you are working through the rest of *The Writer's Portable Mentor*. This exercise will plunge you into the work of writing a piece. No more chewing on the pencil. No more staring at the page or the computer screen. In the space of an hour, the exercise generates a rough draft, gives you something first to type and then to work on. In this exercise you set the timer and write through your hesitations. Do this by yourself or do it with a writing buddy or in a writing-practice group. Write continuously without stopping. If you become stuck, write, "I am stuck" or write out your hesitations: "Let's see, what else do I want to say, perhaps…" Don't stop writing and don't worry about being correct or neat or about whether or not it's going to be any good. Just write without pausing, without lifting your pen from the page.

1. Five minutes — I want to write an essay (story) on… (In this write, spin out a number of ideas.)
2. Five minutes — The essay that attracts me most right now is…
3. Ten minutes — List ten items, in no particular order, that I certainly would want to cover in this essay (make a list of ten items). Note that this one is not exactly a writing practice because you are making a list, and you can pause.
4. Five minutes — Take the most interesting thing on the list and write for five minutes on it. Do this three or four times.
5. Five minutes — Does this piece have a central dramatic conflict? If so, who is the antagonist? What is at stake?
6. Five minutes — If the piece has a central dramatic conflict, write a trial opening paragraph that includes the central dramatic conflict.
7. Five minutes — How is the conflict resolved?
8. Five minutes — What does the main person in question (protagonist if it's a story, the "I" if memoir) *do* to resolve the conflict?
9. Ten minutes — What important questions emerge from this subject matter? (If this is fiction, what are the character's questions? What are your questions about the character?)
10. Now go home and type up these "writes." Leave a good amount of space between each paragraph — put them in chronological order if you want — but at this point you have not necessarily discovered an order.

This exercise will give you a draft of a story or essay to work on. In the space of an hour or two you will be much further along than you would be by chewing on your fingernails for that same amount of time. You're on your way!

2.

Working with Language

And so in the last light, at the end of the day, what matters is language.
—Eavan Boland

IT IS REMARKABLE HOW MANY VIRTUOSO ESSAYISTS are also poets. I am thinking of Diane Ackerman, Anne Carson, Floyd Skloot, Seamus Heaney, Heather McHugh, Eavan Boland, John Haines, Mary Oliver, John Updike, Anne Michaels, et al. These poets collect words the way some numismatists collect coins. They work sounds constantly and consciously. The music in their prose functions as a magnet to draw readers into their thoughts, memories, reflections, reports. The music vibrates in the lines but it's not rock music; it's a subtext, a whisper that runs along under the text, inaudible to readers with no need to concern themselves with the technical aspects of writing they love.

This chapter is about how to get nearer to language. It is about how to vastly increase your resource base in the language, and how to play words like music.

GATHERING WORDS

I have known writers who have worked hard for years doing pretty good work. They may aspire to art, but the writing never comes close to the most brilliant writing being done today. All that hard work should give more back to the writer, yet the quality of writing remains merely competent.

Often this hard-working writer is approaching language passively, different from the way Barry Lopez or Mary Oliver or William T. Vollmann or Alistair MacLeod approach language. This writer is using only words that come to mind, or words he grew up with, or words she stumbles upon while reading *The New York Times*. Naturally this writer looks up the occasional unfamiliar word in a dictionary, as any educated person would do. But he strives for expression with rather general, conventional diction that has little to offer in the way of echo, color, or texture. Unlike Annie Dillard:

> Nature is like one of those line drawings of a tree that are
> puzzles for children: Can you find hidden in the leaves a
> duck, a house, a boy, a bucket, a zebra, and a boot?
> (Annie Dillard, "Seeing," 694)

Dillard's list of nouns calls no attention to itself; the words are short and plain, yet the echoing effects, the musicality (duck, bucket, the *b*'s in zebra, boy, boot) are part of what sucks the reader in.

The writers of deep and beautiful works spend real time gathering words. They learn the names of weeds and tools and types of roof. They make lists of color words (ruby, scarlet, cranberry, brick). They savor not only the meanings, but also the musicality of words. They are hunting neither big words nor pompous words nor Latinate words but mainly words they like. They are not "improving their vocabulary" or studying for the SAT or the GRE. They are not trying to be fancy or decorative. This is a different kind of thing. Annie Proulx:

> I use an old Webster's Unabridged. I do collect dictionaries and I do read them and I do keep word lists and I do make notes of language. I have big notebooks, page after page of words that I like or find interesting or crackly or whatever. And from time to time I will, if I feel a section is a bit limp, take a couple of days and just do dictionary work and recast the sentences so that they have more power because their words are not overused. And often the search for the right word can consume a lot of time, but usually it can be found.*

First-rate writers get an enormous amount of capital out of putting accurate names on things. Barry Lopez makes splendid sentences merely by naming trees and tools. Here he is cutting firewood:

> The owners had felled big-leaf maple, Douglas fir, Lombardy poplar, red cedar, that black locust, and a little cherry. I cut about three cords of locust, maple, and cherry, using my truck like a tractor to skid the big logs free of one another and swamping them out with a limbing ax and a bow saw. (Barry Lopez, "Effleurage: The Stroke of Fire," 158)

---

* Annie Proulx interviewed by Michael Upchurch, *The Glimmer Train Guide to Writing Fiction*, 248.

Lopez favors words with Old English or Old German roots —
truck, split, bolt, skid, log, big, black, cord — and he favors concrete
words (black locust, tractor) that can be seen, smelled, touched, tasted,
or heard. For Lopez, language is a musical instrument: *truck, tractor,
cut, cords.*

May Sarton never wrote of a dog, tree, cat, flower, or food except
by name:

> Tamas, Pierrot, and I had swordfish for supper — what
> an extravagance! But we all three agreed that it was very
> good indeed, and for me the added pleasure of a glass of
> the Vouvray Pat Keen gave me.
> (May Sarton, *After the Stroke*, 130)

May Sarton writes *Tamas*, not *my dog*; she writes *Pierrot*, not *the cat*; she
writes *swordfish*, not *fish*; she writes *Vouvray*, not *white wine*; she writes
Pat Keen, not *my friend.*

Open any anthology of excellent stories or essays. How many town
names, street names, dog names, plant names, actual prices, actual dates,
proper names of persons do you see? Yet these pieces eschew writing that
is merely decorative. They are vibrant with nouns and verbs:

> The Reverent Francis Kilvert, an English curate in the Welsh
> border region, kept a journal of his life — where he went,
> what he did, what he dreamt, who he knew, and what he
> thought — from 1870 to 1879.
> (Bret Lott, "Toward a Definition of Creative Nonfiction," 79)

DICTION PRIMER

Concrete words are words that can be perceived through a sense organ: eyes, nose, skin, tongue, ears. You can always specify *which* sense organ has perceived a concrete word (*yellow*: eyes; *rotten eggs*: nose). Proper names are concrete. A proper name can turn general words like *street* or *river* into specific concrete words: *Everett Avenue*; the *Nooksack River*. Because you are perceiving the thing in question through one of your sense organs, it is typically one thing. You can't see "the world's rivers." You *can* see the Duwamish River. You can see the Snake and Columbia rivers at their confluence. You can't see "cities" but you can see Chicago.

Abstract words like *love* or *gentle* or *inscrutable* or *freedom* cannot be perceived through a sense organ.

There are, it seems to me, degrees of concretion. Thus *yellow* is concrete (you perceive it through your eyes). But *mustard-yellow* or *yellow ochre* are more concrete (the words make a closer match to the actual color).

Work that attains universality is usually quite specific, reflecting the situation that things don't happen in general. "War is burdensome to soldiers" just doesn't do it. It's not that we should avoid abstract words entirely but that in excellent writing they are typically embedded in a matrix of concrete words. Concrete diction makes writing more visual. Tim O'Brien makes war visual. He also makes it stink and itch.

> They carried diseases, among them malaria and dysentery.
> They carried lice and ringworm and leeches and paddy algae
> and various rots and molds. They carried the land itself —
> Vietnam, the place, the soil — a powdery orange-red dust
> that covered their boots and fatigues and faces. They carried
> the sky. The whole atmosphere, they carried it, the humidity,

the monsoons, the stink of fungus, all of it, they carried gravity. They moved like mules.

(Tim O'Brien, *The Things They Carried*, 14–15)

Yet virtuoso writers experiment with strategies rather than following rules. It is true that less skilled writers tend to use many more abstract, general words like *gentle* or *abuse* than do first-rate writers. But details put in for their own sake can be distracting. Sometimes a character can simply get in a car and drive away; to learn that the car is a red Honda Civic coupe may do nothing to further the story. Writers like Amy Hempel and Mark Strand use *car* and *tree* to great effect.

Think of a detail as an index to something else — a situation, a character trait, a town, an era. A man's mismatched socks may be an index to his lifestyle (up early to do the milking, nobody here but the cows). A woman's progression from feedbag dress to Armani suit can index her upward mobility.

How much language to use is the writer's choice, always. But to use a limited vocabulary because in reality you only command a limited vocabulary produces a result entirely different from what you might produce in a spare style spun out of an ample and ever-growing word list.

WHERE TO FIND GOOD WORDS

No writer should be without a Very Large dictionary. Would you hire a carpenter to build you a house who had for tools a single pair of pliers? Would you begin a cross-country road trip with one gallon of gas in the tank? No you wouldn't, but many writers go for years with nothing more in hand than their little college dictionary.

Hint for the true fanatic: The very largest Very Large dictionary, and the most delicious, is *Webster's New International Dictionary*, Second

Edition, Unabridged, with a 1934 copyright. Note that it's the Second Edition we want. (The sensible, cost-conscious, and ever so *reasonable* editors of the Third Edition dumped out 100,000 words.)

The 1934, Second Edition of this dictionary has 600,000 words. It has words like croodle, which is mildly obsolete but which feels comfortable with cradle or crook and which can be brought back into use. This dictionary even has extra words on the bottom of each page, and numerous words come with elaborate illustrations (a wooden sailing ship, with every rope, spar, and crossbeam named). It can be had for a fairly large chunk of change on the used-book market (Some time in 2005 I bought mine for $60, a steal. I bought another as a wedding gift for two dear writer friends for $125).

As you know, *The Oxford Dictionary of the English Language* is also an indispensable resource. This dictionary traces a word back to when it first entered English (a Germanic language that came into existence in the centuries after Germanic tribes, including Angles, invaded England in the fifth century and suppressed the Celt-speaking Britons). The dictionary gives instances of a word's use from its earliest appearance to the present. The verb *to write* for example can be found in an Old English sentence of the year 835: "This mid episcopus rodetacne [ic] festnie & write." Many university and public libraries subscribe to *The Oxford Dictionary of the English Language*. The Seattle Public Library, for example, provides it online to anyone who has a (free) library card.

At least one ample, argumentative grammar-and-usage book is a necessity, since most dictionaries describe but do not prescribe. Usage manuals prescribe. They fight to retain the difference between insure and ensure, between that and which, between alumnae and alumni. They insist and recapitulate that "And" and "But" are excellent ways to begin a sentence, favored by first-rate writers the world over, approved and even advocated by even the most conservative grammarians. The original Fowler's (*A Dictionary of Modern English Usage* by H. W. Fowler) is an entertaining and enlightening read. For a contemporary work, I would not be without my *Garner's Modern American Usage* by Bryan A. Garner. It is also essential to have a grammar book. One I like is *The Deluxe Transitive Vampire* by Karen Elizabeth Gordon.

What guidebooks are to the world traveler, dictionaries, grammars, and usage manuals are to the writer. But gathering words should take you beyond these reference works to other compendiums of words. Clothing catalogs name clothes (chinos, cords, boot-cut jeans). Tool catalogs — try leevalley.com — name tools (ripsaw, bucksaw, coping saw, band saw). Go to an art store for types of brushes and names of pigments (bone black, burnt umber). Go to the United States Geological Survey for geographical features such as shrub-steppe, bog, or slough and for spooky proper names such as the Great Dismal Swamp. You get the idea.

THE LEXICON PRACTICE

For most virtuoso writers, collecting words is a definite, specific, regular habit. Leonardo da Vinci ended up with more than 9,000 words in his lexicon.* James Joyce gathered words and phrases in a fat notebook: After he used one in the book he was writing — *Ulysses* — he would cross it out.** Mary Oliver ventures outdoors with pen and pad, ready to record any bug or old bone. If such writers do their lexicon work, so also should we.

What I call the Lexicon Practice is the specific process by which you put actual time — regular time — into collecting words and phrases. There are two parts to the practice. One is to make your own Lexicon (word book) and the other is to collect words and phrases in a list that pertains to the piece you are currently working on. I call this second part

---

* Michael J. Gelb, *How to Think Like Leonardo da Vinci*, 73.
** "Ireland Buys a Trove of Joyce Notebooks," *The New York Times*, May 31, 2002, E5.

the word trap, because trapping words is like trapping fish in a net. The words are out there. Time to bring them in.

I have been teaching these practices for a decade and what impresses me is how I can, years later, read the writing of a former student and tell whether or not he or she is doing the Lexicon Practice. I can tell by her writing. Writers who do the Lexicon Practice have left in the dust what I call "conventional received diction." Writers who don't do it in one way or another are pretty much stuck with television words, newspaper words, cereal-box words.

Conventional received diction is the language of belief rather than the language of recorded sensory experience. For example, to speak of "buying a home" rather than "buying a house" or better, "buying a California bungalow" is to speak in the conventional diction of the real-estate business. This term is based not on sense perception but on an agenda: If we long for a home then we will be more likely to "buy a home" than to "buy a house." To speak of hair color as blonde (or blond) is often to wander into the beige-curtained suburb of convention and stereotype rather than to put a specific person's head of hair on the page:

> The mother: that severe chignon, pewter tinged with bronze.
> (Edith Pearlman, "Her Cousin Jamie," 43)

I discovered my own form of Lexicon Practice in the following way. For twelve years during the 1970s and early 1980s, I worked as a printer in Boston. During those years I began getting up at 4 or 5 a.m. to write before leaving for work at 7. My thermos of hot strong coffee was at the ready. I would sit to write in my nightgown and robe; my big old black-and-white cat, Frisky, would jump into my lap and curl up and watch my moving pen with intense interest, occasionally batting it with his paw. My then-husband, Peter Irons, would be fast asleep in the next room. A carpenter friend had made me a simple, built-in, L-shaped desk with a black-Formica handwriting surface and, to my right, when I swiveled the chair, a place for my IBM Selectric typewriter. I will never forget the pleasure of those silent mornings of writing.

At the time I had written nothing about my childhood growing up on a dairy farm on the Eastern Shore of Maryland. That part of who I was was put away: Perhaps I was not ready to face the traumas of childhood. In any case my friends, pals, coworkers, comrades, and various buddies had all emerged from radically different backgrounds. Childhood was for me a distant country. But for unknown reasons, words began coming to me, and I began entering them into a black-and-white composition notebook. I titled my notebook *Memories of Underdevelopment* after the great Cuban film of that name. During a season of winter mornings I filled the notebook with the language of my childhood, words with no currency whatever in my post-childhood life — greenbriar, dirt road, Neil Lindsey's pig, 4-H Club, teats, stanchions, silage, milkers, mastitis, calf barn, gutter, manure pile, manure spreader, marsh grass, muck, eels, eel trap, watermen, field hands, tizzylish cake... What amazed me was how the words themselves held that time and that place. I went on to remember small stories, which became "Snapshots: The Eastern Shore of Maryland," which ultimately appeared in *North Dakota Quarterly*. That first lexicon was for me a turning point as a writer.

And the point is that every childhood has a lexicon. Place names, certain trees and buildings, the toys of 1934 versus the toys of 1964 versus the toys of 1984, they all make vivid a particular place, a particular era, a particular person, a particular experience. It is astonishing how much language itself holds, with no meanings added by the writer, no interpretations, no sentences, no writing.

HANDS ON: MAKE YOUR OWN LEXICON

Buy a small bound and sewn blank book, with fine paper. This is your Lexicon.

Put in words you like, words that strike your fancy, words you want to own. I suggest giving each word half a page. Put in the word — lickspittle — and draw a horizontal line dividing the page in half. This way you can put in a word and look it up later. (Under lickspittle write: a contemptible, fawning person; a flatterer or toady.) You will end up with two words per page.

This is not a typical vocabulary list full of horrible Latinate words you don't know and don't want to know.

The rule is, put in only the good words, the juicy words, the hot words. From time to time, savor this book. Look up words you've put in (something from your reading) and haven't looked up yet. Be sure to investigate the root. Put in familiar words along with new words. Play with sounds right in your Lexicon: kitchen matches; cord/weird/word/fired/turd.

From time to time read a big dictionary hunting for a new good word, any word that strikes your fancy: galoot.

On some pages make word lists. Fiddle parts — peg box, button, side rib, bridge. Words for blue — cobalt, woad, sapphire, smalt. Words from an art exhibition you especially loved — bone, tin plate; cotton, cord, silk ribbon, silver, galloon; coconuts, shells, ostrich eggs (from Moscow Treasures).

Put down things you don't know the names of. Do you know the parts of a window? (Muntin? Sash?) Do you know the parts of a rocking chair? Draw or describe the thing in your Lexicon and then set about looking (in a book on house repairs or on furniture) for splat or spindle or stile. Do not order your list in any way. If you try to order it alphabetically, you will have nowhere to put words that sound good together and you will have nowhere to draw an object — a tool or roof or chair — that you will later put a name to. Do you know the names of the weeds in your garden? Look in Alexander C. Martin's *Golden Guide to Weeds*. Identify the ones you see — spatterdock, chickweed, pokeweed. Write them in your Lexicon.

Do nothing more. Do not try to force the words into your writing. Just work on the Lexicon on a regular basis, as a form of play. It is remarkable how the words you put in your own Lexicon have a way of creeping into your writing.

Your Lexicon becomes part of the resource base you create for yourself as a writer. We writers accumulate large vocabularies that are constantly expanding. We take pleasure in learning the names for things. The Lexicon holds new words and words that please you. It forever ends the in-one-ear-out-the-other problem as it pertains to putting a name on a thing.

The Lexicon is a blank book with a pleasing feel, a permanent little book that you keep beside your dictionaries. Eventually you will accumulate several lexicons. It's fun to play with them, of an evening, to look up a word, to list the kinds of stones or guns or stars or shoes.

HANDS ON: MAKE A WORD TRAP

The second part of the Lexicon Practice is to make a word trap — a list of words and phrases — for every story or essay, not to mention novel, you work on. Most should be concrete words like *tomato* or *horse manure* that can be perceived by one of the senses. Write twenty-five numbers on twenty-five lines in your notebook. Each numbered item in the list will end up with two or three or four words. Here is the beginning of my list for a piece I am writing called "Composition in Yellow":

1. yellow, pall, pillowcase
2. yearning, urine, yams

3. "yellow peril," pearls, pee
4. sulfur, turmeric, yellow toad
5. pear, peach, yellow pansy
6. Yellow Springs; Yellowstone Park, yellow brick road
7. mildew, mold, buttermilk

These items sound good together. Individual words within items have no need to connect with each other in any narrative sense. I like the way *turmeric* chimes with *yellow toad* and have no clue as to whether one or both or neither will end up in the piece. The list has no need whatever to make any sense whatever.

I work on my list before I begin a piece and during the whole time I am working on it. Work in your writer's notebook — this list will start out being too messy for your Lexicon. First simply make a list of twenty-five or even a hundred words and phrases, not necessarily big words or new words, but simply vocabulary associated with that time and place and character and activity. Just making the list will help you sink deeper into the subject matter. First write the list in your writer's notebook, and then type it. After it's typed, work on it some more. Put words together that sound good. Keep naming things more and more accurately. When you've completed the piece that this word trap pertains to, write your favorite words in your Lexicon for future reference.

For an essay called "Housekeeping" (set in my own house) I list objects in my house, for example:

dropleaf table
blender
black buckram covered journal books
lamp

Working on the list means naming things more accurately and working with sounds: I added a hyphen too, which pleases me.

> Pembroke table
> Osterizer blender
> black buckram-bound journals
> black metal gooseneck lamp

Can a verb be concrete? Conventionally, a concrete word is a noun and indeed the usual phrase is "concrete noun." But I include verbs because I think that to *trudge* to work is more vivid and more concrete than to *go* to work or to *walk slowly to work*.

Persons have lexicons. The list alone can evoke a person with remarkable vividness. My Grandfather Henry: ice water, salted butter, Pennsylvania Dutch, "the wooden hill" (staircase)...

Places have lexicons. The Pacific Northwest: crow, Puget Sound, Steilacoom Tribe, western red cedar, Smith Tower, Emmett Watson's Oyster Bar, Starbucks, Northwest jellyfish, geoduck (pronounced *gooey duck*), Stillaguamish River...

You get the idea. Here is a passage from Henry Louis Gates Jr. that shows the obvious use of some sort of lexicon work:

> I used all the greases, from sea-blue Bergamot and creamy vanilla Duke (in its clear jar with the orange, white, and green label) to the godfather of grease, the formidable Murray's. Now, Murray's was some *serious* grease. Whereas Bergamot was like oily jello and Duke was viscous and sickly sweet, Murray's was light brown and *hard*. Hard as lard and twice as greasy, Daddy used to say. Murray's came in an orange can with a press-on top. It was so hard that some people would put a match to the can, just to soften the stuff and make it more manageable. Then, in the late

sixties, when Afros came into style, I used Afro Sheen. From Murray's to Duke to Afro Sheen: that was my progression in black consciousness.

(Henry Louis Gates Jr., "In the Kitchen," 121)

Every craft, trade, profession, or job has a lexicon. Here's a passage from Annie Tremmel Wilcox's beautiful book on conserving books.

> This book's major problem is that it doesn't have any covers. All that remains attached to the text block is the original leather spine of the binding with its label. The leather appears to be calf and has red rot, a condition of older leather that causes it to turn red and crumble at the slightest touch. As I examine it, the spine leaves leather smudges all over my hands. Since this is a tight-back book where the leather cover is glued directly to the back of the text block, I will probably not be able to save the spine piece. With luck, however, I will be able to remove and reuse the label.
>
> (Annie Tremmel Wilcox, *A Degree of Mastery*, 3)

An interesting exercise is to take a passage that attracts you and make a reverse lexicon from it — a list of its most quirky or interesting words. This can lay bare the effects of diction (word choice) on the piece. A reverse lexicon for Wilcox's passage on bookbinding would include:

covers	red rot
text block	tight-back book
leather spine	leather cover
calf	spine piece
label	smudges

WORDS AS NOTES

Whenever we write, we work with sound. Every word, every sentence emits sound. The question is, is it a musical sound, whether plain or ornate, or is it the interminable drone of a washing machine?

Here is a sentence written by Edward Abbey:

> I want to be able to look at and into a juniper tree, a piece of quartz, a vulture, a spider, and see it as it is in itself, devoid of all humanly ascribed qualities, anti-Kantian, even the categories of scientific description.
> (Edward Abbey, *Desert Solitaire*, 7)

That *anti-Kantian* — how nice! And listen to the echoing *k* sounds: *quartz, ascribed, anti-Kantian, categories*. Now listen to the long *e*'s: *tree, piece, qualities, categories*. Listen to *juniper, vulture, spider* (the *er* sound). Note that any random list of specific examples opens the door to working with sound. He might have picked other words to echo: *mule deer, tool, toad, bird*.

Working sound is about creating echoes and pleasing resonances. Resonance: intensification and prolongation of sound, especially of a musical tone, produced by sympathetic vibration.

Here is a passage from the poet Mary Oliver:

> There are pickerel in the ponds. Other fish too, I do
> not know their names. But I have seen them, on misty
> mornings, leaping from pewter water.
> (Mary Oliver, "The Ponds," 38)

Listen to the alliteration (same first consonant) in *pickerel...ponds... pewter* and in *misty mornings*. Now listen to the assonating (echoing vowel sounds) short *i* in *pickerel, fish*, and *misty*. The words *pewter* and

water chime their *er* sound. Finally, note the rhyme of *too* and *I do.* Yet
how plain, how unadorned those three sentences seem.

Here is poet and essayist Eavan Boland:

> From painting I learned something else of infinite value
> to me. Most young poets have bad working habits. They
> write their poems in fits and starts, by feast or famine. But
> painters follow the light. They wait for it and do their work
> by it. They combine artisan practicality with vision. In a
> house with small children, with no time to waste, I gradually
> reformed my working habits. I learned that if I could not
> write a poem, I could make an image, and if I could not
> make an image, I could take out a word, savor it and store it.
> (Eavan Boland, "The Woman Poet: Her Dilemma," 253)

Note how *fits and starts* jams together two one-syllable words that each
ends in a *ts* sound. Note the echo in *artisan* and *vision.* The words *feast,
famine,* and *follow* alliterate. So do *wait* and *work. Savor it and store it*
alliterates and also repeats the *it.* Finally, *time to waste* repeats *t* sounds
and sounds two notes (long *i* and long *a*) high on the vowel scale. *Make*
and *write* does the same.

And here is John Haines, poet:

> There are shadows over the land. They come out of the
> ground, from the dust and tumbled bones of the earth. Tree
> shadows that haunt the woodlands of childhood, holding
> fear in their branches. Stone shadows on the desert, cloud
> shadows on the sea and over the summer hills, bringing
> water. Shapes of shadow in pools and wells, vague forms in
> the sand-light.
> (John Haines, "Shadows," 149)

Listen to how the word *shadow* echoes five times in this short passage. Note the rhyme of wood/hood in *woodlands of childhood*. Hear how *dust and tumbled bones* assonates its short *u* sounds and echoes its *b*'s in *tumbled* and *bones*. Note the *ls* sound in *hills/pools/wells* (all one-syllable words). Finally, note the sibilants (*s* sounds) in *Stone shadows on the desert, cloud shadows on the sea and over the summer hills...*

This passage that opens Amy Hempel's story "The Annex" uses alliteration and repetition, but sticks to plain and simple words. Nothing decorative here:

> The headlights hit the headstone and I hate it all over again.
> It is all that I can ever see, all that I can ever talk about.
> There is nothing else to talk about.
> (Amy Hempel, "The Annex," 57)

SOUND-EFFECTS

Poets know what a slant rhyme is, and poets, at least the lyrical poets, know alliteration, assonance, the vowel scale, and various other ways to make words echo. Here are some main types of sound-effects that are just as effective in prose, when used with a good ear. (See ahead for a note on how to develop that good ear.)

SLANT RHYME

Slant rhyme is also called off-rhyme or imperfect rhyme or near rhyme. It is not new. Emily Dickinson — who was of course way ahead of her time — used it a lot. She would put together words like *violet* and *light* or *Heaven, even, given*. Slant rhyme can sound more modern than perfect rhyme (*white, height*) and modern poets use it profusely.

Here are examples of perfect rhymes followed by a slant rhyme:

some/hum	home
cash/flash	flesh or wish
flood/blood	glad or Trinidad or mood
blue/shoe	blow, maybe shawl
dust/rust	roost
change/range	orange or hinge
word/bird	bored

ALLITERATION

Alliteration occurs when first consonants make the same sound and thus set up an echo. Many slogans alliterate: *Power to the People*. Alliterating can be overdone and sometimes, once you begin enthusiastically alliterating, it is necessary to tone it down, to revise against it. But first, do alliterate. Here is a sentence by Phillip Lopate:

> The personal essay has historically sought to puncture the
> stiffness of formal discourse with language that is casual,
> everyday, demotic, direct.
> (Phillip Lopate, *The Art of the Personal Essay*, xxv)

In this sentence *personal* and *puncture* alliterate, as do *demotic* and *direct*. Note other echoes too: the *d* sound picked up in *everyday*. Listen also to *personal* and *casual*.

ASSONANCE

Assonance is the echoing of vowel sounds. In Lopate's sentence above, *historically*, *stiffness*, and *discourse* assonate in their *hiss-stiff-ness-dis* sound.

Here is Ira Sadoff, writing on the saxophonist Ben Webster:

> His tone is thick and reedy, almost as full of air as note.
> (Ira Sadoff, "Ben Webster," 255)

Note how the *o* sounds assonate: *tone, almost, note.* There are other echoes too, such as the *t* sounds in *tone* and *note.*

THE VOWEL SCALE

Sounds have frequency. Sound travels in waves that come at more frequent or less frequent intervals. The shorter the wave, the higher the frequency. Eek! is a high-frequency sound. The longer the wave, the lower the frequency. Blue is a low-frequency sound.

It is useful to think of the high-frequency vowels as high-energy vowels. Pie in the sky! Let's get high! Dream on! Scream! Hey, hey! In his great villanelle, Dylan Thomas makes conscious use of vowels high on the vowel scale: "Rage, rage against the dying of the light."

Low-frequency vowels are low-energy vowels. They bring us down. We have the blues (not the greens). We are lonely. We feel moody, we moon about, we moan and groan. We feel low.

Certain words are riveting because (I think) they combine lowest- and highest-frequency sounds and thus contain both shadow (low) and light (high): *moonlight.*

Here's your primer:

Lowest Frequency	Highest Frequency
long *o* (boo)	long *e* (bee)
long *o* (bone)	long *a* (bay)
short *o* (book)	long *i* (buy)

The Scale from Low to High
boo
bone
book
aw (thought)
oi (boy)
ow (bough)

ah (bar)
bud
bird
bat
bet
bit
buy
bay
bee

We all use the vowel scale semiconsciously (it may be partly physiological), but it is a delight to begin using it consciously. If your character has the blues, try revising the diction of her thoughts to lower on the vowel scale. For an excited, high-energy feel, try making more words shriek naked in the night trees.

HANDS ON: WORKING WITH SOUND

Begin working with sound. Try all kinds of sounds. Many poets eschew blatant perfect rhymes (slow, blow, show), but some writers can make them work. If this is your cup of tea, try putting the rhymes here and there rather than only at the end of lines. And use slant rhymes too. In prose and poetry, try all the sound-effects. It will likely feel awkward at first, but gradually your ear will improve. The point is not to go fancy or to indulge in false rhapsody or fussy hyper-description. The simplest-sounding prose can be playing words as notes.

∿ Develop your ear. Read, reread, and read out loud the lyrical writers, including the prose and poetry of lyrical poets. Keep in mind that poetics in our culture is vastly diverse: Some poets write against conventional lyricism and strive for an anti-lyrical voice. Other poets use engines other than sound to drive their poems. Besides which, there's such a thing as a "prosy" poem with diction dull and gray. This is a common fault of unrealized poems but it may be a technique of some writers. Whatever the case, reading them only deadens your ear. To train your ear, read the lyric poets. Gerard Manley Hopkins is a must. Try Yeats and John Haines. Try Muriel Rukeyser, Theodore Roethke, Kenneth Rexroth, and Heather McHugh, lyric poets all.

∽ Develop a keen awareness of word roots, and include them in your Lexicon. You can chime and ding Old English words — wood, God, bed, clock, work — much easier than Latinate words — approximately, judicious, interim, attention. But there are no absolute rules. Use Latinate words whenever you want to, but do so with cognizance and consciousness.

∽ Learn the rudiments of sound-effects in language. A short list would include the vowel scale, slant rhyme, assonance, alliteration, sibilants (the *s* sound), and repetition. Music is related to echo. No need to master the names of the sounds that echo in *thick* and *smoke*, but find them and use them.

∽ Sentences that have lists in them are a prime place to work sounds. The list should ding and bop. Consider this lovely sentence composed by John Updike:

> As a lecturer he was enthusiastic, electric, evangelical.
> (John Updike, "Nabokov's Lectures," 231)

∽ Take something you are working on, that you have on your computer. Take one of your paragraphs and write it by hand back into your writing-practice notebook. Consider it a "before" paragraph. Now work it to improve sound (honing to extreme accuracy as well). Then type the changes back into the piece itself. Keep on doing this, paragraph by paragraph. Here is a paragraph I worked from a book I am writing on artists and creativity:

Before

> A forceful and original artist, Münter was socially insecure, and in her relationship with Kandinsky, lived outside what would have been her preferred (and more protected) way of life within a marriage.

After

> Gabriele Münter was a forceful and original artist, but socially diffident and emotionally dependent on Kandinsky. She was too Bohemian or too conventional or too timid to tell him outright that she longed to marry him.

∾ Take a paragraph that holds a lot of emotion. Make that a "before" paragraph. Then work on an "after" paragraph that pushes the words lower in the vowel scale (for a sad scene) or higher in the vowel scale (for a tense or exciting scene).

REPETITION

Good writers delight in repeating good words. Poor writers, timid writers, average writers, many teachers including writing teachers, and some editors despise a repeated word. Their philosophy is: Use once and discard. To them words are like dental floss, toilet paper, chewing gum.

To first-rate writers, a good word is a note to be chimed. Begin looking for repetition in your reading and you will see it everywhere:

A **poem does invite**, it does require. What **does** it **invite?**
A **poem invites** you to feel. More **than that**: it **invites**
you to respond. And better **than that**: a **poem invites** a
total response.
(Muriel Rukeyser, *The Life of Poetry*, 11)

Rukeyser's repetitions roll from one to the next, rather like a relay race. The words *poem* and *does* and *invite* repeat and repeat. In this short passage we have *poem* three times, *invite* five times, and the roll from *more than that* to *better than that*.

Now look at a passage composed by Judith Kitchen:

Time is the trickster. I woke up half a century old. I am not
ready. **Too much** yet to do. **Too much** everyday living. **Too
much** left unsaid, unimagined.
(Judith Kitchen, "Culloden," 28)

Not only do we have *too much, too much,* and *too much,* but also the chime of *un* in *unsaid, unimagined.* Note the pleasing alliterations of *time, trickster,* and *too.*

Here is a paragraph from a work of natural history that won the Pulitzer Prize. Jonathan Weiner is writing about cactus finches that live on the Galapagos Islands:

The black cocks that Rosemary trapped this morning are
cactus finches. **Cactus** finches do more with **cactus** than
Plains Indians did with buffalo. They nest in **cactus**; they
sleep in **cactus**; they often copulate in **cactus**; they drink
cactus nectar; they eat **cactus** flowers, **cactus** pollen, and
cactus seeds. In return they pollinate the **cactus**, like bees.
(Jonathan Weiner, *The Beak of the Finch*, 17)

Note how the sounds of *black, cock, copulate,* and *nectar* pick up the clacking of *cactus* (eleven repetitions).

Here is Susan Sontag repeating the word *most* four times in a fourteen-word sentence:

> Poetry stands for literature at its **most** serious, **most** improving, **most** intense, **most** coveted.
>
> (Susan Sontag, "The Wisdom Project," 49)

And just look at this gorgeous and profound passage composed by John Edgar Wideman. It depends on repetition:

> For a people who have endured a long, long history of **waiting** — **waiting** at the Jordan River, **waiting** chained in stone forts on the west coast of Africa, **waiting** for slavery and discrimination to end, **waiting** for justice and respect as first-class citizens, **waiting** for prison gates to open, **waiting** eternities in emergency wards and clinic lines of sorry urban hospitals — **silence** is an old, familiar companion. Time and **silence, silence** and time. The **silence** attending **waiting, waiting** through times of enforced **silence. Silence** the ground upon which wishes are inscribed while the endless **waiting** continues. **Silence** a dreaming space where what's **awaited** is imagined and, when it doesn't come, the space where dreams are dismantled, dissolving again into **silence.** Dreams born and dying and born again in the deep womb of **silence,** and **silence,** tainted though it is by disappointment and **waiting,** also a reservoir of hope.
>
> (John Edgar Wideman, "In Praise of Silence," 114)

And here is Philip H. Red Eagle's gripping Vietnam War novel, *Red Earth*:

> For now he was still stuck in this **red earth** country, in this **red earth** place, in the **red** sky world, **far from** home, **far from** life, **far from** anything. On top of that he felt **slightly** worn. **Slightly** old now. **More than slightly** seasoned. And **more than** anything else, used up.
> (Philip H. Red Eagle, *Red Earth*, 16–17)

Finally, the peerless Zora Neale Hurston:

> Who Flung had taken her to a **shabby** room in a **shabby** house in a **shabby** street and promised to marry her the next day.
> (Zora Neale Hurston, *Their Eyes Were Watching God*, 114)

HANDS ON: LEARNING TO REPEAT

If you have trained yourself not to repeat, learning to do the opposite takes practice and it takes developing your ear. Hint No. 1: Three is the magic number. Repeating a word once looks like you ran out of words. Repeating it twice signals confidence and intention.

Hint No. 2: Repeat a word as soon as possible after you first use it. Immediately is better than soon.

Now try this. Do a five-minute writing-practice session describing a place or person. Circle the hot words and put them in a list.

What is a hot word? Hot words zing. They hold what may be emotionally strong, emotionally hot. Use impulse and instinct to find your hot words.

Now that you have circled the hot words, choose one, and do the practice again, writing on the same subject. *Write for a full ten minutes.* In every line of writing, force yourself to repeat the word you have chosen.

I repeat, in every *line* of writing, force yourself to repeat the hot word. I did not say repeat the word in every sentence. I said repeat the word in every line. Every time you return with your hand to the left side of the page, you are obliged to repeat your hot word before you get to the end of the line. Now, at a certain point you will become desperate. Keep writing anyhow. Past the point of desperation lies inspiration.

This exercise is fascinating. In a group of ten writers we do the exercise, and then read what we've written. Invariably there are amazing passages that go deeper and deeper into the emotion of the situation.

Now take what you have written and compose a paragraph. Try repeating more than one word, as in many of the models presented in this chapter.

Read aloud the passage you have written. Work on it for sound. Read it aloud again, and then again, until it sounds just right.

The practice of repeating, though, requires a cautionary note. Soon after you begin, you will hit the wall of teachers, editors, and peer writers who wish to stamp out repetition. Admit that your passage may not be well rendered — yet — and keep on working your ear. Show your peer writers passages by Susan Sontag and other virtuoso writers and ask if they think these writers were in error. Show them this part of your *Writer's Portable Mentor.*

As for teachers and editors, it depends on your relationship. Don't fight with them. Go ahead and trade your repetitions for a grade or a paycheck. But in your other work, keep the faith and keep on perfecting your skill at repeating words.

VERB WORK

Verbs carry the action, they carry the story, they carry character, feeling, a sense of doom, a sense of hope. Question every adverb because adverbs modify verbs. Consider whether "She ate her soup noisily" could be changed to "She slurped her soup."

The simple act of circling and questioning every verb in a passage you have written can result in radical improvements.

> When she cooked the entire kitchen was galvanized by the strength she put into it; the dishes, pans, knives, everything bore the brunt of her strength…. The fruit was stabbed, assassinated, the lettuce was murdered with a machete.
> (Anaïs Nin, *Ladders to Fire*, 7–8)

At least once in every piece you write, consciously make a sentence using multiple verbs. Here is Alice Walker:

> We must cherish our old men. We must revere their wisdom, appreciate their insight, love the humanity of their words.
> (Alice Walker, "Duties of the Black Revolutionary," 135)

And here is Anthony Doerr, in Rome for the first time, with his wife and baby twins:

> We descend a steep alley, slip beneath an archway, skirt some shuttered restaurants.
> (Anthony Doerr, *Four Seasons in Rome*, 27)

Here is a beautiful sentence that multiplies — and keeps on multiplying — verbs. It is from an essay written in defense of MFA programs and their graduates by D. W. Fenza, the executive director of the Association of Writers and Writing Programs (AWP). The sentence refutes the charge that MFA graduates lead uneventful lives.

> Graduates of writing programs have gone to war, sequestered themselves in monasteries, planted cannas and zinnias for hummingbirds and butterflies, sold drugs at both the retail and wholesale levels, worked in paper mills, reported as journalists, built latrines in the Peace Corps, inseminated cows, gone to prison, bred and raced horses, managed restaurants, hitchhiked across North America, raised children, lived in communes, caught marlins, wahoos, and mahi mahi, toured with rock bands, snorkeled through coral reefs, suffered rape, worked night shifts at hospitals, endured prejudices, launched new companies, practiced martial arts, acted in plays, sold antiques, cuckolded their best friends, developed screenplays, tended beehives, nursed their suicidal or damaged friends, sold their souls, saw the towers fall, deranged their senses, remarried, practiced law, staggered out of casinos just after dawn, recovered from cancer, and worked as roustabouts, waiters, cooks, bartenders, and wine stewards and as every other kind of minion.
> (D. W. Fenza, "Who Keeps Killing Poetry?" 16–17)

Here the poet Colleen McElroy, traveling in Madagascar, is being conveyed in a questionable vehicle over a questionable road:

> We jiggedy-hicked past a scattering of farmhouses that were bricked in rust colored adobe, tall and narrow as New York walk-ups.
> (Colleen McElroy, *Over the Lip of the World*, 74)

HANDS ON: WORKING VERBS

∽ Take a page of a piece you've written. Circle the verbs. Question each one. Change at least one verb per page.

∽ Circle every adverb. (Adverbs modify verbs.) Can you take out an adverb by making the verb do more work? (Change "She cut vigorously" to "She whacked." Change "He ran fast" to "He raced" or "He sprinted." Change "She turned around quickly" to "She spun around.")

∽ In every piece, write at least one sentence with multiple verbs.

∽

This is more than you need to know to begin working with sound.

You can begin to play the vowel scale. You can make consonants clack and sibilants swish. You can ring words like bells, dinging the hot words.

But don't forget truth and don't forget accuracy. That is your brake on flowery, over-alliterated, hyper-decorative, false language. Don't forget image. Eschew adjectives. Adore verbs and nouns. Keep it simple. *Omit needless words.*

3.

Writing to See:
Training in Observation

Your beliefs will be the light by which you see, but they will not be what
you see and they will not be a substitute for seeing.
—Flannery O'Connor

WE WRITE TO BRING INSIGHT TO THE PAGE. We hope to be perceptive. We hope to discern the essential nature of the matter at hand. Very well. The truth is that insight begins with sight — with seeing what is there. Perception, writes Joan M. Erikson in *Wisdom and the Senses,* begins with sense perception.

Sense perception requires really looking, really listening, really paying attention. It requires time. Henry James famously said that a writer is one upon whom nothing is lost. But, writer or not, it's easy to become one upon whom most everything is lost as we rush to get to work or get the kids to school on time. Our days full of duties and distractions, not to mention way too much chitchatting on the cell phone, tend to dull our senses. Under these circumstances, it's a good idea to spend regular time each week training ourselves in observation. For a writer, observation becomes a habit and a way of life. And it really can't be cranked up for special circumstances (such as the piece you happen to be working on) and then let drop.

A visual artist may attend a life class and sit and draw the figure for an hour or two hours a week. John Berger describes the drawing process this way: "For the artist, drawing is discovery. And that is not just a slick phrase, it is quite literally true. It is the actual act of drawing that forces the artist to look at the object in front of him, to dissect it in his mind's eye and put it together again; or, if he is drawing from memory, that forces him to dredge his own mind, to discover the content of his own store of past observations."*

The Here and Now exercise is the writer's version of drawing.

OBSERVING THE HERE AND NOW

Go to a café. Or go to a park. Or go to a library. Or go down to the river. Write for fifteen minutes at a steady pace without stopping. (Use a timer, or write down your start time.) Describe what's in front of you. You can describe the whole scene, or just one object.

Don't write about anything except what you see, hear, touch, taste, or smell. Don't write your feelings, opinions, or reflections. Write color and shape. Write sound. You might describe the damp air or the hard desk. The taste of coffee. The smell of exhaust fumes. No feelings. No opinions. No thoughts.

These writings connect you to the world, to where you are. The more you do them, the more aware you become. They are pure training

---

* John Berger, "Drawing," in *John Berger: Selected Essays*, 10.

in sensory observation; you can also type them and compose them into settings, poems, pieces of essays. They are concrete-word farms.

Doing this exercise, you will inevitably come across objects, gizmos, thingamajigs, doohickeys, and doodads, not to mention any number of plants, that you can't put a name to. Write these down in your Lexicon, not the word, which you don't know, but the thing that awaits its word. Write "the vertical center piece in the back of a straight-back chair." In your Lexicon you can also draw the chair. The definition will be there waiting for the word *splat*.

Now a warning: When you first do the Here and Now exercise, and then compose it into a setting or a poem, you may have a rather adjective-laden paragraph. First do your lexicon work (make that chair into a ladder-back chair, make the table a Pembroke table). Then work at reducing adjectives and increasing concrete nouns and verbs. Make a list sentence, and make the list a list of nouns. Work to make the nouns more specific: not *small house*, but *cottage*; not *roof*, but *mansard roof*; not *container*, but *Mason jar, flowerpot, rucksack*. Work to make the verbs contain their adverbs: not *slowly walk*, but *stroll*.

You can do the Here and Now exercise from memory. Write continuously but slowly to recall every detail of a kitchen, an evening at the movies, a family meal. Here is a scene from *Huckleberry Finn* written out of acute, extended observation:

> The first thing to see, looking away over the water, was
> a kind of dull line — that was the woods on t'other side;
> you couldn't make nothing else out; then a pale place in
> the sky; then more paleness spreading around; then the
> river softened up away off, and warn't black any more, but
> gray; you could see little dark spots drifting along ever
> so far away — trading-scows, and such things; and long
> black streaks — rafts; sometimes you could hear a sweep
> screaking; or jumbled up voices, it was so still, and sounds

come so far; and by and by you could see a streak on the
water which you know by the look of the streak that there's
a snag there in a swift current which breaks on it and makes
that streak look that way; and you see the mist curl up off
of the water, and the east reddens up, and the river, and
you make out a log cabin in the edge of the woods, away
on the bank on t'other side of the river, being a wood-yard,
likely, and piled by them cheats so you can throw a dog
through it anywheres; then the nice breeze springs up, and
comes fanning you from over there, so cool and fresh and
sweet to smell on account of the woods and the flowers; but
sometimes not that way, because they've left dead fish laying
around, gars and such, and they do get pretty rank; and next
you've got the full day, and everything smiling in the sun,
and the song-birds just going it!
(Mark Twain, *Huckleberry Finn*, 163)

And this passage by the poet John Haines is a Here and Now of
sorts, written from memory:

It is evening in the kitchen of the roadhouse at Richardson,
past dusk of a winter day. A gas lantern is burning overhead,
throwing strong light on the white enamel of the shelves
and cupboards, a brightness on the hanging pots and pans.
A white oilcloth marked with a well-rubbed floral pattern
gleams on the long table in the center of the room.
(John Haines, "Stories We Listened To," 30)

HANDS ON: WRITING THE HERE AND NOW

- Look over the piece or pieces you are working on. Can you go to an actual setting and capture it in your notebook by setting your timer and writing it down? Do so.
- Or set your timer and do a Here and Now from memory: Capture every detail you can remember of a childhood room; a synagogue, church, or mosque you once attended; a beach; a street.
- On a regular basis, do the Here and Now exercise just to train your capacity to observe. Look and write and look again. Or write while looking.
- Try this: For thirty days in a row, do the Here and Now exercise for fifteen minutes a day in the same place. Do lexicon work each day so that gradually you can put a name on everything you are looking at. I once did this in my living room. At first it was interesting. Following that: excruciating boredom. I wrote through that and one day, like magic, I saw the room in a way I never had before, its wood and earth colors intensely glowing, a glint of sunlight on the maplewood rocker turning it almost white...

SEEING COLOR

Look up from this page. Look around you. What colors do you see? What if you were to paint the scene before your eyes, just as you see it? What pigments would you squeeze from the tube? Look at your hand. How many colors do you see? Can you put them into words?

We've heard the phrase "gray prose." Gray prose is general prose, colorless prose. Put color into your prose. Some nouns — rubies, urine — carry color onto the page without further elaboration. These concrete nouns are especially good because nouns are stronger than adjectives, and in becoming aware of color you don't want to inadvertently begin proliferating adjectives. Remember the color verbs: to blacken; to yellow; to purple.

Become aware of color. If you are color blind, or so I understand, you can see certain things better, greens against green. If you are color blind, write a piece that puts on the page what the world looks like to your way of seeing.

To comprehend what it could mean to become acutely cognizant of color, we can turn to Vincent van Gogh's letters to his brother Theo:

> But if only you had been with us on Sunday, when we saw a red vineyard, all red like red wine. In the distance it turned to yellow, and then a green sky with the sun, the earth after the rain violet, sparkling yellow here and there where it caught the reflection of the setting sun.
> (Vincent to Theo, Arles, early November 1888, *The Letters of Vincent van Gogh*, 300)

Or, we can turn to that lyrical classic of the Harlem Renaissance, *Cane*, by Jean Toomer. *Cane* is more than color — it's metaphor, music, mojo — but colors glow on every page. Here is a town called Sempter:

> Sempter's streets are vacant and still. White paint on the wealthier houses has the chill blue glitter of distant stars. Negro cabins are a purple blur. Broad Street is deserted.
> (Jean Toomer, *Cane*, 105)

How is your color lexicon? Go to any art-supply store. Purveyors of pigments such as the firm Winsor & Newton provide sample sheets with daubs of paint painted on. These sheets name the pigments, which have over the centuries evolved stable names (burnt umber, Payne's gray, yellow ochre), unlike the colors of house paints and printing inks, which are dyes named by advertising writers. The hues of a house paint by Pittsburgh Paints called "Twilight Purple" or one by Benjamin Moore called "Autumn Purple" are not traditional and there's no way to know what they look like without looking at them. Burnt sienna, though, refers to a traditional pigment, a clay containing the red iron oxide and manganese oxide. Burnt sienna is burnt sienna no matter who manufactures it.

Any common object, substance, or living thing that has a stable color can be used as a color word. In a home-furnishing catalog the color of a washcloth may be "wheat" or "blackberry." But you can't color something "river" and you really can't color something "stone" (although it's done anyway), because rivers continuously change color and stones come in reds (iron oxide) and grays (granites) and blues (bluestone) and yellows (calcite). Ebony, that hard, blackish heartwood of *E. ebenum* originating in Asia and Africa, has a stable color and it has become a common color word, detached from its tree of origin.

Color brightens (or purples or yellows or greens) any sort of writing. Consider the surgeon Richard Selzer's description of cutting into an abdomen:

> Deeper still. The peritoneum, pink and gleaming and
> membranous, bulges into the wound. It is grasped with
> forceps, and opened. For the first time we can see into
> the cavity of the abdomen. Such a primitive place. One
> expects to find drawings of buffalo on the walls. The sense
> of trespassing is keener now, heightened by the world's light
> illuminating the organs, their secret colors — maroon and
> salmon and yellow.
> (Richard Selzer, "The Knife," 708)

Note *maroon* and *salmon* — color words outside a short list of red, green, yellow, and blue.

Colors derived from objects or living things become instantly metaphorical in that they compare one thing to another. Instantly then, the writer needs to work to make the metaphor intensify the character or setting or situation rather than detract from it. No snow-white objects in the tropics! Here is a passage I wrote about my childhood, part of a memoir:

> They stink of hay and sweat. The father is there, his face
> burnt dark-orange like a Jersey calf. And the twins, with
> their pale yellow braids and pink faces. They get paid a
> quarter an hour by the father's boss. The field hands, Neil
> Lindsey and Buck Washington, have worked on the farm
> longer than anyone. Neil is a coppery-dark man, large and
> kindly, who lives at the end of the lane. Buck is bony and
> reserved, with dusty black skin the color of a bible.
> (Priscilla Long, "Snapshots: The Eastern Shore of Maryland," 98)

To state the obvious, had my father been a Wall Street lawyer, I would not compare his face-color to a Jersey calf. If Buck Washington had been a Buddhist, I would not compare his face-color to a bible.

HANDS ON: WRITING COLOR

Do the Here and Now exercise, this time paying close attention to color. Write slowly and mention the color of everything you see. Use as many different words for colors as you can think of. Words meaning brown: dun, auburn, burnt sienna, umber, chocolate, turd-colored, straw-colored. Her eyes the color of molasses.

Run comparisons. Write thinking of objects in the world that are the same color as this person's hair. You might write in your notebook: "His eyes were blue sort of like the sky, no brighter, maybe like blue thistles or maybe robin's eggs. Bleach." Later, choose the most accurate one for color but also for the character, the situation. A character who has steel-blue eyes will differ considerably from one with pale blue eyes.

Finally, remember this: Nouns and verbs are strong. Adjectives and adverbs are weak cousins, hangers-on. Do not use your color practice to proliferate adjectives in your writing. Use color verbs: Dusk reddens the sky. Use nouns that emit their colors — walnut, eggplant, cherrywood, chocolate milk. Add a color adjective, but force it to earn its keep by deleting two adjectives and one adverb.

OBSERVING PERSONS

We prose writers are always writing persons, whether a historical figure, a fictional character, or the shopkeeper down the street. No doubt it is one of the first things we learn to do. Still, it's easy to neglect one or more aspects of putting a person on the page. As a writer, I need these reminders, and I hope they are useful to you.

To write a telling portrait is to observe a person closely, to recognize who that person is. It is to observe the person in his or her body as well as in his or her actions, opinions, achievements, derangements, or whatever. It is to hear the quality of voice, to remember his or her habitual expressions or startling expressions. Portraits, even brief ones, usually include body type, dress, gesture (body language), color (hair, skin, neon-pink spikes), and sometimes voice. In memoir, essay, or fiction, when a person comes on stage, he or she needs some kind of portrait (unless you are writing from his or her point of view). Call it a visual. Writing is a visual art. Consider this passage from Tobias Wolff's *This Boy's Life*. The man who has just come on stage is a guy the boy's mother is about to pick up:

> The man she'd been talking with turned to me. He was the
> older of the two, a tall angular man with ginger-colored
> hair and a disjointed way of moving, as if he were always off
> balance. He wore Bermudas and black socks. His long face
> was sunburned, making his teeth look strangely prominent.
> "Let's ask the big fella," he said. "What say, big fella? You
> want to watch the fun from my place?" He pointed at a large
> brick house at the edge of the park.
>   I ignored him. "Mom," I said. "I'm hungry."
> (Tobias Wolff, *This Boy's Life*, 51)

The man is tall, angular (body type). He has "a disjointed way of moving, as if he were always off balance" (body language or gesture). He wears "Bermudas and black socks" (dress). His hair is "ginger-colored" (coloration). In other words, you can see him.

And here is Melissa Fay Greene's memorable portrait of Thurnell Alston, who comes on stage in an essay she wrote on how she came to write *Praying for Sheetrock*, about a community in Georgia:

> I saw Thurnell Alston for the first time that night. A tall,
> thin, ebony man with a long face and wild frizzy hair,
> he wore formal attire — a green suit with diagonally cut
> pockets and lapels trimmed in dark green velvet, and a light
> green shirt with a frilly front — he looked like a bridegroom
> or one of the Temptations. He was the first to stand and
> face the suddenly subdued crowd. He was by nature a jittery
> man, a chain-smoker, with a nervous stammer and sudden
> movements, so he stood as calmly as it was possible for him
> to stand, shifting his weight from foot to foot and trying his
> hands in this or that decorative pocket.
> (Melissa Fay Greene, "On Writing Nonfiction," 234)

Here again. The man comes onstage. He is "tall, thin" (body type). His skin color is ebony. He is dressed. He is "shifting his weight from foot to foot" (gesture).

The very split-second a character (whether fictional or actual) enters the page, he or she should get a portrait. Think of it as theater. When an actor makes an entrance you can *see* the character.

The more important a character is, the more space on the page his or her visual should take up. A long description of a character clues the reader that this one will be significant. For a minor character, the doorman or server or bus driver, give a glimpse, just a line or half a line. Still, they are visually present. Here is a minor character from a Jack Remick story from his collection *Terminal Weird:*

> Archer felt a tap on his shoulder. A man in a white coat with
> a name tag that said Superintendent smiled at him.
> (Jack Remick, "The Machine," 25)

And here is Mary Gordon buying Arpege perfume in a duty-free shop at the London airport. This is the saleswoman's only appearance in the piece:

> The young saleswoman is thin, in a short black skirt, black
> shirt, and black pumps with something called kitten heels.
> (Mary Gordon, "My Mother's Body," 68)

A portrait can be salted down through lines of dialogue. Lines of dialogue spoken by non-point-of-view characters should have gestures (body language) as well as other sorts of visuals. Here's an example from Raymond Chandler's *The Big Sleep.* The "she" speaker is guarding detective Philip Marlowe, who comes to consciousness to find himself handcuffed and tied to the couch:

"You're a little light-headed," she said with a grave stare.

"Would you mind moving this light?"

She got up and went behind the davenport. The light went off. The dimness was a benison.

"I don't think you're dangerous," she said. She was tall rather than short, but no bean-pole. She was slim, but not a dried crust. She went back to her chair.

(Raymond Chandler, *The Big Sleep*, 128–129)

Later in the passage, her blue eyes flash. She glares at him, swings her head sharply, looks down at the floor. Her voice is embodied and her body language accompanies everything she says.

Philip Marlowe, the detective describing his captor, is looking out of his own eyes (he is the point-of-view character) so he will not, of course, describe himself. A point-of-view character can peer into a mirror or someone else can remark on his appearance ("You haven't shaved for days — is something wrong?"), or she can choose a dress ("She pulled on her skimpy, slinky red dress"). Only in such ways can a point-of-view character view himself or herself. Reserve most of your portrait work for your non-point-of-view characters.

HANDS ON: PUTTING PERSONS ON THE PAGE

In this practice you separate a person's or character's qualities in order to focus on each one in turn. Do each timed write in the spirit of exploration. Allow yourself to stall and stammer in the writing in order to dwell, in order to stay with something. ("He waves his arms when he talks, sort of up and down, like he's trying to flag a taxi or something, or give signals to an airplane, what do you call that...") Write for three to five minutes on each element. If you feel stuck, use negatives: She's not obese, not short, not a redhead. Then move in closer: Her hair is the color of a Chestnut horse.

∿ Write down twenty concrete words associated with this person. The words might pertain to clothing, foods, hobbies, occupation or trade, or favored objects.

∿ Give a macro-portrait: In quick strokes give an overall picture of the person you are going to portray: "a tall angular man with ginger-colored hair and a disjointed way of moving." The macro includes body type, and then simply the most noticeable things about the person at first glance.

∿ Coloration: Color of hair, skin tones (everyone's skin has coloration and no person's skin has only one tone). Use comparison as you write; slow down in order to dwell. Write: "His face was reddish, not like strawberries but maybe more like raw beef, pink beef, well, there is a purple splotch, like purple grapes on the side of his nose. The red is a sunburned red, it has rust in it, I'm thinking of the red stones in New Mexico but it's darker than that. His hair is the exact color of an Irish setter." And so on. Expand your range of color description by using comparisons to common (and uniformly colored) fruits, dogs, birds, gems, stones, vegetables, horses, etc.

∿ Body language: Put the person's habitual gestures on the page. The way the person walks, moves his or her hands, weeps, laughs, talks. Consider open and shut, looseness and tightness, defended and undefended. Consider energy, agitation, stillness. The foot tapping. Arms hanging to the sides motionless.

∿ What the person said: Write down a few of his or her exact phrases.

∿ Dress the person. Dress reveals character. The way people dress reveals who they are or who they think they are.

∿ Write for ten minutes to reflect on this person or character. What insights can you come to?

∾ Write a ten-minute biography of the person.

∾ Now compose a portrait of the person, using the most telling attributes from each of the various categories. It can be long or short, two lines or two pages.

OBSERVING GESTURE

Body language is as ubiquitous as speech. More ubiquitous, because it continues through silence, and in dialogue it is a form of speech. Body language can either contradict or intensify what is said verbally:

> "What do you mean?" His lips quivered.
> "What do you mean?" He slammed the book down.
> "What do you mean?" He knit his brow.
> "What do you mean?" He grinned at her.

Or this:

> "I love you," she said, and turned away.
> "I love you," she said, and raised the gun.
> "I love you," she said. Tears streamed down her face.

Body language can hold things not consciously felt by the speaker:

> "I'd love to go," she said, looking at the ground.

Look at how excellent writers use body language at every turn. Here is a passage from Paul Bowles's novel *Up Above the World:*

> "How're you weathering lap two?" he asked her.
> "What?" She squinted up at him.
> "The second lap of the Slade anniversary expedition?"

"Oh." She stretched with pleasure and waited a while before saying, "I meant to tell you. We're having drinks with Mrs. Rainmantle at six. Down in the bar."

He was mystified. "What for?" he asked, but his wife merely looked at him.

(Paul Bowles, *Up Above the World*, 55)

The woman in this doomed couple squints, stretches, looks. Her gestures become part of the language of the interchange.

HANDS ON: WRITING GESTURE

෨ Go to a café or to some other place where people hang out and you can write about them. Choose two people sitting together. You are going to open your notebook, set your timer for fifteen minutes or a half-hour, and observe them while writing continuously. Observe their postures and gestures, the way they hold themselves, the way they move their hands, where they place their feet. Use this strategy taken from the visual arts: Look, memorize what you see, then turn to the page and write. Then look again. Note position of hands, torso, elbows. Note movements (jiggling foot, smiling, eyes, position of hands). Just detail the body language, no opinions or speculations about them. And don't worry. You'll become a pro at averting your eyes just as someone looks over. People are extremely absorbed in their own affairs: It is remarkable how easily you can write on and on without being observed.

෨ Only *after* you've completed the observation exercise without opinion or speculation, *then* see if you can arrive at any insights on the body language you have observed. Decide on degree of intimacy. Decide who has more power. (Defended? Wide open? Leaning back? Leaning forward?) Give evidence for your decisions. Record how far apart or close the pair sits within a half-hour period. Is there a space barrier (how wide is it?) or has the barrier been crossed? Think about:

tension vs. ease
defended vs. open
happy vs. depressed
wary or aware vs. oblivious
intimacy vs. distance
power relations: Who has more power? Or, are they equals?
low self-esteem vs. centered, confident

Gesture work begins to give you a vocabulary of body language. The task is to work on rendering stances and gestures, to learn to name body parts — Is it "put out her hands" or "turned up her palms"? — and to become adept at including body language in dialogue and portrait.

Gesture work is also character work. One man, when he talks, strokes his beard and looks into the distance. Another stares solemnly into your eyes. Yet another looks anywhere *but* into your eyes.

OBSERVING VOICE

Particular people have particular voices. Particular characters have particular voices. Certain works of fiction and nonfiction are entirely voice-driven. But even essays and stories not voice-driven are given authenticity by voice. People do not have neutral voices, just as they do not always say what they mean. Voices have age and region, but also individual characteristics. Paying attention to voice in the grocery store and in your reading will repay you many times.

Alice Adams, in "Roses, Rhododendron," portrays two precocious 10-year-old girls who have just met. They are discussing literature:

> "I love Virginia Woolf!"
> "Yes, she's very good. Amazing metaphors."
> (Alice Adams, "Roses, Rhododendron," 524)

And here's a teenage voice, from Tobias Wolff's *This Boy's Life*. This boy has just stolen items from a drugstore:

> I collected some Old Spice aftershave, brass plated fingernail clippers, a hairbrush, and a package of pipe tobacco. As I approached the cash register she smiled and asked me how I was today.
> "Grand," I said. "Just grand."
> She added up my bill and asked if I wanted anything else.
> "I believe that will do the trick," I said and put my hand in my right pocket and frowned. Still frowning, I patted my other pocket. "Wouldn't you know it," I said. "I seem to have left my wallet at home. Drat! Sorry for the inconvenience."
> (Tobias Wolff, *This Boy's Life*, 194)

And here, in a James Alan McPherson story, which, like Alice Adams's "Roses, Rhododendron," reads like a memoir, is a well-educated young writer who has taken a janitorial job. He is black and in conference with the building's crusty Irish janitor-in-chief:

> "Sit down, for Chrissake, and take a load off your feet," he told me.

I sat on the red bench next to him and accepted the wilted cigarette he offered me from the crushed package he kept in his sweater pocket.

"Now, I'll tell you something to help you get along in the building," he said.

I listened attentively.

"If any of these sons of bitches ever ask you to do something extra, be sure to charge them for it."

I assured him that I absolutely would.

"If they can afford to live here, they can afford to pay. The bastards."

"Undoubtedly," I assured him again.

"And another thing," he added. "Don't let any of these girls shove any cat shit under your nose. That ain't your job. You tell them to put it in a bag and take it out themselves."
(James Alan McPherson, "Gold Coast," 479)

Finally, Dagoberto Gilb's "Victoria" is entirely voice-driven:

I'll even blame the heat for my inability to remember which year it was — 1986, give or take. It was hot like never before, my skin so porous it was hard to distinguish which side of it I was on. Like I could sweat and become a puddle. A dirty puddle because I'd absorbed that construction site. And because this was Los Angeles and it was smoggy too. But you know what, it wasn't the smog or the dirt or the cement, it was the heat....
(Dagoberto Gilb, "Victoria," 103)

How do you write distinct voices, whether in stories or nonfiction pieces? Partly, it is a matter of learning to hear voice. Once again, observation deepens insight. In your carry-about notebook, write down exact scraps of talk you hear at the office, in a café, on the bus, in your own kitchen. On an airplane, one flight attendant asks another, "Tom, did you talk to the overwing exits?" That's flight-attendant lingo (passengers sitting beside exit doors must be willing to perform certain duties in an emergency). On this flight my 23-year-old niece Joanna said to her mother, "Don't you just love the scene in *The Red Violin* where the old man unravels the sweater?" "Don't you just love…" — that's voice. Think about it. Would your grandfather ever say, "Don't you just love?" Place, time, gender, generation all influence a person's voice.

Listen for voice, and write it down. Do not plan to do anything else with such scraps, just accumulate them. You will begin listening in a new way. You will begin to hear voice.

Here's a voice I captured of a middle-aged, white, bulky, rather jovial construction-worker type. He and I were both waiting for our appointments in a clinic. He had just explained that on a construction job-site he could remember the names of all 748 men on the job (his job involved meeting with each one each week). But, he said: "Sittin' down at school and tryin' to learn out of a book, I'm no good at it."

Lee Gutkind, writer and editor of the journal *Creative Nonfiction*, advises that when conducting an interview for an article, the most important things to write down are the interviewee's specific expressions. You will remember the gist of the conversation very well, but actual speech — the housepainter reminding the homeowner to "exercise the windows," the bridge engineer speaking of excavating "in the dry" — tends to slip away. Yet that expression more than any gist captures that person and her world.

HANDS ON: WRITING VOICE

Do writing practices to capture voices you know well:

↜ Fifteen minutes: Write a bitter complaint in your own most colloquial voice.

↜ Five minutes: "My father always used to say…"

↜ Can you capture the voice of one of your friends or family members? Try. Then, next time you get together, check it out. Try again. Now use elements of what you've learned in a story or essay.

↜ Do a writing practice in which you tell something that happened to you in the most colloquial version of your own voice. Make this into a story.

Continue to observe the voices of people around you. Write it down. Can this voice (especially if it's close to a voice you know well) be turned into a character's voice?

A final word. Writing regional and ethnic voices is a nice skill. Study the masters, study the stories of Grace Paley, Tim Gautreaux, Dagoberto Gilb. Note how the great majority of words in these voiced sentences are actually written in Standard English. There is something about a sentence in which every word is bent out of standard that makes it seem caricatured.

4.

Object and Setting

The gathered, crumpled, slewed sheet, its folds like gray twigs woven together to make a nest, and its highlights like falling water, is unambiguously eloquent about what has happened on the bed.
—John Berger, on a Frans Hals painting of a nude.

IN REAL LIFE, OBJECTS AND SETTINGS carry strong meanings. No knickknack, no set of car keys, no room is neutral or random. Compare your own living room with that of your great aunt or your best friend. The chair, the rug, the photos speak — even if obliquely — about who that person is. If you've ever had occasion to deal with a person's effects after death, you know how powerfully these trinkets and packets of letters and ironed cotton handkerchiefs bare a particular person's particular life. And so it is with fictional characters. Rooms stand for lives; objects hold history.

Compare two characters, portrayed through their respective suppers. The first is the ex-convict Socrates, the protagonist in Walter Mosley's *Always Outnumbered, Always Outgunned*:

> He boiled potatoes and eggs in a saucepan on his single hotplate and then cut them together in the pot with two knives, adding mustard and sweet pickle relish. After the meal he had two shots of whiskey and one Camel cigarette.
> (Walter Mosley, *Always Outnumbered, Always Outgunned*, 69)

Now here, in *After the Stroke*, is May Sarton partaking of her supper:

> The table looked beautiful with a white cloth strewn with violets — the pattern is violets — two deep red roses in the center with the silver candlesticks and tall white candles. The tenderloin roast about which I felt terribly anxious turned out perfectly.
> (May Sarton, *After the Stroke*, 226)

Though one supper is fiction, the other fact, the techniques of detailing the suppers are identical. Far from taking up room as meaningless description, the objects — the single hotplate, the silver candlesticks — stand in for the characters themselves. Socrates with his hotplate is no corporate lawyer. May Sarton with her silver candlesticks is no ex-con cooking on a hotplate. We can take our own work to the next level by giving our character objects that represent his sorry past or her essentially European aesthetic or whatever lies at the heart of who he is.

Settings work to intensify the emotion of the story, and settings characterize. Here is an alley, seen through the eyes of the above-mentioned Socrates:

> The sun was coming up. The alley was almost pretty with
> the trash and broken asphalt covered in half light. Discarded
> wine bottles shone like murky emeralds in the sludge.
> (Walter Mosley, *Always Outnumbered, Always Outgunned*, 23)

The alley holds a feeling of tranquility. It also holds the character of Socrates. The alley is beautiful not because trash is beautiful but because this is a man who, despite his hard life, can see the beauty in things.

A person's room is an index to his or her life. Here is V. S. Pritchett writing about the novelist Forrest Reid, who lived in Belfast:

> I found him living alone on the top floor of a shabby house
> in a noisy and dirty factory district. His room was bare and
> poor, and only packed shelves of books, carefully bound in
> white paper covers to protect them from smoke and smuts,
> suggested the bibliophile and the scholar.
> (V. S. Pritchett, "Forrest Reid: Escaping from Belfast," 111)

Settings mirror lives. If you merely list out words here — alone, shabby, noisy, dirty, bare, poor, smoke, smuts — you can see what powerful vehicles they are for carrying the hard life of this creative genius.

Settings ought to do double duty to deepen a story emotionally. Look at the world a bummed-out character is passing through in that great novel *Wide Sargasso Sea*:

> Meanwhile the horses jogged along a very bad road. It
> was getting cooler. A bird whistled, a long sad note. What
> bird is that? She was too far ahead and did not hear me.
> The bird whistled again. A mountain bird. Shrill and sweet.
> A very lonely sound.
> (Jean Rhys, *Wide Sargasso Sea*, 70)

Because objects occur in settings, settings and objects are interrelated. It is useful to speak of them in the same breath. They resonate metaphorically: Socrates' rudimentary room and his hotplate stand for themselves but they also stand for Socrates' circumstances, his history, his occupation. I read somewhere that the great Russian writer Isaac Babel, understanding how revealing objects can be, used to pay women to show him the entire contents of their pocketbooks. Here is a passage from Aleksandar Hemon's short story, "Blind Jozef Pronek." Pronek, having just arrived to Chicago from the terror of war in Eastern Europe, enters his new girlfriend's pungent, smoke-filled apartment:

> "My roommate is a slob," she said. Pronek panned the room:
> a sofa with stuffing hatching from its cushions, a stereo, and
> a TV stacked with CDs and videos. There was a small table,
> its surface buried under McDonald's bags, crushed cigarette
> packages, and ashtrays brimming with butts and ashes. The
> window looked out on a brick wall. A porcine black cat
> glanced at Pronek and then turned away. On the kitchen
> table was a throng of beer bottles with their labels torn off,
> huddled together as if awaiting execution.
> (Aleksandar Hemon, "Blind Jozef Pronek," 168)

This setting carries the chaos, the war, and Pronek's state of mind, not to mention his girlfriend's character.

The psychoanalyst Christopher Bollas perceives objects as expressions of self. In *Being a Character* he suggests that we evoke "self experiences" by choosing objects. So, for example, you might pick up a softball mitt on one occasion, a sonnet on another. A different person will pick up a flat of petunias or a pistol. We choose not only an activity but also the self we want to inhabit while carrying out that activity. What object does our protagonist pick up? Does the object tend to change as our protagonist changes?

Objects carry both history and desire. Feng shui is greatly concerned with objects, and feng shui coach Karen Rauch Carter writes in *Move Your Stuff, Change Your Life* that again and again she encounters relationship-seeking single women whose walls are covered with images of solitary, single women. She advises replacing these with images of couples and coupling. The idea is to portray not the reality but the intention and the desire. We writers might concern ourselves with what our protagonists put on their walls. Does this taxidermed moose-head represent who the character is or does it represent what he wishes to be?

Did I mention that settings and objects carry strong meanings? A room can stand for a character's mood — it can look dreary or the dust can dance. Objects carry cultural meanings as well as personal meanings less accessible to an outsider. If you walked into my house you would see on the mantelpiece a carved African bowl. It was carved in Liberia some time during the mid-1960s. Considered at length it may raise cultural and historical questions and suggest a lot of history. For me personally it is also a relic of my late sister, who brought it back from the Peace Corps long ago. Does your character possess a relic of lost love or a memento of a distant place?

We writers can deepen our work by observing settings and objects — deeply and at length — and using them to enrich every page.

HANDS ON: OBJECTS AND SETTINGS

Make objects do work. Make settings do work. What is that blue bowl on that yellow tablecloth good for? Why is that room dusty and why does that dust darken that room? Make settings carry the emotion, the drama, the mood, the character's situation or past or wish.

ᑫ Describe a room of your house. Describe it from the point of view of someone who is totally depressed, has lost the love of his life, his money, his home, his wallet, his job, etc. Do not mention any of these circumstances. Only describe the room. Now describe the same exact room again, from the point of view of a happy person. (This is, essentially, John Gardner's exercise from *The Art of Fiction*.)

∾ Now describe your character's kitchen. Make the kitchen say everything about your character's life. Open your character's bottom drawer, the drawer where she keeps mementos. What are they? How do they carry her past?

∾ Make a list of objects for each of the characters in your novel (or memoir or story). Specify the objects to the utmost. Not just chewing tobacco but Elephant Butts chewing tobacco.

PART
II

Getting There:
Finding a Structure

I copy what I admire. I pinch. I read not only for pleasure, but as a journeyman, and where I see a good effect, I study it and try to reproduce it. Like an actor will study a senior character and learn an effect of make-up or a particular slouchy walk for a role he's not thought of himself. He doesn't regard that as being particularly influenced by the actor, but as a trick of the trade which he owes it to himself to pick up.

—Lawrence Durrell

5.

Writing into a Structure

The search for models, in my terms, becomes a search for alternatives.
—C. D. Wright

WORK HABITS OF HIGHLY SUCCESSFUL AUTHORS was the title of an excellent panel at the July 2004 Pacific Northwest Writers Association Conference. Sitting on this panel were three hyper-productive writers: Carolyn See (six novels, three nonfiction books, and co-author of five more books), Donald E. McQuinn (nine novels), and Terry Brooks (twenty-three novels). These many-book authors had never before met and neither did they cheat and compare notes to get their stories straight. Their advice was identical. They each did two things. They wrote 1,000 words every day (with, I think, one day off a week). And they wrote into a structure. Write every day, each advised, one after the other. And, each elaborated, write into a structure.

Does writing into a structure (setting aside for a moment the question of *what* structure) conflict with writing practice — writing continuously without stopping until the timer goes off?

It doesn't conflict because you can write into a structure in the writing-practice manner. Besides, writing into a structure should be done in tandem with "discovery writing," that is, writing to learn what you have to say, writing to work out your thoughts, writing to find out what your antagonist thinks (by writing from her point of view in your notebook, even though in the finished story you are never going to be in her point of view).

Skipping discovery writing, deciding on a structure and then forcing material into it like stuffing a sausage may result in writing that is too thin, with a forced or contrived feel. Discovery writing — a term coined by Jack Remick and Robert Ray — in the writing-practice notebook makes the work richer and more layered and more insightful. But doing writing practice endlessly with no structure in mind puts you on the road to Never Never Land — never finishing, never publishing.

You write in your writer's notebook to find out what you have to say and then you deliberate on how to structure it and then you write it again, into its structure. In the midst of shaping and revising you may go back to your notebook to explore another aspect or to write for a second or third time to get to the bottom of it. There are writers who write entire novels, scene by scene, in their writer's notebook. Then, of course, they go home and type.

Writing to a form strikes some writers as a strange idea. But think of an assignment to write a sonnet. There are hundreds of sonnets, poems structured the same way, but which differ radically from one another in subject matter, language, image, tone. The form is the vessel. What goes into it is up to the writer.

These chapters on structure offer four prose structures, with models to illustrate each one. For each type of structure, we'll take a close look at a model and work through the steps of separating its structure from its content. This is a core skill that, with practice, will enable you to comprehend the structure of any piece of writing, much as an x-ray makes visible the skeleton, leaving in the dark all that these bones support.

Our four structures are:

THEME STRUCTURE
Diane Ackerman, "Mute Dancers: How to Watch
a Hummingbird"
Michael Ondaatje, "7 or 8 Things I Know About Her"

COLLAGE STRUCTURE
David Shields, "Spider's Stratagem"
Rebecca McClanahan, "Considering the Lilies"

TWO- OR THREE-STRAND (BRAID) STRUCTURE
Robert Bergman, "Blue Notes: Poetry and Psychoanalysis"
Albert Goldbarth, "Farder to Reache"

DRAMATIC STORY STRUCTURE
Tim Gautreaux, "Welding with Children"

When I set out to write a new piece into a structure that I've extracted from a model, I spend a large amount of time cogitating on what to write about. This rumination may take as much time as generating the first draft of the piece. It is helpful to pick a subject different from that of the model, because you will be living closely with the model for some time and you don't want to inadvertently ingest image or idea. You must work on material that is truly your own, of central importance to you. These are vital moves when you consciously put yourself under the influence of another writer. When we absorb the lessons of our models we incorporate neither subject matter, nor word, nor image, nor idea, but structure and technique. That we are working our own most urgent material acts as a counterweight to the model, allowing us to ultimately pull our own piece away altogether, with only scents or tints of its influence remaining. Finally, it is important that we use as models the work of a great variety of writers, because we are in the process of exploring, evolving, and speaking in our own voices. The last thing we want is to become a weak imitator of a predecessor writer.

Nothing here is offered in the spirit of an academic exercise. Who among us has time to waste? Everything here is intended to assist you in completing and polishing excellent, original, publishable works. There is no better way to build a body of work than to give yourself the assignment of writing into a particular structure, then writing into another structure, then into another...

FINDING THE RIGHT STRUCTURE

How to approach this part of your learning? I suggest reading this section of *The Writer's Portable Mentor* straight through and then going back and choosing a form to write a piece into. First study the structure and then choose a subject matter from among your concerns that is both different from that of the model and that might possibly fit the structure.

How to match content with structure? Think about the content. Does it suggest a narrative? That is, does it have a character in trouble or want (whether actual or fictional) with enough grit to fight his or her way out, for better or worse? If so the dramatic story structure illustrated by Tim Gautreaux's "Welding with Children" in Chapter 9 suggests itself. For example, I had a character, a woman in her forties, who'd spent her life not writing her own Ph.D. dissertation but instead helping her brilliant professor husband, who has now deserted her for another woman, a fellow professor. This is a significant complication, worthy of a story, I thought, and so the dramatic story structure seemed right.

("Living for Robert" appeared in *The Chaffin Journal*.) On the other hand, for a piece called "Stonework," I had my stone collection, my fascination with stones, the book I'd written on the rock that burns (coal), a collection of persons I might call "emotional stones," in other words, a little of this, a little of that. No real protagonist, but something to say. A collage suggested itself. Remember that this process is not arbitrary, but rather, organic. Think of molding your material into its most natural shape.

Practice abstracting the structure of works you read — essays or articles or short stories. This involves the skill of looking at the piece literally. Structure is carried in the following sorts of moves:

- What are the literal divisions — sections separated by a subtitle, a number, or by white space?
- How many paragraphs does each section contain? What are the transitional devices?
- Mark out the scenes. A scene takes place in one setting. If you shift settings you are writing a new scene. A scene is one episode, in which there is dialogue and/or some sort of action. Think of a scene as happening on stage in a theater. A scene shows you what is happening, when it is happening, where it is happening. Summary is different. Summary explains, summarizes what happened, but doesn't show it happening.
- New character comes on stage (Antagonist? Helper? Protagonist?) What is this character's role? That is structural.
- Dialogue carries the essential dramatic action and thus is structural.
- Shifts from concrete description or narration to passages of philosophy, insight, or metaphor are structural shifts.
- Compare the beginning to the end. Does the beginning mirror the end? This is structural.

~ Note all actions, whether mental or physical. Actions tend to
move a story forward and are structural.

The rewards of comprehending structures are great. Consider a new structure as an invitation to write not only a new piece but, for your own body of work, a new kind of piece. Some structures, such as the seemingly simple collage structure, can actually be quite challenging.

How many different structures are there for short fictions or nonfictions? That is impossible to say. Some writers have little interest in new structures, writing their great stories and fine essays into traditional structures. Others constantly try to find new structures, which sometimes work and sometimes begin to seem a bit gimmicky. Thinking about structure, reading *for* structure, and becoming savvier about writing *into* structures is an ongoing process that lasts for all the years of writing. The guideline, the goal for any given structure is that it fit or even intensify its content.

INVENTING A STRUCTURE

There is no need to invent a structure. Most works that are original in their ideas and fresh in their language use a traditional structure. Original works do not require an original structure.

But it's fun to invent structures. How to begin doing such a thing? Think first of what the content is asking for. Form exists to intensify meaning.

For example, I invented a creative nonfiction titled "Archaeology of Childhood." I grew up on a commercial dairy farm where my father was employed as the dairyman. The farm was our home. We children grew up there and returned there to visit our parents for two decades after we'd moved away. We felt that the farmhouse, barns, windmill, machine shed, and silo were "ours," though not in the sense of a property right.

Eventually, due to falling milk prices, the farm went out of business. The original owner died and the land was sold to a non-farmer who used its fields, woods, creeks, and marshes for duck hunting. The duck blinds were kept in repair but the other buildings stood in desuetude.

Decades later, with the permission of the new owner, we returned to see our old place. We walked down the rutted mile-long dirt road, now impassable by most vehicles. The farmhouse was still there, overgrown with Virginia creeper, uninhabited except by field mice. The barns, too, were extant, but collapsing, roofs caving in. The milkhouse, machine shed, rusting windmill — everything was there. It was eerie, like returning in a dream to the ruins of childhood. The word *archaeology* came to mind.

To shape "Archaeology of Childhood," about our return journey to that place and its memories, I used the form of an academic archaeology article. My bookish friend Greg Lange left two shopping-bagsful of archaeology tomes on my doorstep. From them I took the form, which includes numbered sections, lists of artifacts, descriptive paragraphs, and so on. Within the different sections, I used different kinds of sentences, sentences that reflected the feel of that section.

The content, you see, can suggest its own form.

Francine du Plessix Gray wrote a masterpiece essay titled "The Work of Mourning." It is a big, wide-ranging piece in which, among much else, she elaborates Elizabeth Kübler-Ross's five stages of grief: Denial, Anger, Bargaining, Depression, Acceptance. Gray's work is shaped in five parts. In the first part we don't even learn that the essay is actually about the death of her adored father when she was 10 years old. (First stage: Denial.)

I wrote a piece called "Genome Tome," which had twenty-three (very short) "chapters" — just as we have twenty-three pairs of chromosomes. The structure was not arbitrary but suggested by the content. One of the chapters comprises twenty-three questions pertaining to the meanings and implications of the Human Genome Project. The only alternative structure that suggested itself was one with forty-six "chapters," one for each chromosome (rather than *pair* of chromosomes), but that seemed a bit much.

One way to invent a form is to think of nonliterary texts. I think of Annie Proulx's *Postcards,* Michael Martone's "Contributor's Note," and many epistolary stories. I have yet to see a short-short based on milk-carton copy or cereal-box text but maybe soon I will.

STRUCTURING A BOOK

Are you writing a novel? A memoir? A how-to book? Collect ten examples of your genre (some you've read before, some new ones) and read them for structure. Write out these structures in your notebook. Then choose one that fits your story or design a fitting hybrid. Begin your own book by employing one of your found structures, modifying as you work along. By the time you finish your own work, it will have found its own shape.

Past reading counts for nothing here. When we remember a book we've read, even recently, we typically don't remember the structure, if we even noticed it in the first place. We remember the character or a tense moment or the setting or something that happens. So, for this work, it is necessary to reread for structure. To write down the structure, start with obvious divisions — paragraphs, sections, scenes, chapters.

This work will repay you many times. Making a serious study of structure is an indispensable stage of writing any full-length book. Many nonfiction books have a rather simple structure that you can discover by looking at the Contents page. In fact writers writing a nonfiction book should write the book into a simple list of chapters. Keep in mind that a nonfiction book is an object made up of chapters. It has a title page and a contents page. (If your book manuscript in progress has no title page and/or no contents page, put them in immediately! To be writing a book for years with no title page and no Contents is to be structurally oblivious. You may write until death and then we could bury your 1,000-plus pages with you.) It is my own belief that it is folly to make an outline with its Roman numerals, its Arabic numerals, its capital letters and lowercase letters, its endless permutations and degrees of hierarchy. Instead, make a simple list of chapters. Then write the book, chapter by chapter.

Here is the structure (the Contents) of a fine book by David B. Williams titled *The Street-Smart Naturalist: Field Notes from Seattle*:

1. The Eagles
2. The Fault
3. The Plants
4. The Creek
5. The Stone
6. The Geese
7. The Bugs
8. The Weather
9. The Hills
10. The Invaders
11. The Water
12. The Crows

Each chapter in *The Street-Smart Naturalist* is essentially an essay on its topic. Each chapter comprises an interesting mix of human and natural history along with the writer's personal experience.

Certain guidebooks contain indispensable instructions on deep structure. Novelists can learn to plot from Robert J. Ray and Bret Norris's *Weekend Novelist*, and no mystery writer should even begin without Robert J. Ray and Jack Remick's *The Weekend Novelist Writes a Mystery*. Nonfiction writers can grasp dramatic story structure from Jon

Franklin's *Writing for Story*. These books will save you years of trial and error. Read them. Do the exercises suggested. Master their contents.

Developing a structure is a core task required for writing a book. Begin exploring structure as you begin doing discovery writing and research. The structure is the framework you write into, your security blanket, your assurance that all your hard work will result in a completed manuscript.

WORD COUNTS

How long should a piece be? How many words? (In the world of professional publishing, we speak of word count, not numbers of pages.) How long is a book? How long is a newspaper article? How long is a short story? Here are some guidelines.

Articles in newspapers and magazines run from 500 to 1,000 words. A feature may be as long as 2,000 words. Among the many newspapers and magazines that use submissions from freelancers are (at this writing) *Newsweek*'s "My Turn" column (1,000–1,100 words); *The Smithsonian*'s back-page humor column (700 words); *The New York Times Magazine*'s "Lives" column (900–1,000 words); an article in the Travel section of *The New York Times* (1,400 words); and an opinion essay about a moral dilemma that appears in *The Christian Science Monitor* (600 words).

Micro-fictions are fun. The famous example is the six-word novel created by Ernest Hemingway on a bet: "For sale: baby shoes, never used." Flash fictions run from 25 words to 200 words. Typical short stories, personal essays, or creative nonfictions run from 1,000 to 6,000 words. (Diane Ackerman's "Mute Dancers" is 1,097 words. Tim Gautreaux's "Welding with Children" is 6,023 words.) A piece may run as long as 7,000 words, but it has to be rather spectacular to earn that much space in an issue.

Books have gotten shorter. An average-length book, whether novel or nonfiction, once ran to 100,000 words. But many books are now 60,000 words or 80,000 words. A book entered into the well-known Association of Writers and Writing Programs (AWP) prose competition (fiction or creative nonfiction) must have at least 50,000 words.

Word count is another way to think about deep structure. Let's say you are writing a set of creative nonfictions in which personal matters intersect with science. Or let's say you are writing a book of interconnected stories about the members of a single Chicago-based family. To complete your book you need ten 5,000-word pieces or you need twenty 2,500-word pieces, or some other combination that gets you up past 50,000 words.

There. You've got your assignment. Go for it!

HANDS ON: WRITING INTO STRUCTURES

After you've chosen a structure to try, make a list of the model's sections and, if it is not too long, its paragraphs. If you are looking at a short story, make a list of the scenes. Now make analogous paragraphs (if an essay) or scenes (if a story) for your own piece.

Write the paragraphs one by one in your writing-practice notebook. Type them up, and then begin working your language, extending a thought, eliminating, or further elaborating. Do the necessary research, write, and rewrite. After you've completed a draft, take one last look at your structure-model to make absolutely certain that you have not unconsciously taken word, image, or idea from your "teaching" piece, your model.

Then put the model aside and work on your own piece on its own terms.

6.

Theme Structure

Working within the self-imposed discipline of a particular form eases the prospect of having to reinvent yourself with each new piece.
—David Bayles and Ted Orland

THE THEME STRUCTURE IS A COMMON TRADITIONAL FORM. It is a perfect salad bowl for a remarkable variety of salads. It is a simple form that often states its subject in the title.

Let's begin by looking at Diane Ackerman's nine-paragraph piece on hummingbirds. Actually, let me rephrase that. Let's begin by reading "Mute Dancers" out loud, rather slowly. This is how, in the Advanced Short Forms Seminar, we take in a new piece. We read it paragraph by paragraph, each taking a turn to read. Read "Mute Dancers" this way with a buddy or read it out loud to yourself. To skim a piece is to get its gist but miss its structure. So we read out loud, as if we were schoolchildren.

Mute Dancers: How to Watch a Hummingbird
by Diane Ackerman

A lot of hummingbirds die in their sleep. Like a small fury of iridescence, a hummingbird spends the day at high speed, darting and swiveling among thousands of nectar-rich blossoms. Hummingbirds have huge hearts and need colossal amounts of energy to fuel their flights, so they live in a perpetual mania to find food. They tend to prefer red, trumpet-shaped flowers, in which nectar thickly oozes, and eat every 15 minutes or so. A hummingbird drinks with a W-shaped tongue, licking nectar up as a cat might (but faster). Like a tiny drum roll, its heart beats at 500 times a minute. Frighten a hummingbird and its heart can race to over 1,200 times a minute. Feasting and flying, courting and dueling, hummingbirds consume life at a fever pitch. No warm-blooded animal on earth uses more energy, for its size. But that puts them at great peril. By day's end, wrung-out and exhausted, a hummingbird rests near collapse.

In the dark night of the hummingbird, it can sink into a zombielike state of torpor; its breathing grows shallow and its wild heart slows to only 36 beats a minute. When dawn breaks on the fuchsia and columbine, hummingbirds must jump-start their hearts and fire up their flight muscles to raise their body temperature for another all-or-nothing day. That demands a colossal effort, which some can't manage. So a lot of hummingbirds die in their sleep.

But most do bestir themselves. This is why, in American Indian myths and legends, hummingbirds are often depicted as resurrection birds, which seem to die and be reborn on another day or in another season. The Aztec god of war was named Huitzilopochtli, a compound word meaning "shining one with weapon like cactus thorn," and "sorcerer that spits fire." Aztec

Mute Dancers

warriors fought, knowing that if they fell in battle they would be reincarnated as glittery, thuglike hummingbirds. The male birds were lionized for their ferocity in battle. And their feathers flashed in the sun like jewel-encrusted shields. Aztec rulers donned ceremonial robes of hummingbird feathers. As they walked, colors danced across their shoulders and bathed them in a supernatural light show.

While most birds are busy singing a small operetta of who and what and where, hummingbirds are virtually mute. Such small voices don't carry far, so they don't bother much with song. But if they can't serenade a mate, or yell war cries at a rival, how can they perform the essential dramas of their lives? They dance. Using body language, they spell out their intentions and moods, just as bees, fireflies or hula dancers do. That means elaborate aerial ballets in which males twirl, joust, sideswipe and somersault. Brazen and fierce, they will take on large adversaries — even cats, dogs or humans.

My neighbor Persis once told me how she'd been needled by hummingbirds. When Persis lived in San Francisco, hummingbirds often attacked her outside her apartment building. From their perspective she was on *their* property, not the other way round, and they flew circles around her to vex her away. My encounters with hummingbirds have been altogether more benign. Whenever I've walked through South American rain forests, with my hair braided and secured by a waterproof red ribbon, hummingbirds have assumed my ribbon to be a succulent flower and have probed my hair repeatedly, searching for nectar. Their touch was as delicate as a sweet bee's. But it was their purring by my ear that made me twitch. In time, they would leave unfed, but for a while I felt like a character in a Li'l

Mute Dancers

Abner cartoon who could be named something like "Hummer." In Portuguese, the word for hummingbird (*Beija flor*) means "flower kisser." It was the American colonists who first imagined the birds humming as they went about their chores.

Last summer, the historical novelist Jeanne Mackin winced to see her cat, Beltane, drag in voles, birds and even baby rabbits. Few things can compete with the blood lust of a tabby cat. But one day Beltane dragged in something rare and shimmery — a struggling hummingbird. The feathers were ruffled and there was a bit of blood on the breast, but the bird still looked perky and alive. So Jeanne fashioned a nest for it out of a small wire basket lined in gauze, and fed it sugar water from an eye dropper. To her amazement, as she watched, "it miscarried a little pearl." Hummingbird eggs are the size of coffee beans, and females usually carry two. So Jeanne knew one might still be safe inside. After a quiet night, the hummingbird seemed stronger, and when she set the basket outside at dawn, the tiny assault victim flew away.

It was a ruby-throated hummingbird that she nursed, the only one native to the East Coast. In the winter they migrate thousands of miles over mountains and open water to Mexico and South America. She may well have been visited by a species known to the Aztecs. Altogether, there are 16 species of hummingbirds in North America, and many dozens in South America, especially near the equator, where they can feed on a buffet of blossoms. The tiniest — the Cuban bee hummingbird — is the smallest warm-blooded animal in the world. About two and one-eighth inches long from beak to tail, it is smaller than the toe of an eagle, and its eggs are like seeds.

Mute Dancers

Hummingbirds are a New World phenomenon. So, too, is vanilla, and their stories are linked. When the early explorers returned home with the riches of the West, they found it impossible, to their deep frustration, to grow vanilla beans. It took ages before they discovered why — that hummingbirds were a key pollinator of vanilla orchids — and devised beaklike splinters of bamboo to do the work of birds.

Now that summer has come at last, lucky days may be spent watching the antics of hummingbirds. The best way to behold them is to stand with the light behind you, so that the bird faces the sun. Most of the trembling colors aren't true pigments, but the result of light staggering through clear cells that act as prisms. Hummingbirds are iridescent for the same reason soap bubbles are. Each feather contains tiny air bubbles separated by dark spaces. Light bounces off the air bubbles at different angles, and that makes blazing colors seem to swarm and leap. All is vanity in the end. The male's shimmer draws a female to mate. But that doesn't matter much to gardeners, watching hummingbirds patrol the impatiens as if the northern lights had suddenly fallen to earth.

~

Now, how do we extract the structure — separate the structure from the hummingbird content — of this piece? The key to abstracting structure is looking at the physical page. We count sections and paragraphs, quite literally. Ackerman, very likely, was writing to a word count ("Mute Dancers" with its 1,097 words, appeared in *The New York Times Magazine*). But for our purposes, it works better to count paragraphs: nine. So we have our structure assignment: Write a nine-paragraph piece on one thing.

"Mute Dancers" has no sections, whether numbered or subtitled or indicated by an extra space between blocks of type. Duly noted.

I like counting paragraphs instead of using a word count because a paragraph is a structural unit. A paragraph has one controlling idea, more or less. You can make a list of paragraphs by making a list of controlling ideas. It's like lining up a row of canning jars, each to be filled with tomatoes, beans, corn, or peaches. The paragraph-as-jar way of thinking about the task makes it seem quite doable. It's especially effective to take a daunting subject, one that seems unmanageable because emotionally tricky or because just too big, and give yourself the assignment: Write a piece on this subject in nine paragraphs. A big subject gives you plenty of material to work with and nine paragraphs gives you a good harness within which to do that work. You have now sidestepped one big problem with many short pieces: They are too slight, not meaty enough, too insubstantial. A short piece need not be slight, and it need not be the last word on the subject either. Writers return to subjects again and again. So you need not worry about wasting your big subject on one nine-paragraph piece.

When "copping a structure," I keep strictly to the given number of paragraphs, although this might cause one or more of my paragraphs to puff out rather big in its effort to contain everything I want to say. As the last step in this process, we discard the model and shape our piece however it wants to be shaped. At that time I break up my ballooning paragraphs into two or sometimes three paragraphs. But this makes only a minor variation on the structure: I'm still not writing a thirty-paragraph piece. To disregard the number of paragraphs at the beginning is to disregard the structure.

Indeed, because the theme structure is a non-dramatic structure that lacks the driving energy of a dramatic story in which there is a protagonist to identify with and high stakes and obstacles to overcome, it may require its very short length to work well. To take the nine-paragraph "Mute Dancers" and make it thirty paragraphs may doom it to the wastebasket.

Now, with assignment in hand, a nine-paragraph piece, what will your subject be? First principle: We will stay away from birds! We will stay as far from Ackerman's subject as possible because we don't want to consciously or unconsciously take word, image, or idea. Those are *her* words, *her* images, *her* experiences, and *her* ideas.

We do note that her subject matter is about a concrete (able to be perceived by a sense organ) creature. It is not about freedom, or nature, or love, or racial prejudice or the homeless — abstract subjects. It has a concrete object (the specific bird) to talk about. Here is the suggestion contained in her piece: If you want to write about nature, write about an earthworm or a walnut tree. If you want to write about love, write about your kid or your sweetheart. If you want to write about agribusiness, write about the 3,000-cow farm down the road with its huge manure lagoon that is stinking up the town.

So, our assignment is to write a nine-paragraph piece focused on something concrete. And, we make it a subject that is somehow core to our own concerns and experiences. This is a good guideline in any case, but it's especially important when we are consciously putting ourselves under the influence of another writer.

It is now time to return to the piece. Let's list the paragraphs in terms of what they are about. In other words, we will make a list consisting of the controlling idea of each paragraph.

Paragraph 1. Facts about hummingbirds (living fast, heartbeat).

Paragraph 2. Elaboration of the last fact enumerated in paragraph 1 (sleep slow).

Paragraph 3. Subject matter as seen by an ancient civilization (Aztecs).

Paragraph 4. More facts (body language for mating behavior).

Paragraph 5. Two personal stories (anecdotes) on subject matter, one a neighbor's, one the author's, ending with a sentence about the etymology of the name of the subject matter.

Paragraph 6. Another personal story (anecdote) from a different person (Beltane the cat).

Paragraph 7. Metafacts: species, statistics, number of miles of flight…

Paragraph 8. A second historical story (vanilla, early explorers).

Paragraph 9. A rhapsody about the subject matter that puts the author back in the story.

There are a couple of things to note here. Ackerman has written a natural-history piece about a bird, but she nevertheless includes three anecdotes relating experiences with the bird (hummingbird attack, cat bringing in bird, and her own red-ribbon experience). Two paragraphs look at the bird in terms of myth and history (the Aztec relationship to the bird and the explorers and vanilla plant). Ackerman puts herself into the piece twice (in the jungle and in the last paragraph, perhaps obliquely, when she writes, "Lucky days may be spent watching.…" Thus she makes personal a non-personal natural-history piece. She reaches out from the core story to connect to a wider world, while sticking strictly to her subject matter.

This is Ackerman's piece. Now, how do *I* proceed?

I want to write a piece (as of this writing, not yet written) on the color purple. Why purple? I came to purple, not arbitrarily, but while doing a writing practice on what my next work should be. It has emotional resonance because my beloved grandmother Olive Henry loved the color purple and had among her possessions many purple objects — purple pumps, vases, dresses, powder boxes, hairbrushes. Once I knitted her a purple shawl and I have a snapshot of her wearing that shawl. So I have picked a subject that I have an emotional connection to. It's not an arbitrary subject picked to complete an assignment. I have started to do discovery writing on the piece, which I will call "Purple Prose."

Now, using Ackerman's nine-paragraph structure, here is my initial list of paragraphs for "Purple Prose." This is not carved in stone but it gives me direction for writing a complete draft.

1. Facts about purple (lacks its own light-wave, red plus indigo).
2. Origin of the term "purple prose" written, I hope, in purple prose.
3. Cleopatra and her wearing of purple-dyed robes, the dye extracted from mollusks.
4. Further facts: purple pigment?
5. Anecdote: Mimi Weiss, a person I once knew, whose entire wardrobe was purple; Grandma Henry, her love of purple, the purple shawl I knitted for her.
6. Another personal story (do I have one?). Perhaps instead this could be about Alice Walker's novel *The Color Purple,* which meant a lot to me.
7. Metafacts: Modern purple dyes? Mystical notions about purple? Purple gems?
8. Second historical story: Han dynasty, or Aztecs and purple dye.
9. Some personal return to purple (my grandmother again?).

Here I have a structure to write into. It's not rigid. It could change. I am also in the process of doing the lexicon work and doing research. I have lists of purple things such as "Purple People Eater," which appear nowhere in the structure list but which may enter at some point. My work is nicely laid out. This is no longer a vague something-or-other on the color purple. It has a direction. I have a harness. And trust me. Even before it is written I can tell you it will look nothing like Diane Ackerman's marvelous piece on hummingbirds.

Now let's look at Michael Ondaatje's very different piece, a portrait of sorts. It is an example of a thematically structured piece with subtitled sections. It is, certainly, "creative nonfiction" though it occurs in a book of poems. Read it out loud.

7 or 8 Things I Know About Her: A Stolen Biography by Michael Ondaatje

The Father's Guns

After her father died they found nine guns in the house. Two in his clothing drawers, one under the bed, one in the glove compartment of the car, etc. Her brother took their mother out onto the prairie with a revolver and taught her to shoot.

The Bird

For a while in Topeka parrots were very popular. Her father was given one in lieu of a payment and kept it with him at all times because it was the fashion. It swung above him in the law office and drove back with him in the car at night. At parties friends would bring their parrots and make them perform what they had been taught: the first line from *Twelfth Night,* a bit of Italian opera, cowboy songs, or a surprisingly good rendition of Russ Colombo singing 'Prisoner of Love.' Her father's parrot could only imitate the office typewriter, along with the *ching* at the end of each line. Later it broke its neck crashing into a bookcase.

The Bread

Four miles out of Topeka on the highway — the largest electrical billboard in the State of Kansas. The envy of all Missouri. It

7 or 8 Things I Know About Her

advertised bread and the electrical image of a knife cut slice after slice. These curled off endlessly. 'Meet you at the bread,' 'See you at the loaf,' were common phrases. Aroused couples would park there under the stars on the open night prairie. Virtue was lost, 'kissed all over by every boy in Witchita.' Poets, the inevitable visiting writers, were taken to see it, and it hummed over the seductions in cars, over the nightmares of girls in bed. Slice after slice fell towards the earth. A feeding of the multitude in this parched land on the way to Dorrance, Kansas.

First Criticism
She is two weeks old, her mother takes her for a drive. At the gas station the mechanic is cleaning the windshield and watches them through the glass. Wiping his hands he puts his head in the side window and says, 'Excuse me for saying this but I know what I'm talking about — that child has a heart condition.'

Listening In
Overhear her in the bathroom, talking to a bug: 'I don't want you on me, honey.' 8 a.m.

Self-Criticism
'For a while there was something about me that had a dubious quality. Dogs would not take meat out of my hand. The town bully kept handcuffing me to trees.'

Fantasies
Always one fantasy. To be traveling down the street and a man in a clean white suit (the detail of 'clean' impresses me) leaps into her path holding flowers and sings to her while an invisible

---

7 or 8 Things I Know About Her

orchestra accompanies his solo. All her life she has waited for this and it never happens.

Reprise

In 1956 the electric billboard in Kansas caught fire and smoke plumed into a wild sunset. Bread on fire, broken glass. Birds flew towards it above the cars that circled round to watch. And last night, past midnight, her excited call. Her home town is having a marathon to benefit the symphony. She pays $4 to participate. A tuxedoed gentleman begins the race with a clash of cymbals and she takes off. Along the route at frequent intervals are quartets who play for her. When they stop for water a violinist performs a solo. So here she comes. And there I go, stepping forward in my white suit, with a song in my heart.

≈

How do we analyze the structure of Michael Ondaatje's strangely evocative piece? (Note that his punctuation is in British form, as befits a Canadian writer.) First, as always, we look at the physical page. There are eight parts, each with a title. Of what does each consist? Each part consists of a telling anecdote about the "her" of the title. The anecdotes relate to essential matters: father, father's bird, bread (nourishment, young love), subject as infant, a piece of dialogue, another piece of dialogue (both germane to who she is), the fantasy, and then the fantasy become reality.

The very shortness of the sections are key. The fact that the anecdotes seem to relate to something essential: birth, death, love. This piece is about a person; could such a form work for a place? Could it work for a dog or an elephant? It seems essential that it is about one individual being. We also note that there are two repeated icons, the white suit and the bread billboard.

HANDS ON: WRITING THE PIECE

Most any idea or ideal, place, plant, animal, or building, or any number of other matters work within this structure. Among the theme-structured pieces I've composed are "Solitude," "Studio," and "Nooks, Caverns, and Corners." A stunning example of a titled theme piece is Emily R. Grosholz's "On Necklaces."

What might work for you using this structure? Do a writing-practice session for twenty minutes or a half-hour. If you had only five years to live, what subject matters would you certainly want to write about? After doing this discovery writing, make a list of every subject that came up. Now which of these might work as a theme-structured essay?

Choose the one that attracts you and begin writing it by "Jump-Starting an Essay or Story" (page 18). And consider, Could you do one of these per month?

Finally, build your own collection of models based on this structure. You will see how delicious and commodious a form it can be.

7.

Collage Structure

The meeting of two or more distant realities on an unfamiliar plane.
—Artist Max Ernst's definition of collage.

IN THE VISUAL ARTS, A COLLAGE IS AN AMALGAMATION of disparate objects — fruit labels, burlap, magazine cutouts, words printed on newspaper, wood, a nail, a spoon. The elements composing a collage may have little or no obvious relationship before they are brought together within the collage. Often the elements are found objects — not themselves generated by the artist. The German artist Kurt Schwitters was one of the early masters of the form and another was Joseph Cornell with his black-painted boxes fitted with objects hoarded from flea markets and junk shops to reveal an inner world. The Swiss artist Meret Oppenheim, a master collagist most famous for her fur-covered teacup, is yet another. Spend real time gazing at the work of these and other collagists to get inspired and get ideas. The found objects found in visual-arts collages may be simulated in a literary collage by using quotations — words found elsewhere.

But what does "amalgamation of distant objects" mean when your materials are words, words, and more words? Well, think of the different shapes words can take: list, haiku, joke, anecdote. Scripture. Lecture. Yarn, story, poem.

David Shields is a leading proponent and practitioner of literary collage. Here is one of his, with its elements being mostly quotations drawn from a variety of sources.

Spider's Stratagem by David Shields

"If you grow up not with toys bought in the shop but things that are found around the farmyard, you do a sort of bricolage. Bits of string and wood. Making all sorts of things, like webs across the legs of a chair. And then you sit there, like the spider. The urge to connect bits that don't seem to belong together has fascinated me all my life." (W. G. Sebald)

~

"The line of beauty is the line of perfect economy." (Emerson)

~

"Collage is a demonstration of the many becoming the one, with the one never fully resolved because of the many that continue to impinge upon it." (Donald Kuspit)

~

"While we tend to conceive of the operations of the mind as unified and transparent, he [Daniel Dennett, author of *Consciousness Explained*] suggests that they are chaotic and opaque. There is no invisible 'boss' in the brain, no 'central meaner,' no unitary self in command of our activities and

Spider's Stratagem

utterances. There is no internal spectator of a 'Cartesian theatre' in our heads to applaud the march of consciousness across its stage." (Adam Zeman)

~

"...the law of mosaics: how to deal with parts in the absence of wholes." (Ronald Sukenick)

~

"To tell a story has become strictly impossible. In short, it is not the anecdote that is lacking, only its character of certainty, its tranquility, its innocence." (Alain Robbe-Grillet)

~

Story seems to say everything happens for a reason, and I want to say, no, it doesn't.

~

"Plots are for dead people." (Lorrie Moore)

~

The absence of plot leaves the reader room to think about other things.

~

"All definitions of montage...imply that meaning is not inherent in any one shot but is created by the juxtaposition of shots. Simply and dramatically, this basic principle of editing was demonstrated by an experiment conducted by Lev Kuleshov, an early Russian filmmaker. He intercut images of an actor's expressionless face with images of a bowl of soup, a woman in a coffin, and a child with a toy. Audiences who saw the film praised the actor's performance; they saw in his face, emotionless as it was, hunger, grief, and affection. They saw, in other words, what was not really there in the separate images. Meaning and emotion, then, were created not by the content of the individual

Spider's Stratagem

images, but by the relationship of the images to each other."
(Vivian and Thomas Sobchack)

~

"Everything I wrote, I believed instinctively, was to some extent
collage. Meaning, ultimately, seemed a matter of adjacent data."
(William Gibson)

~

For Kuleshov, montage meant a juxtaposition of disparate,
or clashing, scenes. But as Eisenstein used the term, it didn't
refer strictly to clashing scenes, but to the use of individual
and separate scenes that "added up" to a meaning or an overall
context — a context that isn't contained in any individual scene.

~

Renata Adler's collage-novel *Speedboat* captivates by tension,
its jagged and frenetic changes of pitch and tone and voice. She
confides, she reflects, she tells a story, aphorizes, undercuts it,
then undercuts that. If she's cryptic in one paragraph, she's clear
in the next. She changes subjects like a brilliant schizophrenic,
making unpredictable leaps that make a kind of irrational sense.
Bed talk, uninhibited by conventions. Ideas, experiences, and
emotions are inseparable. She's always present, teasing things
apart. There's very little that's abstract. I can feel her breathe.
"The point has never quite been entrusted to me," she says, and
so we must keep reading, for we know there will be another way
of looking at everything. The book has suspense and momentum.
She's promising us something; something is around the corner.
How long can she go on this way? I don't know, but timing
is everything. She has to quit before we do, and still give an
oblique, sly sense of satisfaction, of closure. You can see her
working hard in the last paragraph.

Spider's Stratagem

~

"A great painting comes together, just barely." (Picasso)

~

Momentum, in literary mosaic, derives not from narrative but the subtle, progressive build-up of thematic resonances.

~

"...the shapely swirl of energy holding shattered fragments in place, but only just." (Sven Birkerts's description of John Edgar Wideman's novel *Philadelphia Fire)*

~

Collage is pieces of other things. Their edges don't meet.

~

"The collage technique, that art of reassembling fragments of pre-existing images in such a way as to form a new image, is the most important innovation in the art of the [twentieth] century.... Found objects, chance creations, ready-mades (mass-produced items promoted into art objects) abolish the separation between art and life. The commonplace is miraculous if rightly seen, if recognized." (Charles Simic)

~

"You don't make art, you find it." (Simic)

~

"The question is not what you look at, but what you see." (Thoreau)

~

"...plunged into a world of complete happiness in which every triviality becomes imbued with a significance..." (Joseph Cornell)

~

"...the singular obsessions endlessly revised..." (Thomas Lux)

Spider's Stratagem

~

"The task is not primarily to have a story, but to penetrate the story, to discard the elements of it that are merely shell, or husk, that give apparent form to the story, but actually obscure the essence. In other words, the problem is to transcend the givens of a narrative." (Deborah Eisenberg)

~

As a moon rocket ascends, different stages of the engine do what they must to accelerate the capsule. Then each is jettisoned until only the capsule is left with the astronauts on its way to the moon. In linear fiction, the whole structure is accelerating toward the epiphanic moment, and certainly the parts are necessary for the final experience, but I still feel that we could jettison all the pages leading to the epiphany, so I'm left with Gabriel Conroy and his falling faintly, faintly falling, and I'm heading to the moon in the capsule. In collage, every fragment is a capsule: I'm on my way to the moon on every page.

~

"Method of this project: literary montage. I need say nothing. Only exhibit. I won't filch anything of value or appropriate any ingenious turns of phrase. Only the trivia, the trash — which I don't want to inventory, but simply allow it to come into its own in the only way possible: by putting it to use. This project must raise the art of quotation without quotation marks to the very highest degree." (Walter Benjamin)

~

"In collage, writing is stripped of the pretense of originality and appears as a practice of mediation, of selection and contextualization, a practice, almost, of reading."
(Shelley Jackson)

Spider's Stratagem

~

"There are two kinds of filmmaking: Hitchcock's (the film is complete in the director's mind) and Coppola's (which thrives on process). For Hitchcock, any variation from the complete internal idea is seen as a defect. The perfection already exists. Francis's approach is to harvest the random elements that the process throws up, things that were not in the filmmaker's mind when he began." (Coppola's editor Walter Murch)

~

"The usual reproach against the essay, that it is fragmentary and random, itself assumes the givenness of totality and suggests that man is in control of totality. The desire of the essay, though, is not to filter the eternal out of the transitory; it wants, rather, to make the transitory eternal." (Theodor Adorno)

~

"...nonlinear, discontinuous, collage-like, semi-fictional, semi-nonfictional assemblage..." (David Markson's description of his own work)

~

Alain Robbe-Grillet's *Ghosts in the Mirror,* which he calls a "Romanesque," is a quasi-memoir with philosophical reflections, intimate flashes, and personal addresses to the reader. The problem of scale is interesting. How long will the reader stay engaged? I don't mean stay dutifully but stay charmed, seduced, and beguiled. About this length, I think. In his case, 174 pages.

~

"The purpose of art is to impart the sensation of things as they are perceived and not as they are known. Art exists that one may recover the sensation of life; it exists to make one feel things, to make the stone stony." (Victor Shklovsky)

Spider's Stratagem

~

"It may be that nowadays in order to move us, abstract pictures need, if not humor, then at least some admission of their own absurdity — expressed in genuine awkwardness, or in an authentic disorder." (Adam Gopnik)

~

"Any opportunity that a writer has to engage the reader intimately in the very act of creating the text is an opportunity to grab onto. White space does that…. I don't ever want to be bored, and I certainly don't ever want any of my readers to be bored. I'd much rather risk them getting annoyed and frustrated than bored." (John D'Agata)

~

"I use the example of a grandfather clock, a wristwatch, and one of these new liquid-crystal watches. The grandfather clock is the reflection of its historical period when time was orderly and slow. Tick-tock. Tick-tock. Tick-tock. When there was something monumental and solid about time. It stood there in the front hall in its great, carved case, with a pendulum like the sun or the moon. By the 1930s and '40s, my era, we had wristwatches that were neurotic and talked very fast, tick-tick-tick-tick — with a sweep-second hand going around. Today, we have watches that don't show any time at all until you press a button. Then the numbers show up. And when you take your finger off, time disappears." (Robert Dana)

~

"If fiction has a main theme, a primary character, an occupation, a methodology, a criterion, a standard, a purpose (is there anything left for fiction to have?), it would be time itself. One basic meaning of narrative, then: to create time where there was

Spider's Stratagem

none. A fiction writer who tells stories is a maker of time. Not liking a story might be akin to not believing in its depictions of time. To the writer searching for the obstacle to surpass, time would look plenty worthy a hurdle. If something must be overcome, ruined, subverted in order for fiction to stay matterful (yes, maybe the metaphor of progress in literary art is pretentious and tired *at this point* (there's time again, aging what was once such a fine idea)), then time would be the thing to beat, the thing fiction seemingly cannot do without, and therefore, to grow or change, must. Time must die." (Ben Marcus)

∽

"Stephen Dobyns has said that every lyric poem implies a narrative. What he means is a sequence of past events, left out of the poem, that brought the speaker to the present, intensified moment in the poem.... But the lyric poet might just as easily say that every narrative poem obscures a lyric. The man in the restaurant crushing a wine glass in his hand acts out an emotional complex not wholly explained by a hard day at the office, or being cheated in the taxi, or what his companion just said. If the narrative writer is instinctively curious about the individuating 'story,' the distinct sequence of events preceding that table and that wine glass, the lyric poet may be as naturally drawn to the isolated human moment of frustration, the distilled indelible peak on the emotional chart." (Ellen Bryant Voigt)

∽

When plot shapes a narrative, it's like knitting a scarf. You have this long, long piece of string and many choices about how to knit, but we understand a sequence was involved, a beginning and an end, with one part of the weave logically and sequentially

Spider's Stratagem

connected to the next. You can figure out where the beginning is and where the last stitch was cast off.

Webs look orderly, too, but unless you watch the spider weaving, you'll never know where it started. It could be attached to branches or table legs or eaves in six or eight places. You won't know the sequence in which the different cells were spun and attached to each other. You have to decide for yourself how to read its patterning, but if you pluck it at any point, the entire web will vibrate.

~

Shields's spiderweb collage defending collage as a literary form in a sense works also as a theme piece — each of the components separated by a dingbat speaks to an aspect of the form. Many of the quotes are "found," lifted out of another context, and these are interspersed with Shields's own comments. The meaning of any given block of type is elaborated and complicated by adjacent blocks of type.

Certainly, there are similarities between a theme piece with titled sections and a collage. One could argue that Michael Ondaatje's "7 or 8 Things I Know About Her" is a collage. Yet each section is an anecdote and each is written by the author. None is a found object, introduced from a context foreign to the new piece being composed. The form of each section is similar: A list does not sit next to a poem. Think of cows lined up in their stanchions in a milking barn. Each cow is an individual but each is also a cow. So the titled sections in a theme piece vary in what they say but not in how they say it. In contrast, the elements in a collage may be more like a cow, a pencil, a rope, a doll.

Definitions aside, what subject matters might work well in this structure? Certainly one in which there are a number of discrete objects pertaining to the same theme, about which you have no desire to create a narration. You have no story with a complication or serious situation at the beginning, a protagonist who sets out to do something about it, a series of actions progressively rising in dramatic tension.

A form of the collage is the abecedarium, the A to Z familiar from childhood alphabet books. This type of collage has twenty-six sections, one for each letter of the alphabet. One I wrote titled "My Brain on My Mind" progresses from A for Alphabet, to B for Brain, to C for Consciousness, down to Z for Zero. Dinty W. Moore composed one on fathers, with twenty-six titled sections that include D for Divorce and F for Father Knows Best. William Boyd's abecedariums include one on the great Russian writer Anton Chekov (A for Anton, C for Critics).

What is this form good for? It is a cathedral form, a considerable space to contain and thankfully to restrain a large subject. As I began building "My Brain on My Mind," I felt the need for even more constraint, so required each section to conclude with the opening word of the following section, a move I learned from William Boyd.

When you first become entranced with this form, you will find it a bit like a puzzle. You'll have three *l*'s, four *d*'s, and no *x*'s. You keep working until the puzzle resolves. (Which *A* is most essential? Could *Alzheimer's* become *Dementia*?)

Another type of collage proceeds by means of numbered sections. (The numbered sections of a collage must be short. Many essays that are completely un-collagelike comprise rather long numbered sections.) In a numbered collage, the numbers, it seems to me, should have some bearing on the subject. Could you write a forty-part piece on turning 40?

Our second example of a collage is "Considering the Lilies" by Rebecca McClanahan.

Considering the Lilies by Rebecca McClanahan

If God had wanted us to be nudists, we would have been born that way. That's what a woman's voice was saying, right there on the *Joe Pyne Show*. Thirty years later I remember her flustered reply. She had called in to register indignation at a nudist — clothed for the camera — who had been stating his case.

~

In the long stretch between wives, my brother dated women who, in his words, *could wear clothes*. Doesn't everyone wear clothes, I wondered, failing to see that the emphasis was on *wear* — an active word, something a woman's body did to the clothes. He came dangerously close to falling in love with a secretary with whom he spent lunch hours, marveling as she modeled before the three-way mirrors of posh shops. She always left with a shopping bag full.

How can you afford it? he asked one day.

She smiled wryly, as if amused at the question. He recalls that her reply struck him like a sexual betrayal: I shoplift, of course. Don't tell me, after all this time, you haven't known.

~

If you're a woman who doesn't *wear* clothes, you know it. There is always something amiss — off-toned stockings, a lining that grabs. You check yourself in the mirror, once, twice. Turn to the side, girdle your abdomen, rehearse a subtle smile. You think this moment will hold. Fifteen minutes into the party, the moment-before-the-mirror unravels. Something is amiss, you're not sure what. Something is not holding.

~

In an early Woody Allen film, a poor and lovely girl sits opposite him at a table, her skin flawless as a petal. It's their first date, and she wears a hat with a small feather.

Considering the Lilies

Nice hat, he says. I've seen them around, in those big bins.
She shakes her head, confused. She had hoped to please him.
Yes, I'm sure, he insists. Whole bins of them. All over
the city.

~

Somewhere in this city is a woman with my body and my taste
in clothes. She can afford the taste. I shadow her, snatching up
her discards a season after she steps out of them. *Gently worn,*
the proprietor calls the clothes in her shop. She tells me there is
a celebrity consignment store in Beverly Hills where women pay
thousands of dollars for a dress that belonged to Liz or Barbra.
The woman I am shadowing is client number sixty-eight. I don't
know her name and don't wish to, but I would know her clothes
anywhere. The proprietor watches as I enter. She says she can
predict which jacket I will approach, which pair of slacks. I like
to imagine the phantom woman. Does she shop in my grocery
store? Has she passed me in the aisles and recognized herself in
this stranger wearing her clothes?

~

My friend, a stylish gay man in his late seventies, has beautiful
hands and always wears a bandanna at his neck. Twice a month
we go to dinner. His eyes are shutters clicking on the most
elegant man or woman in the restaurant. In his youth he was a
fashion photographer.

They were exquisite, he recalls of the models from the
forties. Simply exquisite.

He's arriving within the hour to pick me up. I search my
closet. Once, years ago, he complimented me: it was a plain black
dress with large lapels, and I'd paid too much for it. I wore it

THE WRITER'S PORTABLE MENTOR

Considering the Lilies

with my favorite necklace, a loop of pearls my father had given
me when I turned eighteen.

My friend said, You should see yourself in this light, with
your head turned just so.

~

We wear what we wore when we were happiest, the fashion
consultant says. The boardwalk at Atlantic City is littered
with the past — cigarette-leg capris on aging tanned women,
lacquered bouffants under pastel nets. In the upscale mall of my
city, young wives shop for pinafore-bibbed dresses that tie in
the back. From birth to death, and all stations between, we are
swaddled and bound. Even the bible has a dress code. Ashes and
sackcloth for mourning, white linen for angels and the newly
resurrected. Rich men wear soft clothing, Job wears worms on
his flesh. You can spot a virtuous woman by the purple silk, an
enemy by his sheepish clothing. Promises and threats abound:
I will clothe you in riches and honor. Then, in your lamentation,
rend and tear what covers you.

~

Here, my father would say, handing my mother some bills. Buy
yourself something. You're worth it. Splurge. My father loved
beautiful clothes, and wanted a wife who loved them too. While
he was stationed in Japan, he commissioned a tailor to fashion
two suits for my mother. One was blue silk, the other boiled wool
the color of milk chocolate. Both were lined in maroon taffeta on
which her initials were stitched in gold thread.

My mother always took the money he offered. Hours later,
she returned with skirts for her daughters, trousers for her
sons, sometimes a bolt of stiff fabric from which she would sew
curtains, tablecloths, house dresses.

Considering the Lilies

~

We put an outfit on layaway, my best friend wrote. It was 1963
and the news was important enough to warrant the 3,000-
mile mail route from the town our family had recently left.
She enclosed intricate sketches of an olive-green three-piece
ensemble, exclaiming over its versatility, how it would carry her
through several seasons. Reading the letter, I remembered all the
Saturdays I'd walked to the department store with her, visiting
an item that would be released after the first or fifteenth of the
month, when her widowed mother got paid. I was small then, so
I didn't notice — until many years later — how small their house
was. Her mother was small, too, and worked long hours to buy
the clothes her daughter coveted.

~

The day shift is ending. Three women shuffle from the mill's
gray exterior, wearing names and younger faces on identification
badges. Shoulder bags, weighted with the day's needs, hang
nearly to their knees. One woman has tucked stretch pants
into high-heeled boots. One matches all over. The third wears a
beaded belt cinched so tight that her stomach blooms beneath
and above. Their efforts make me sad. How many bins have I
rummaged with these women? In dreams we tumble together
in huge bargain barrels, smothered in ginghams, tweeds, tartan
plaids. We dive deep, searching for logos. I have a butcher knife
and I'm thinking when I find a label that matters I will slash it
into shreds — This one's for you, Pierre, and for you, Donna —
but it's too late, they've arrived ahead of us again, vandalizing
their names as if ashamed to be linked with us: seconds, slightly
irregular, imperfect. We crawl from the bin, grasping our prizes.

~

Considering the Lilies

Laura Ashley, the comedian says. For the woman whose goal in life is to look like wallpaper.

~

The magazine photographer lights upon some woman on the street, a school teacher this time. She will appear in next month's issue, beneath the heading *Fashion Don'ts,* her eyes x'ed out as if she's been caught in a crime beyond belief. The blindfold is a gift, the kindness of an executioner who cancels out the prisoner's last view: *She never knew what hit her.*

~

Condemned girls, under SS guard, spent their last days ripping sleeves off coats and replacing them with sleeves of different colors. They painted the back of each coat with a red bull's-eye for the marksman stationed above the electric fence. Some prisoners threw themselves against it. In the morning the girls tied belts around the ankles of the dead and dragged the bodies to the meadow. If a dress suited, if a pair of shoes fit, they took it.

~

If we were in the chemo ward, we would sadden or sympathize, but here in this uptown Bohemian restaurant, our young waitress is beautiful and admired, her white scalp visible, black hair bristling from each follicle. Fashion, I decide, is mostly context.

Stunning, says a middle-aged man seated with a forgettable woman at a nearby table. He can't take his eyes off the waitress.

Fashion also implies option, choice. The same runway frame a designer hangs dresses on, holds up the gown of the dying woman I visit each week. She sucks on ice chips, her cheekbones the kind that plump girls reading magazines would die for.

~

Considering the Lilies

In the dream I am standing with my dead mother before her closet, arguing about what she should wear for eternity. I suggest the blue silk with maroon lining. She pulls out a pair of paint-speckled dungarees.

Mother! I cry.

I don't see why it matters, she says. As long as it's comfortable.

～

My friend, a middle-aged man recently divorced, tells me how simple it once seemed — how, as a young man, all he wanted was a woman who looked good in a suit. One afternoon thirty years into the marriage, his wife walked out of a dressing room *wearing* a suit. He was stunned to realize he not only possessed his desire, but had possessed it all these years. In the same moment, he realized it was not enough.

It was the saddest day of my life, he said.

～

It's 1965, and I'm sharing a bed with my cousin the night before her wedding. She's eight years older, petite and boyish, still a virgin.

In the dark she says to the ceiling, I have the kind of body that only looks good naked. The tone is half lament, half expectation. For years she's been hiding beneath her clothes a lovely secret which is about to be spoken.

～

Rebecca McClanahan's "Considering the Lilies" repays the effort not only to count the seventeen sections, but to note the location of dreams, anecdotes, and passages with dialogue. Note that there is a frame: It begins and ends with nakedness. Note how the mood sinks (the low point being the girls in the death camp) and then rises again.

HANDS ON: MAKING A COLLAGE

For the creator, forms open doors. Discovering the collage has catalyzed a number of works for me, and this is what happens when you begin working within any specific form. The form itself opens up the subject matter in unique and interesting ways.

Think of a collage as a type of patchwork quilt. The first step may be to begin a literary ragbag — a file for quotes and your own thoughts around a subject. Currently, for example, I am filling such a ragbag with thoughts and quotes on teaching writing. Then the juxtaposing may be a matter of matching or contrasting colors, of likes and opposites, of elaborations and contradictions.

How do you sustain interest? What about closure, since a collage could in principle dribble on forever? (Consider matching beginning and end.) How long should individual sections be? Overly long sections will undermine the form. If, while making a quilt, you include as one piece a bedsheet, you have shifted into a different form.

Collect your own examples of the form to study and learn from. Brilliant collages that have recently come under my eyes include Patrick Madden's "On Laughter," C. D. Wright's "Hidebound Opinions, Propositions, and Several Asides from a Manila Envelope Concerning the Stuff of Poets," and "Grace Notes" by Brian Doyle (who calls this lovely form a mosaic).

8.

Two- or Three-Strand (Braid) Structure

You don't really have a workable idea until you combine two ideas.
—Twyla Tharp

THE TWO-STRAND STRUCTURE TAKES TWO TOPICS and weaves them. Each pulls on the other, stretches the other, pushes against the other. It is a useful way to work your way into a new piece because the technique itself pulls you, the writer, along. Thinking of Thread No. 1 in a certain way forces you to consider Thread No. 2 in that way too. Like so many writing strategies, it is not only a writing plan but also a thinking plan.

Comparing something that interests you to something else that also interests you can open the door to several new pieces. You look at the first through the lens of the second, and then turn it around and look at the second through the lens of the first.

Our first model, "Blue Notes: Poetry and Psychoanalysis," compares poetry and psychoanalysis, as specified by the title, but Robert L. Bergman introduces a third thread, music, in the first paragraph. A hallmark of this structure is that both or all three threads are introduced immediately. Bergman begins his piece with a poem by T. S. Eliot.

Blue Notes: Poetry and Psychoanalysis
by Robert L. Bergman

In T. S. Eliot's "Four Quartets," a fragment in Part 1, "Burnt Norton," reads:

Words move, music moves
Only in time; but that which is only living
Can only die. Words, after speech, reach
Into the silence. Only by the form, the pattern,
Can words or music reach
The stillness, as a Chinese jar still
Moves perpetually in its stillness.
Not the stillness of the violin, while the note lasts,
Not that only, but the co-existence,
Or say that the end precedes the beginning,
And the end and the beginning were always there
Before the beginning and after the end.
And all is always now. Words strain,
Crack and sometimes break, under the burden,
Under the tension, slip, slide, perish,
Decay with imprecision, will not stay in place,
Will not stay still.

Blue Notes

Poetry and psychoanalysis strain words to their limits. Poets, analysts and analysands need to express the almost inexpressible. We try to convey the essence of our experience, including the pertinent facts, the associated memories and the passions. An approach to a complete account of any moment in the life of one person, let alone two together, would require hours of saying or chapters of writing unless some method could force meaning upon meaning into a few symbols. Music is wonderful in that way. Beethoven's 16th quartet op. 135 or Louis Armstrong and His Hot Seven playing *West End Blues* compress whole worlds into sound. The limitation of music, though, is its leaving out the concrete details. Richard Strauss did claim that he could describe anything, even the taste of lager beer, in music, but even he needed the poet and librettist Hugo van Hofmannsthahl to supply some of the specifics.

Words are wonderfully specific. Sentences like "Turn left at the third traffic light and go two blocks" are perfect in their lack of ambiguity, but it is the very lack of ambiguity that cripples speech in its attempt to express anything like the subtlety, contradictoriness and many-layeredness of actual life. Words are like pianos, organs or xylophones that can only play tones that are exactly a half-step apart. Voices and many instruments can produce an infinite gradation of pitches, but our system of notation is like the piano: the worlds of sound between the lines are hard to express. The African ancestors of jazz include quarter-steps or simply unstable tones, and so jazz players need to find ways of producing blue notes, the ones that occur in the crack between two piano keys. Sometimes pianists hit those adjacent keys together to render something like the note between them. When we speak and write, to get the whole palette of existence

Blue Notes

we have to somehow hit the notes in the cracks between adjacent words, because words tend to be stuck in place without the give that, say, a trombone has. One of the simplest ways of hitting the meaning in the crack is through the simple juxtaposition of words that are on either side: an oxymoron like "make haste slowly." Other tropes are more complicated, but each is a method of locating meaning between, around and over the words as tent poles and stakes hold a tent in place but are not the tent.

Fortunately, we have practiced this sort of expression every night of our lives. All people are poets when they make their dreams. Writers can do it when they are awake, too. Freud seems to have had relatively little appreciation of one of his great achievements: the recognition of dreams as poems, and the resulting expansion of the freedom of written poetry to be dreamlike. Nine years after the publication of Freud's *The Interpretation of Dreams,* T. S. Eliot wrote: "Let us go then, you and I / When the evening is spread out against the sky / Like a patient etherised upon a table." What few early readers the poem found mostly said that the lines meant nothing, as many people before 1900 had said that dreams meant nothing. In demonstrating that dreams mean something, Freud needed only to demonstrate single meanings. He appreciated but did not emphasize that dreams are little things that mean a lot. Eliot and other poets of the early twentieth century broke loose from the custom of having any obvious meaning, and so were able to write poems whose dreamlike nature emphasized how many more things than one they meant. In "The Love Song of J. Alfred Prufrock," the word *evening* is stretched beyond its usual limits by its including the concept of sunset along with many other connotations. We often use *sunset* to imply evening, but not

Blue Notes

commonly the reverse as here, where clearly what is spread is the last light spreading from the sun to clouds all along the horizon. But then there is the startling simile of the anesthetized surgical patient. Prufrock announces at the beginning of his love song that he sees everywhere a torturous pull between beauty and the customs and qualities of the machine age. He is timidly stuck in a role determined by his place in an affected and artificial society, but longs for real contact with the natural and the transcendent. He is helpless against the forces at work on him, and can only long for something more genuine and vigorous. "I should have been a pair of ragged claws / Scuttling across the floors of silent seas." The strangeness and ambiguity of everything from the start forces all kinds of questions: What kind of love song is this, and to whom is it addressed? Among the answers that satisfy me is that it is a song of someone to himself, someone afraid to sing out loud. Eliot lived his life backwards. When he was young he seems to have been like the timid old Prufrock, and when he was old he became the vigorous lover of his young wife, and instead of writing about the wasteland he wrote about quite energetic cats. In his uncertain youth he must have feared never being able to say what he meant and be understood, and of not being able to appeal to others as one who heard them well:

And I have known the eyes already, known them all—
The eyes that fix you in a formulated phrase,
And when I am formulated, sprawling on a pin,
When I am pinned and wriggling on the wall,
Then how should I begin
To spit out all the butt-ends of my days and ways?
And how should I presume?

Blue Notes

...

It is impossible to say just what I mean!
But as if a magic lantern threw the nerves in patterns on a
  screen:
Would it have been worth while
If one, settling a pillow or throwing off a shawl,
And turning toward the window should say,
  "That is not it at all,
  That is not what I meant at all."

He was intent on writing in a way that could not be formulated, and created a great work that still leaves us finding new significance almost a century later.

In my opinion, formulations are the bane of psychoanalysis and of criticism of poetry. Though I don't like Archibald MacLeish's poem very much (because it has a tendency to mean), I agree with his famous lines: "A poem should not mean / but be." Neither poems nor dreams are ciphers to be decoded. Someone conveys some part of existence in a form that someone else can appreciate; that is, the audience when fully responsive to the created expression has a similar intuition of experience as the writer / dreamer had. Art does not relate to existence as hat-check relates to hat, but as soup relates to soup bone. One is not a token of the other but an essence of the other. It is useful sometimes for an analyst to say about a dream or some other creation, "I think one of the things you mean is..." but to imply that only one thing is meant not only misses all the other points, but worse yet implies that the analysand has put his meaning into code only to avoid facing something squarely. Of course, we do disguise our meaning for that reason all the time,

Blue Notes

but that is not the only thing we are up to. Every dream, joke, memory and so forth expresses so much that a full analysis of it would be similar to the whole analysis of which it is a tiny part.

Our analytic heritage tends to lead us into the error of formulation. Freud had what seems to me an odd idea that he expressed in *The Interpretation of Dreams*. He said that dreams were largely visual images which could be translated into verbal dream thoughts, and that the original dream thought existed in words in the dreamer's mind before he or she translated and disguised it in pictures. This cumbersome theory implies that unconscious primary process is in words even though words are poorly suited to expressing the sorts of thinking we infer primary process to be. If the dream thoughts were in words originally, then we would be justified in seeing dreams as coded messages, not as works of art. It seems to me much more lifelike to assume that our moment-to-moment experience exists in every sense modality we possess. Some of our experience is verbal thought and is in words or thought summaries of collections of words, but much of what is on our minds is experienced in touch, taste, nonverbal hearing, bodily tensions and movements and so forth. Dreams, poems and other creations cram all sorts of experience into something that expresses them, and a reader or an analyst needs to respond to many levels of meaning at once.

When we respond we are an appreciative audience, which is satisfying in and of itself, and when it is the creation of an analysand that we are appreciating, the other person's perceiving us as getting her or him is part of what is therapeutic. But beyond that we are in a position to be a useful critic. I do not mean someone who points out what could be better in a work of art, but someone who helps others to appreciate the work.

Blue Notes

Great poetry is not obvious or easy to grasp because it means so much. A good critic is perceptive and practiced in responding to art. Critics need historical knowledge so that they know what various parts of the poem (or dream) refer to. As skilled readers of poetry, we can help others to know poems. As analysts, we are sometimes in the odd position of being the critic who helps the artist appreciate her or his own work.

By our appreciation we also increase our analysands' skill as poets. Some come to us already skilled. Many years ago, I heard a schizophrenic young man say that as he was beginning to fall apart he would go into his family's corn field, where he could see only corn and sky, and imagine that he was hiding there, "the last survivor of a defeated army." But many people who come to see us think at the beginning that they need to tell us the facts in simple and even hackneyed ways. If we can make it safe to say anything to us and respond in ways that are appreciative and, if possible, poetic and playful, analysands will reward us with beautiful evocations of their experience. These can be dreams, images, memories or almost anything. When things are going well, these bits of poetry become leitmotifs that run throughout years of the analysis. Someone I work with told me years ago that one of his favorite movie scenes is from *Monty Python and the Holy Grail*. In order to be allowed to cross a bridge, a traveler must be able to answer questions put by the troll who guards it. The traveler who answers wrong is punished by being plunged into the abyss below. The hapless member of the group is relieved to be asked an easy question, "What's your favorite color?" "Blue," he answers. "Wrong!" the troll shouts, and down he goes. This person's parents consistently acted as if his own idea of himself was wrong, and when something comes up about his

Blue Notes

believing or not in the validity of his own experience, one or the other of us is likely to shout, "What's your favorite color?"

First memories, as Sullivan pointed out, are poems on the subject of who people believe themselves to be. My second psychotherapy patient was an enormous and muscular but anxious young man. When I asked his earliest memory, he said, "A big yellow chicken." Many other memories can be poems expressing a great deal about a person's basic perceptions and dilemmas. Someone told me that her mother, who was highly skilled in generating her own glamorous appearance but had little regard for her daughter, and especially for her daughter's appearance, was wonderful at costumes and makeup. One year when this person was in elementary school, she begged her mother to do her up as a witch for a Halloween party. It was unusual for the daughter to ask for anything, and it took a lot of asking before the mother finally gave in and made her into a wonderful and frightening witch. But when they got to the party, the little witch was struck shy and, much to the mother's dissatisfaction, could not bring herself to go in.

We often hear shorter but still eloquent figures of speech. An analyst with whom I consult told me that her patient, reporting on the onset of a new bout of her terrible self-doubt, said that she had just encountered "the first emissary from the pit of pain."

Besides eloquence, poems and poetic expressions have a certain stillness to them. A work of art is not propaganda or cries of pain or lust. (Even though there is some truth in the remark that the operas of Verdi are battle cries and the operas of Puccinni mating calls.) Making art out of experience distills the experience and puts it into a form that can be contemplated. Two

Blue Notes

people engaged together in that contemplation is analysis at its best. At its worst it is the intrusion into the private experience of one person of the formulating and destroying voice of another.

I have heard the mermaids singing, each to each.

I do not think that they will sing to me.

I have seen them riding seaward on the waves
Combing the white hair of the waves blown back
When the wind blows the water white and black.

We have lingered in the chambers of the sea
By sea-girls wreathed with seaweed red and brown
Till human voices wake us, and we drown.

∼

Bergman's piece is 2,400 words long (eleven paragraphs, some of them quite long), bookended and hinged at the center with lines from two different T. S. Eliot poems. It is here reprinted from a psychoanalytic newsletter, and is an appropriate length for any number of literary journals or magazines (it would be too long for a newspaper piece). Bergman simplifies the concepts by using only one poet (and only two poems) to talk about poetry.

Let's abstract the structure, paragraph by paragraph. We will make a list of paragraphs, making sure to note which threads are in each one.

Paragraph 1. Poetry and psychoanalysis express the inexpressible. Music almost does. This paragraph introduces all three threads. Note that the first sentence includes two of the threads.

Paragraph 2. Words are too unambiguous to express reality. So are piano keys. Psychoanalysis and poetry can play the "blue notes" of jazz, the notes between the two definite piano keys, by putting opposites together. Paragraph includes all three threads.

Paragraph 3. Dreams are poems. Freud liberated poets to write dreamlike poems. Analyzes Eliot's poem for its dreamlike qualities. (No music thread.)

Middle Section: lines from the poem.

Paragraph 4. A comment on the poem.

Paragraph 5. Formulations are the bane of both poetry and psychoanalysis. (No music thread.)

Paragraph 6. Dreams and poems (and all art forms) are experienced with all the senses. (No music thread.)

Paragraph 7. Common characteristics of good literary critics and good analysts: they both appreciate the expression. (No music thread.)

Paragraph 8. Skilled analysands are already poets. Analysts should be an appreciative audience. (No music thread.)

Paragraph 9. First memories (psychoanalysis) are poems (poetry) on the subject of who people believe themselves to be. (No music thread.)

Paragraph 10. Analysts often hear short but eloquent figures of speech. "Figures of speech" is a literary term and thus refers to the poetry thread. (No music thread.)

Paragraph 11. We make art out of experience. This last paragraph brings the music thread back in.

End. More of "The Love Song of J. Alfred Prufrock."

Each paragraph treats an aspect of the similarities between poetry and psychoanalysis, and sometimes music. The generalizations are backed up, always, with evidence — psychoanalytic stories or critical analysis of the poem (with specific examples from music sometimes added). Bergman is extremely familiar with both poetry and psychoanalysis. Thus he has a wealth of specific examples and stories to draw on.

How to think about using this structure? First think about two worlds you know well. How could you bring them together?

I am thinking of writing a piece on farming and writing. I might think of ten ways farming and writing are similar.

1. Farming and writing both require daily work.
2. Farming and writing both have a vast store of knowledge and information attached.
3. Farming and writing were both once learned by apprenticeship and are now often learned in professional educational institutions.
4. Farming and writing both involve a lot of solitude.

And so on. You see how it works.

Our second two-strand model is Albert Goldbarth's ten-paragraph, 500-word "Farder to Reache." Goldbarth compares views on the structure of the universe with views on the structure of verse.

Farder to Reache by Albert Goldbarth

Kepler was born in 1571. He knew about as much of the night sky and its mysteries as anyone alive in his time. We might say his skull contained the sky of the 16th and early 17th centuries, held it in place like a planetarium dome. Today we still haven't improved on his famous Three Laws of Planetary Motion.

Farder to Reache

And yet the notion that the universe might be infinite —
that there wasn't an outermost sphere of stars that bound it all
in — terrified him, filled him with what he termed "secret,
hidden horror.... One finds oneself wandering in this immensity
in which are denied limits and center."

This is, of course, the dread of free verse, that one might
fall into Whitman and freefloat directionlessly forever. Whitman
calls himself "a Kosmos," and in "Song of Myself" the vision
is of a creation whose parts are "limitless" and "numberless" —
these words and their kin are used with manic glee and with
a great intentionality. This is poetry's announcement of the
given of 20th century astronomy: the universe is, so far as we
know, unbounded.

But it isn't easy to walk through a day of fists and kisses,
paychecks, diaperstains, tirejacks, and our buildingblock
aspirations, with the mind fixed on infinity. Every year in
beginning poetry classes hands startle up in protest of free verse,
"it isn't poetry," which is metered and rhymed, and so is a kind
of map of Kepler's universe.

John Donne's poems, for instance — he was born one year
after Kepler. And he praises his lover by placing her at the center
of an onion-ring sky: "so many spheres, but one heaven make,"
and "they are all concentric unto thee."

And yet as early as 1577 — Kepler was only six years old —
the British astronomer Thomas Digges undid the outer sphere,
and published a vision of stars in endlessness: "Of which lights
celestiall, it is to bee thoughte that we onely behoulde sutch as
are in the inferioure partes... even tyll our sighte being not able
farder to reache or conceyve, the greatest part rest by reason of
their wonderfull distance invisible unto us."

Farder to Reache

Perhaps infinity isn't discovered along a timeline of gathering progress, but by certain sensibility, no matter when it lives.

In that land of simultaneous sensibility, I think that I could knock on Kepler's door and invite him out for some beers with Whitman. Really, he's flinging his cloak on now.

It's a foggy night as we sit around the veranda overlooking the lake. The sky is cloudy, and so are my two friends' faces — they don't know each other, are guarded, and rely on me to ease the conversation.

I do, though; or maybe it's the beer. It turns out we can shoot the shit all night, stein after stein, anecdote on anecdote, until the first light swarms over the water like thistledown on fire. Then the fog disappears — which is, of course, the day clearing its throat for clear speech.

~

What can we learn from Goldbarth's humorous and brilliant piece? Instead of bringing together two like things, he brings together two opposite ways of looking at the world, the closed-and-safe way and the open-and-potentially-chaotic way. (Dichotomous ways of looking at the world: wildly romantic and strictly practical; mystical and rational; dutiful and willful; stay-at-home and wanderlust.) Then Goldbarth speaks about these two ways of looking at the world not in general but as personified by specific persons working within two specific realms.

Now, with this piece, I would not, in fact, go through and enumerate Goldbarth's paragraphs and then list my own analogous paragraphs in preparation for writing an analogous piece. Why not? Because Goldbarth's form itself is so original and so extremely short that

I cannot imagine doing so and not ending up with an imitative piece of my own, even given an entirely different subject matter. And that is the last thing I want.

But I will take the underlying idea of considering two opposite ways of looking at the world (perhaps introvert and extrovert) and I will consider the strategy of using actual persons whether living or historical to personify the two outlooks.

HANDS ON: WRITING THE PIECE

The two- or three-strand form invites many sorts of pieces and you will want to explore its riches by adding it to your repertoire of structures.

∽ First, begin your own collection of models. Among those I admire is T. Coraghessan Boyle's "Chicxulub," which alternates between a teenage daughter and the danger she is in, and the danger of a meteor hitting the earth. Jane Kramer's "The Reporter's Kitchen" mixes writing and cooking (this reporter cannot write without cooking and her account of this difficulty is both hilarious and breathtaking in its virtuosity).

∽ Again list out the key subjects that interest you, that would repay research and reflection. Make a list of ten subjects. Now which of these might be compared? Which contain analogous requirements and attributes (like poetry and psychoanalysis). Which contain opposite requirements and attributes (like closed cosmology and formal poetry vs. open cosmology and free verse)? Who whether historical or living stands for this way of looking at the world?

∽ Now, begin a piece in your writer's notebook. Write the piece. Make it the first of a series.

9.

Dramatic Story Structure

Most short stories focus on a main character.... We expect the character's experiences will change him / her, because change is the way we perceive that something has happened.... Readers are also very much interested in the struggle toward that change.

—Charles Brashear

THE LAST STRUCTURE OFFERED HERE, ILLUSTRATED BY Tim Gautreaux's "Welding with Children," is the dramatic story structure ("story" refers to both nonfiction and fiction). It begins with a problem or complication, which the protagonist then attempts to solve in a rising series of dramatic actions (a series of efforts, directed against obstacles, each one more intense than the last). The story has a protagonist, an antagonist, and a helper. The problem or complication is ultimately resolved (a resolution can be happy or unhappy, success or failure).

This is the structure Aristotle was talking about in *Poetics*. For him, plot is "an imitation of an action that is complete, and whole, and of a certain magnitude; for there may be a whole that is wanting in magnitude. A whole is that which has a beginning, a middle, and an end."*

The dramatic story structure is old, reliable, faithful, and remains the structure of choice for any number of short stories, articles, and essays. There are writers who think it is the only way to write a piece. Two instruction books that I would not be without elaborate this dramatic structure for fiction and nonfiction. They are Janet Burroway's *Writing Fiction* and Jon Franklin's *Writing for Story*. It's important for writers to command dramatic story structure if only to comprehend how non-dramatic structures must rely on something *else* to drive them forward. Or to comprehend how, in some cases, a piece constructed in a seemingly different form, such as a collage, can be powered by an underlying dramatic structure.

Note two key strategies that inform successful dramatic stories. First, the story's problem or complication, the thing that sets it off, should be *important* (not "wanting in magnitude," as Aristotle put it). A trivial complication will give you a trivial story, guaranteed. Second, the complication should be something that the protagonist attempts to solve (whether successfully or not) *by his or her own efforts.* Passive protagonists don't make good stories because it is the protagonist's actions to solve the problem that move the story forward. Often, before the protagonist resolves the complication, he or she must arrive at a new understanding of what the complication is. Note how, in "Welding with Children," our model just ahead, the protagonist increasingly, step by step, comes to understand that the problem is *his* problem. Part of the progression

---

* Aristotle, *Poetics,* translated by S. H. Butcher, available online at The Internet Classics Archive website (http://classics.mit.edu/Aristotle/poetics.html).

of the story is his progression in taking responsibility for the mess his grandchildren are in.

Now let's read "Welding with Children" out loud, without speeding.

Welding with Children by Tim Gautreaux

Tuesday was about typical. My four daughters, not a one of them married, you understand, brought over their kids, one each, and explained to my wife how much fun she was going to have looking after them again. But Tuesday was her day to go to the casino, so guess who got to tend the four babies? My oldest daughter also brought over a bed rail that the end broke off of. She wanted me to weld it. Now, what the hell you can do in a bed that'll cause the end of a iron rail to break off is beyond me, but she can't afford another one on her burger-flipping salary, she said, so I got to fix it with four little kids hanging on my coveralls. Her kid is seven months, nicknamed Nu-Nu, a big-head baby with a bubbling tongue always hanging out his mouth. My second-oldest, a flight attendant on some propeller airline out of Alexandria, has a little six-year-old girl named Moonbean, and that ain't no nickname. My third-oldest, who is still dating, dropped off Tammynette, also six, and last to come was Freddie, my favorite because he looks like those old photographs of me when I was seven, a round head with copper bristle for hair, cut about as short as Velcro. He's got that kind of papery skin like me, too, except splashed with a handful of freckles.

When everybody was on deck, I put the three oldest in front the TV and rocked Nu-Nu off and dropped him in the Portacrib. Then I dragged the bed rail and the three awake kids out through the trees, back to my tin workshop. I tried to get something done, but Tammynette got the big grinder turned on and jammed a file against the stone just to laugh at the sparks.

Welding with Children

I got the thing unplugged and then started to work, but when I was setting the bed rail in the vise and clamping on the ground wire from the welding machine, I leaned against the iron and Moonbean picked the electric rod holder off the cracker box and struck a blue arc on the zipper of my coveralls, low. I jumped back like I was hit with religion and tore those coveralls off and shook the sparks out of my drawers. Moonbean opened her goat eyes wide and sang, "Whoo. Grendaddy can bust a move." I decided I better hold off trying to weld with little kids around.

I herded them into the yard to play, but even though I got three acres, there ain't much for them to do at my place, so I sat down and watched Freddie climb on a Oldsmobile engine I got hanging from a willow oak on a long chain. Tammynette and Moonbean pushed him like he was on a swing, and I yelled at them to stop, but they wouldn't listen. It was a sad sight, I guess. I shouldn't have that old greasy engine hanging from that Kmart chain in my side yard. I know better. Even in this central Louisiana town of Gumwood, which is just like any other red-dirt place in the South, trash in the yard is trash in the yard. I make decent money as a now-and-then welder.

I think sometimes about how I even went to college once. I went a whole semester to LSU. Worked overtime at a sawmill for a year to afford the tuition and showed up in my work boots to be taught English 101 by a black guy from Pakistan who couldn't understand one word we said, much less us him. He didn't teach me a damn thing and would sit on the desk with his legs crossed and tell us to write nonstop in what he called our "portfolios," which he never read. For all I know, he sent our tablets back to Pakistan for his relatives to use as stove wood.

Welding with Children

The algebra teacher talked to us with his eyes rolled up like his lecture was printed out on the ceiling. He didn't even know we were in the room, most of the time, and for a month I thought the poor bastard was stone-blind. I never once solved for X.

The chemistry professor was a fat drunk who heated Campbell's soup on one of those little burners and ate it out the can while he talked. There was about a million of us in that classroom, and I couldn't get the hang of what he wanted us to do with the numbers and names. I sat way in the back next to some fraternity boys who called me "Uncle Jed." Time or two, when I could see the blackboard off on the horizon, I almost got the hang of something, and I was glad of that.

I kind of liked the history professor and learned to write down a lot of what he said, but he dropped dead one hot afternoon in the middle of the pyramids and was replaced by a little porch lizard that looked down his nose at me where I sat in the front row. He bit on me pretty good because I guess I didn't look like nobody else in that class, with my short red hair and blue jeans that were blue. I flunked out that semester, but I got my money's worth learning about people that don't have hearts no bigger than bird shot.

Tammynette and Moonbean gave the engine a long shove, got distracted by a yellow butterfly playing in a clump of pigweed, and that nine-hundred-pound V-8 kind of ironed them out on the backswing. So I picked the squalling girls up and got everybody inside, where I cleaned them good with Go-Jo.

"I want a Icee," Tammynette yelled while I was getting the motor oil from between her fingers. "I ain't had a Icee all day."

"You don't need one every day, little miss," I told her.

Welding with Children

"Don't you got some money?" She pulled a hand away and flipped her hair with it like a model on TV.

"Those things cost most of a dollar. When I was a kid, I used to get a nickel for candy, and that only twice a week."

"Icee," she yelled in my face, Moonbean taking up the cry and calling out from the kitchen in her dull little voice. She wasn't dull in the head; she just talked low, like a bad cowboy actor. Nu-Nu sat up in the Portacrib and gargled something, so I gathered everyone up, put them in the Caprice, and drove them down to the Gumwood Pak-a-Sak. The baby was in my lap when I pulled up, Freddie tuning in some rock music that sounded like hail on a tin roof. Two guys I know, older than me, watched us roll to the curb. When I turned the engine off, I could barely hear one of them say, "Here comes Bruton and his bastardmobile." I grabbed the steering wheel hard and looked down on the top of Nu-Nu's head, feeling like someone just told me my house burned down. I'm naturally tanned, so the old men couldn't see the shame rising in my face. I got out, pretending I didn't hear anything, Nu-Nu in the crook of my arm like a loaf of bread. I wanted to punch the older guy and break his upper plate, but I could see the article in the local paper. I could imagine the memories the kids would have of their grandfather whaling away at two snuff-dripping geezers. I looked them in the eye and smiled, surprising even myself. Bastardmobile. Man.

"Hey, Bruton," the younger one said, a Mr. Fordlyson, maybe sixty-five. "All them kids yours? You start over?"

"Grandkids," I said, holding Nu-Nu over his shoes so maybe he'd drool on them.

The older one wore a straw fedora and was nicked up in twenty places with skin cancer operations. He snorted. "Maybe

Welding with Children

you can do better with this batch," he told me. I remembered then that he was also a Mr. Fordlyson, the other guy's uncle. He used to run the hardwood sawmill north of town, was a deacon in the Baptist church, and owned about 1 percent of the pissant bank down next to the gin. He thought he was king of Gumwood, but then, every old man in town who had five dollars in his pocket and an opinion on the tip of his tongue thought the same.

I pushed past him and went into the Pak-a-Sak. The kids saw the candy rack and cried out for Mars Bars and Zeroes. Even Nu-Nu put out a slobbery hand toward the Gummy Worms, but I ignored their whining and drew them each a small Coke Icee. Tammynette and Moonbean grabbed theirs and headed for the door. Freddie took his carefully when I offered it. Nu-Nu might be kind of wobble-headed and plain as a melon, but he sure knew what an Icee was and how to go after a straw. And what a smile when that Coke syrup hit those bald gums of his.

Right then, Freddie looked up at me with his green eyes in that speckled face and said, "What's a bastardmobile?"

I guess my mouth dropped open. "I don't know what you're talking about."

"I thought we was in a Chevrolet," he said.

"We are."

"Well, that man said we was in a —"

"Never mind what he said. You must have misheard him." I nudged him toward the door and we went out. The older Mr. Fordlyson was watching us like we were a parade. I was trying to look straight ahead. In my mind, the newspaper bore the headline, LOCAL MAN ARRESTED WITH GRANDCHILDREN FOR ASSAULT. I got into the car with the kids and looked back

Welding with Children

out at the Fordlysons where they sat on a bumper rail, sweating through their white shirts and staring at us all. Their kids owned sawmills, ran fast-food franchises, were on the school board. They were all married. I guess the young Fordlysons were smart, though looking at that pair, you'd never know where they got their brains. I started my car and backed out onto the highway, trying not to think, but to me the word was spelled out in chrome script on my fenders: BASTARDMOBILE.

On the way home, Tammynette stole a suck on Freddie's straw, and he jerked it away and called her something I'd only heard the younger workers at the plywood mill say. The words hit me in the back of the head like a brick, and I pulled off the road onto the gravel shoulder. "What'd you say, boy?"

"Nothing." But he reddened. I saw he cared what I thought.

"Kids your age don't use language like that."

Tammynette flipped her hair and raised her chin. "How old you got to be?"

I gave her a look. "Don't you care what he said to you?"

"It's what they say on the comedy program," Freddie said. "Everybody says that."

"What comedy program?"

"It comes on after the nighttime news."

"What you doing up late at night?"

He just stared at me, and I saw that he had no idea of what *late* was. Glendine, his mamma, probably lets him fall asleep in front of the set every night. I pictured him crumpled up on that smelly shag rug his mamma keeps in front of the TV to catch the spills and crumbs.

When I got home, I took them all out on our covered side porch. The girls began to struggle with jacks, their little ball

Welding with Children

bouncing crooked on the slanted floor, Freddie played tunes on his Icee straw, and Nu-Nu fell asleep in my lap. I stared at my car and wondered if its name had spread throughout the community, if everywhere I drove people would call out, "Here comes the bastardmobile." Gumwood is one of those towns where everybody looks at everything that moves. I do it myself. If my neighbor Miss Hanchy pulls out of her lane, I wonder, Now, where is the old bat off to? It's two-thirty, so her soap opera must be over. I figure her route to the store and then somebody different will drive by and catch my attention and I'll think after them. This is not all bad. It makes you watch how you behave, and besides, what's the alternative? Nobody giving a flip about whether you live or die? I've heard those stories from the big cities about how people will sit in an apartment window six stories up, watch somebody take ten minutes to kill you with a stick, and not even reach for the phone.

I started thinking about my four daughters. None of them has any religion to speak of. I thought they'd pick it up from their mamma, like I did from mine, but LaNelle always worked so much, she just had time to cook, clean, transport, and fuss. The girls grew up watching cable and videos every night, and that's where they got their view of the world, and that's why four dirty blondes with weak chins from St. Helena Parish thought they lived in a Hollywood soap opera. They also thought the married pulpwood truck drivers and garage mechanics they dated were movie stars. I guess a lot of what's wrong with my girls is my fault, but I don't know what I could've done different.

Moonbean raked in a gaggle of jacks, and a splinter from the porch floor ran up under her nail. "Shit dog," she said, wagging her hand like it was on fire and coming to me on her knees.

Welding with Children

"Don't say that."

"My finger hurts. Fix it, Paw-Paw."

"I will if you stop talking like white trash."

Tammynette picked up on fivesies. "Mamma's boyfriend, Melvin, says *shit dog.*"

"Would you do everything your mamma's boyfriend does?"

"Melvin can drive," Tammynette said. "I'd like to drive."

I got out my penknife and worked the splinter from under Moonbean's nail while she jabbered to Tammynette about how her mamma's Toyota cost more than Melvin's teeny Dodge truck. I swear I don't know how these kids got so complicated. When I was their age, all I wanted to do was make mud pies or play in the creek. I didn't want anything but a twice-a-week nickel to bring to the store. These kids ain't eight years old and already know enough to run a casino. When I finished, I looked down at Moonbean's brown eyes, at Nu-Nu's pulsing head. "Does your mammas ever talk to y'all about, you know, God?"

"My mamma says *God* when she's cussing Melvin," Tammynette said.

"That's not what I mean. Do they read Bible stories to y'all at bedtime?"

Freddie's face brightened. "She rented *Conan the Barbarian* for us once. That movie kicked ass."

"That's not a Bible movie," I told him.

"It ain't? It's got swords and snakes in it."

"What's that got to do with anything?"

Tammynette came close and grabbed Nu-Nu's hand and played the fingers like they were piano keys. "Ain't the Bible full of swords and snakes?"

Welding with Children

Nu-Nu woke up and peed on himself, so I had to go for a plastic diaper. On the way back from the bathroom, I saw our little book rack out the corner of my eye. I found my old Bible stories hardback and brought it out on the porch. It was time somebody taught them something about something.

They gathered round, sitting on the floor, and I got down amongst them. I started into Genesis and how God made the earth, and how he made us and gave us a soul that would live forever. Moonbean reached into the book and put her hand on God's beard. "If he shaved, he'd look just like that old man down at the Pak-a-Sak," she said.

My mouth dropped a bit. "You mean Mr. Fordlyson? That man don't look like God."

Tammynette yawned. "You just said God made us to look like him."

"Never mind," I told them, going on into Adam and Eve and the Garden. Soon as I turned the page, they saw the snake and began to squeal.

"Look at the size of that sucker," Freddie said.

Tammynette wiggled closer. "I knew they was a snake in this book."

"He's a bad one," I told them. "He lied to Adam and Eve and said not to do what God told them to do."

Moonbean looked up at me slow. "This snake can talk?"

"Yes."

"How about that. Just like on cartoons. I thought they was making that up."

"Well, a real snake can't talk, nowadays," I explained.

"Ain't this garden snake a real snake?" Freddie asked.

"It's the devil in disguise," I told them.

Welding with Children

Tammynette flipped her hair. "Aw, that's just a old song. I heard it on the reddio."

"That Elvis Presley tune's got nothing to do with the devil making himself into a snake in the Garden of Eden."

"Who's Elvis Presley?" Moonbean sat back in the dust by the weatherboard wall and stared out at my overgrown lawn.

"He's some old singer died a million years ago," Tammynette told her.

"Was he in the Bible, too?"

I beat the book on the floor. "No, he ain't. Now pay attention. This is important." I read the section about Adam and Eve disobeying God, turned the page, and all hell broke loose. An angel was holding a long sword over Adam and Eve's downturned heads as he ran them out of the Garden. Even Nu-Nu got excited and pointed a finger at the angel.

"What's that guy doing?" Tammynette asked.

"Chasing them out of Paradise. Adam and Eve did a bad thing, and when you do bad, you get punished for it." I looked down at their faces and it seemed that they were all thinking about something at the same time. It was scary, the little sparks I saw flying in their eyes. Whatever you tell them at this age stays forever. You got to be careful. Freddie looked up at me and asked, "Did they ever get to go back?"

"Nope. Eve started worrying about everything and Adam had to work every day like a beaver just to get by."

"Was that angel really gonna stick Adam with that sword?" Moonbean asked.

"Forget about that darned sword, will you?"

"Well, that's just mean" is what she said.

Welding with Children

"No it ain't," I said. "They got what was coming to them."
Then I went into Noah and the Flood, and in the middle of
things, Freddie piped up.

"You mean all the bad people got drownded at once?
All right!"

I looked down at him hard and saw that the Bible was
turning into one big adventure film for him. Freddie had already
watched so many movies that any religion he would hear about
would nest in his brain on top of *Tanga the Cave Woman* and
Bikini Death Squad. I got everybody a cold drink and jelly
sandwiches, and after that I turned on a window unit, handed
out Popsicles, and we sat inside on the couch because the heat
had waked up the yellow flies outside. I tore into how Abraham
almost stabbed Isaac, and the kids' eyes got big when they saw
the knife. I hoped that they got a sense of obedience to God out
of it, but when I asked Freddie what the point of the story was,
he just shrugged and looked glum. Tammynette, however, had an
opinion. "He's just like O. J. Simpson!"

Freddie shook his head. "Naw. God told Abraham to do it
just as a test."

"Maybe God told O. J. to do what he did," Tammynette sang.

"Naw. O. J. did it on his own," Freddie told her. "He didn't
like his wife no more."

"Well, maybe Abraham didn't like his son no more
neither, so he was gonna kill him dead and God stopped him."
Tammynette's voice was starting to rise the way her mother's did
when she'd been drinking.

"Daddies don't kill their sons when they don't like them,"
Freddie told her. "They just pack up and leave." He broke apart
the two halves of his Popsicle and bit one, then the other.

Welding with Children

Real quick, I started in on Sodom and Gomorrah and the burning of the towns full of wicked people. Moonbean was struck with Lot's wife. "I saw this movie once where Martians shot a gun at you and turned you into a statue. You reckon it was Martians burnt down those towns?"

"The Bible is not a movie," I told her.

"I think I seen it down at Blockbuster," Tammynette said.

I didn't stop to argue, just pushed on through Moses and the Ten Commandments, spending a lot of time on number six, since that one give their mammas so much trouble. Then Nu-Nu began to rub his nose with the backs of his hands and started to tune up, so I knew it was time to put the book down and wash faces and get snacks and play crawl-around. I was determined not to turn on TV again, but Freddie hit the button when I was in the kitchen. When Nu-Nu and me came into the living room, they were in a half circle around a talk show. On the set were several overweight, tattooed, frowning, slouching individuals who, the announcer told us, had tricked their parents into signing over ownership of their houses, and then evicted them. The kids watched like they were looking at cartoons, which is to say, they gobbled it all up. At a commercial, I asked Moonbean, who has the softest heart, what she thought of kids that threw their parents in the street. She put a finger in an ear and said through a long yawn that if the parents did mean things, then the kids could do what they wanted to them. I shook my head, went in the kitchen, found the Christmas vodka, and poured myself a long drink. I stared out in the yard to where my last pickup truck lay dead and rusting in a pile of wisteria at the edge of the lot. I formed a little fantasy about gathering all these kids into my Caprice and heading out northwest to start

Welding with Children

over, away from their mammas, TVs, mildew, their casino-mad grandmother, and Louisiana in general. I could get a job, raise them right, send them to college so they could own sawmills and run car dealerships. A drop of sweat rolled off the glass and hit my right shoe, and I looked down at it. The leather lace-ups I was wearing were paint-spattered and twenty years old. They told me I hadn't held a steady job in a long time, that whatever bad was gonna happen was partly my fault. I wondered then if my wife had had the same fantasy: leaving her scruffy, sunburned, failed-welder husband home and moving away with these kids, maybe taking a course in clerical skills and getting a job in Utah, raising them right, sending them off to college. Maybe even each of their mammas had the same fantasy, pulling their kids out of their parents' gassy-smelling old house and heading away from the heat and humidity. I took another long swallow and wondered why one of us didn't do it. I looked out to my Caprice sitting in the shade of a pecan tree, shadows of leaves moving on it, making it wiggle like a dark green flame, and I realized we couldn't drive away from ourselves. We couldn't escape in the bastardmobile.

In the pantry, I opened the house's circuit panel and rotated out a fuse until I heard a cry from the living room. I went in and pulled down a storybook, something about a dog chasing a train. My wife bought it twenty years ago for one of our daughters but never read it to her. I sat in front of the dark television.

"What's wrong with the TV, Paw-Paw?" Moonbean rasped.

"It died," I said, opening the book. They squirmed and complained, but after a few pages they were hooked. It was a good book, one I'd read myself one afternoon during a thunderstorm. But while I was reading, this blue feeling got me. I was thinking, What's the use? I'm just one old man with

Welding with Children

a little brown book of Bible stories and a doggy-hero book.
How can that compete with daily MTV, kids' programs that
make big people look like fools, the Playboy Channel, the shiny
magazines their mammas and their boyfriends leave around the
house, magazines like *Me,* and *Self,* and *Love Guides,* and rental
movies where people kill one another with no more thought than
it would take to swat a fly, nothing at all like what Abraham
suffered before he raised that knife? But I read on for a half hour,
and when that dog stopped the locomotive before it pulled the
passenger train over the collapsed bridge, even Tammynette
clapped her sticky hands.

The next day, I didn't have much on the welding schedule,
so after one or two little jobs, including the bed rail that my
daughter called and ragged me about, I went out to pick up a
window grate the town marshal wanted me to fix. It was hot
right after lunch, and Gumwood was wiggling with heat. Across
from the cypress railroad station was our little redbrick city hall
with a green copper dome on it, and on the grass in front of that
was a pecan tree with a wooden bench next to its trunk. Old
men sometimes gathered under the cool branches and told one
another how to fix tractors that hadn't been made in fifty years,
or how to make grits out of a strain of corn that didn't exist
anymore. That big pecan was a landmark, and locals called it the
"Tree of Knowledge." When I walked by going to the marshal's
office, I saw the older Mr. Fordlyson seated in the middle of the
long bench, blinking at the street like a chicken. He called out
to me.

"Bruton," he said. "Too hot to weld?" I didn't think it was a
friendly comment, though he waved for me to come over.

Welding with Children

"Something like that." I was tempted to walk on, but he motioned for me to sit next to him, which I did. I looked across the street for a long time. "The other day at the store," I began, "you said my car was a bastardmobile."

Fordlyson blinked twice but didn't change his expression. Most local men would be embarrassed at being called down for a lack of politeness, but he sat there with his face as hard as a plowshare. "Is that not what it is?" he said at last.

I should have been mad, and I was mad, but I kept on. "It was a mean thing to let me hear." I looked down and wagged my head. "I need help with those kids, not your meanness."

He looked at me with his little nickel-colored eyes glinting under that straw fedora with the black silk hatband. "What kind of help you need?"

I picked up a pecan that was still in its green pod. "I'd like to fix it so those grandkids do right. I'm thinking of talking to their mammas and —"

"Too late for their mammas." He put up a hand and let it fall like an ax. "They'll have to decide to straighten out on their own or not at all. Nothing you can tell those girls now will change them a whit." He said this in a tone that hinted I was stupid for not seeing this. Dumb as a post. He looked off to the left for half a second, then back. "You got to deal directly with those kids."

"I'm trying." I cracked the nut open on the edge of the bench.

"Tryin' won't do shit. You got to bring them to Sunday school every week. You go to church?"

"Yeah."

"Don't eat that green pecan — it'll make you sick. Which church you go to?"

Welding with Children

"Bonner Straight Gospel."

He flew back as though he'd just fired a twelve-gauge at the dog sleeping under the station platform across the street. "Bruton, your wild-man preacher is one step away from taking up serpents. I've heard he lets the kids come to the main service and yells at them about frying in hell like chicken parts. You got to keep them away from that man. Why don't you come to First Baptist?"

I looked at the ground. "I don't know."

The old man bobbed his head once. "I know damned well why not. You won't tithe."

That hurt deep. "Hey, I don't have a lot of extra money. I know the Baptists got good Sunday-school programs, but..."

Fordlyson waved a finger in the air like a little sword. "Well, join the Methodists. The Presbyterians." He pointed up the street. "Join those Catholics. Some of them don't put more than a dollar a week in the plate, but there's so many of them, and the church has so many services a weekend, the priests can run the place on volume like Wal-Mart."

I knew several good mechanics who were Methodists. "How's the Methodists' children's programs?"

The old man spoke out of the side of his mouth. "Better'n you got now."

"I'll think about it," I told him.

"Yeah, bullshit. You'll go home and weld together a log truck, and tomorrow you'll go fishing, and you'll never do nothing for them kids, and they'll all wind up serving time in Angola or on their backs in New Orleans."

Welding with Children

It got me hot the way he thought he had all the answers, and I turned on him quick. "Okay, wise man. I came to the Tree of Knowledge. Tell me what to do."

He pulled down one finger on his right hand with the forefinger of the left. "Go join the Methodists." Another finger went down and he told me, "Every Sunday, bring them children to church." A third finger, and he said, "And keep 'em with you as much as you can."

I shook my head. "I already raised my kids."

Fordlyson looked at me hard and didn't have to say what he was thinking. He glanced down at the ground between his smooth-toe lace-ups. "And clean up your yard."

"What's that got to do with anything?"

"It's got everything to do with everything."

"Why?"

"If you don't know, I can't tell you." Here he stood up, and I saw his daughter at the curb in her Lincoln. One leg wouldn't straighten all the way out, and I could see the pain in his face. I grabbed his arm, and he smiled a mean little smile and leaned in to me for a second and said, "Bruton, everything worth doing hurts like hell." He toddled off and left me with his sour breath on my face and a thought forming in my head like a rain cloud.

After a session with the Methodist preacher, I went home and stared at the yard, then stared at the telephone until I got up the strength to call Famous Amos Salvage. The next morning, a wrecker and a gondola came down my road, and before noon, Amos loaded up four derelict cars, six engines, four washing machines, ten broken lawn mowers, and two and one-quarter tons of scrap iron. I begged and borrowed Miss Hanchy's

Welding with Children

Super-A and bush-hogged the three acres I own and then some.
I cut the grass and picked up around the workshop. With the
money I got from the scrap, I bought some aluminum paint for
the shop and some first-class stuff for the outside of the house.
The next morning, I was up at seven replacing screens on the
little porch, and on the big porch on the side, I began putting
down a heavy coat of glossy green deck enamel. At lunch, my
wife stuck her head through the porch door to watch me work.
"The kids are coming over again. How you gonna keep 'em off
of all this wet paint?"

My knees were killing me, and I couldn't figure how to keep
Nu-Nu from crawling where he shouldn't. "I don't know."

She looked around at the wet glare. "What's got into you,
changing our religion and all?"

"Time for a change, I guess." I loaded up my brush.

She thought about this a moment, then pointed. "Careful
you don't paint yourself in a corner."

"I'm doing the best I can."

"It's about time," she said under her breath, walking away.

I backed off the porch and down the steps, then stood in
the pine straw next to the house, painting the ends of the porch
boards. I heard a car come down the road and watched my oldest
daughter drive up and get out with Nu-Nu over her shoulder.
When she came close, I looked at her dyed hair, which was the
color and texture of fiberglass insulation, the dark mascara, and
the olive skin under her eyes. She smelled of cigarette smoke,
stale smoke, like she hadn't had a bath in three days. Her tan
blouse was tight and tied in a knot above her navel, which was a
lardy hole. She passed Nu-Nu to me like he was a ham. "Can he
stay the night?" she asked. "I want to go hear some music."

Welding with Children

"Why not?"

She looked around slowly. "Looks like a bomb hit this place and blew everything away." The door to her dusty compact creaked open, and a freckled hand came out. "I forgot to mention that I picked up Freddie on the way in. Hope you don't mind." She didn't look at him as she mumbled this, hands on her cocked hips. Freddie, who had been sleeping, I guess, sat on the edge of the car seat and rubbed his eyes like a drunk.

"He'll be all right here," I said.

She took in a deep, slow breath, so deathly bored that I felt sorry for her. "Well, guess I better be heading on down the road." She turned, then whipped around on me. "Hey, guess what?"

"What?"

"Nu-Nu finally said his first word yesterday." She was biting the inside of her cheek. I could tell.

I looked at the baby, who was going after my shirt buttons. "What'd he say?"

"Da-da." And her eyes started to get red, so she broke and ran for her car.

"Wait," I called, but it was too late. In a flash, she was gone in a cloud of gravel dust, racing toward the most cigarette smoke, music, and beer she could find in one place.

I took Freddie and the baby around to the back steps by the little screen porch and sat down. We tickled and goo-gooed at Nu-Nu until he finally let out a "Da-da" — real loud, like a call.

Freddie looked back toward the woods, at all the nice trees in the yard, which looked like what they were now that the trash had been carried off. "What happened to all the stuff?"

"Gone," I said. "We gonna put a tire swing on that tall willow oak there, first off."

Welding with Children

"All right. Can you cut a drain hole in the bottom so the rainwater won't stay in it?" He came close and put a hand on top of the baby's head.

"Yep."

"A big steel-belt tire?"

"Sounds like a plan." Nu-Nu looked at me and yelled, "Da-da," and I thought how he'll be saying that in one way or another for the rest of his life and never be able to face the fact that Da-da had skipped town, whoever Da-da was. The baby brought me in focus, somebody's blue eyes looking at me hard. He blew spit over his tongue and cried out, "Da-da," and I put him on my knee, facing away toward the cool green branches of my biggest willow oak.

"Even Nu-Nu can ride the tire," Freddie said.

"He can fit the circle in the middle," I told him.

~

Now, let's take a look at this structure.

Everything is told from the protagonist's point of view. The protagonist is the character whose story it is, the one who acts to change things. In this case, the protagonist is also the narrator, the one who tells the story. The protagonist's efforts to solve the problem are separated by passages in which he reflects on the situation. Gradually, he comes to take more responsibility for it: It becomes *his* problem to solve. An interesting aspect of this story is that the antagonist, Mr. Fordlyson, mutates into a helper before the end.

First, there is a problem or complication. The protagonist has to weld and care for four grandkids at the same time. The problem unfolds as a serious and worthy problem: These children are not being cared for as children should be. His junky yard with the engine hung from the tree serves to show immediately that *this is also the protagonist's problem*, at least in part.

Flashback shows protagonist's failure of previous effort at self-improvement. This is a very typical place to put a flashback in a short story, right after the complication has been laid out. We might ask what this story of his attempt at college is doing here? How does it contribute to the story of caring for the children? This is a revealing window into the protagonist's character. It is a past failure, which he blames on the system and on rotten professors (with devastating wit, granted). Although he has already noted the junk in the yard, in the flashback he takes no responsibility for his failure, so this is the starting point, the ground off of which he has to move for the story to go anywhere. It also eliminates the avenue of education as a resolution for this character's complication.

Meeting the antagonist. They travel to the store for "Icees" and meet the antagonists, the two Fordlysons, who intensify the perception of the problem and humiliate the protagonist by speaking of the "bastardmobile." (As Charles Brashear writes in his excellent *Elements of the Short Story,* "Get your fighters fighting.'") Here the fighters start fighting. Also, the children's language and behavior continually bring home the point that these children are not being raised properly. The protagonist-narrator doesn't notice (though the reader might), that Coke and candy are not healthy foods for children.

Protagonist's first effort to overcome problem. He pulls off road to reprimand Freddie for his language. **Weak effort and it fails.**

---

* Charles Brashear, *Elements of the Short Story,* 15.

Protagonist reflects on nature of problem. They get home and protagonist reflects on the nature of the community (thinking about other people's business) and puts his values behind his community. Next he reflects on how this came about, how he and his wife raised his daughters. (This reflection is one of the steps toward taking responsibility for the problem. It also sets up the possibility of listening to Fordlyson later.)

Protagonist's second attempt to overcome problem. The long scene where he tries to teach the children bible stories, ending with the TV program about children cheating and evicting their parents. **Much greater effort, ending with failure.**

Low point. Protagonist takes a drink, notes his paint-spattered shoes, has a fantasy about driving away, sees that you can't drive away from yourself. (He is beginning to take more responsibility.)

Protagonist's third attempt to overcome the problem. He disconnects the TV and brings a storybook. The story "Welding with Children" is still at a low point, there is still little hope, but here it begins to rise. The problems are not solved, but the heroic action of the dog in the story affects the children greatly. Note that this episode is quite short.

Reassessment of the problem with the aid of a helper. The conversation with Mr. Fordlyson under the Tree of Knowledge. Note the rejected alternatives: attempting to change the daughters; sending the children to a Holy Roller church. Note Mr. Fordlyson's advice that he should (essentially) clean up his own act. This scene sets up the resolution: Resolutions of complications often require thinking through the problem once again, gaining insight into it. In particular, the protagonist understands fully that this is *his* problem.

Resolution. Note that his actions are not huge, grand, earth-shattering actions. They are just a beginning. He cleans up the yard. He intends to fix a screen.

Finally note that the beginning and the end — the arrival of the children — match. Thus the story has a frame. Note the large willow oak early on and again at the end.

HANDS ON: WRITING THE PIECE

What is the significant complication? Who is the character with enough grit to fight to resolve it? These are the two key ingredients required for dramatic narrations. Take any volume of *The Best American Short Stories* put out by Houghton Mifflin and go through and reread the stories. Which stories clearly follow this dramatic structure? Can you name the complication? Is it a significant complication? Can you show how the protagonist fights to resolve it? (Whether or not the complication is resolved successfully is not at issue.) If a story seems obscure in terms of this structure, just pass it by. This is not the only structure in existence. To learn dramatic structure, look for stories that plainly use it.

Now turn to a story of your own. What is a significant complication that engages you? Do you have a character (whether yourself or someone else in nonfiction or memoir or a fictional character in a story) with enough grit to fight toward resolution? Passive characters and trivial complications generally do not make good stories.

Beyond that you can proceed to structure just about any dramatic narrative using three or five attempts to overcome the difficulty or achieve the desired object. Who or what is opposed to the success of the protagonist? Add an antagonist. (Writers Jack Remick and Robert J. Ray ask the writers in their classes, Who is the antagonist? The plain implication is, no antagonist, no story.) And who is the helper? And does the resolution come about in part due to the fact that the protagonist comes to better understand the nature of the complication?

10.

How to Open

When in doubt, or wherever possible, tell the whole story of the novel in the first sentence.
—John Irving

A GREAT OPENING WORKS LIKE A BAKED ALASKA: The server lights a match and it bursts into flame. It's mesmerizing, and when the flame dies down, you are ready to eat.

Open with the most important thing you have to say. Spend your capital — fast. Open with a swift, well-placed whack:

> "I steal."
>
> (Mona Simpson, "Lawns," 80)

For five years I was on the team of short-fiction readers for *The Seattle Review*. What an enlightening experience. Above all, I learned — again and again — how a weak opening can kill a piece. Nice writing does not do the job. A nice description does not do the job. A windup explanatory sentence, typically begun with a dependent clause, does not do the job.

Take up one or more anthologies of short masterworks, fiction or nonfiction. Page through. Look at each opening. What can you learn?

∿ Often a good opening consists of a small sentence that concentrates into its short little self the essence (sometimes the central dramatic conflict) of what follows.

> Their plans were to develop the valley, and my plans were to stop them.
> (Rick Bass, "Days of Heaven," 15)

> The first time I cheated on my husband, my mother had been dead for exactly one week.
> (Cheryl Strayed, "The Love of My Life," 291)

> My father drank.
> (Scott Russell Sanders, "Under the Influence," 733)

> We sit in the bull pen. We are all black. All restless. And we are all freezing.
> (Assata Shakur, "Women in Prison: How We Are," 471)

> I have devoted my life to slime molds.
> (John Tyler Bonner, *Life Cycles*, 3)

He always feels hot. I always feel cold.
(Natalia Ginzburg, "He and I," 423)

∽ Begin with an aphorism. An aphorism is a pithy truth that the rest of the piece then proceeds to prove out or defend. Or begin with your conclusion.

Death is ordinary.
(William T. Vollmann, "Three Meditations on Death," 7)

Cinema's hundred years appear to have the shape of a life cycle: an inevitable birth, the steady accumulation of glories, and the onset in the last decade of an ignominious, irreversible decline.
(Susan Sontag, "A Century of Cinema," 117)

War is a racket.
(Major General Smedley D. Butler, "War Is a Racket," 252)

∽ What is the central question of the piece? Ask the question in the first sentence.

What is patriotism?
(Emma Goldman, "Patriotism: A Menace to Liberty," 270)

Why do I fast?
(Wole Soyinka, "Why Do I Fast?" 454)

What is so special about the Greek alphabet?
(Anne Carson, *Eros the Bittersweet*, 53)

Is literary greatness still possible?
(Susan Sontag, "A Mind in Mourning," 41)

❧ An elegant and simple way to begin is to state directly what a
piece (whether short or book-length) is about in the first sentence
or at least by the end of the first paragraph.

> This book attempts to put forward and interpret a tradition:
> the personal essay.
> (Phillip Lopate, *The Art of the Personal Essay*, xxiii)

> This book is about a momentous event in the history of
> Mexico, popularly called La Revolución, a civil war that
> erupted in 1910; before coming to a close, it claimed the
> lives of untold numbers of Mexicans and put to the torch
> millions of dollars of private property. The drama covers the
> years between 1905 and 1924. However, it is not a simple
> chronology but an interpretation of events. It is my view
> of what took place, that Mexico underwent a cataclysmic
> rebellion but not a social revolution.
> (Ramón Eduardo Ruiz, *The Great Rebellion*, ix)

> This is a story about two writers.
> (Kathryn Chetkovich, "Envy," 9)

❧ Immediately establish your own or the protagonist's connection to
the subject matter at hand.

> I stand here ironing and what you asked me moves
> tormented back and forth with the iron.
> (Tillie Olsen, "I Stand Here Ironing," 9)

One day you have a home and the next day you don't, but
I'm not going to tell you my particular reason for being
homeless, because it's my secret story, and Indians have to
work hard to keep secrets from hungry white folks.
(Sherman Alexie, "What You Pawn I Will Redeem," 1)

Before I became a professional historian, I had grown up
in the dankness and dirt of New York tenements, had been
knocked unconscious by a policeman while holding a banner
in a demonstration, worked for three years in a shipyard, and
dropped bombs for the U.S. Air Force. These experiences,
and more, made me lose all desire for "objectivity," whether
in living my life, or writing history.
(Howard Zinn, "Objections to Objectivity," 29)

∾ Begin with a telling anecdote or quote. Remember that the reader
must be completely oriented as to what the essay is about by the
end of the second paragraph, at latest.

Somebody said recently to an old black lady from Mississippi
whose legs had been badly mangled by local police who
arrested her for "disturbing the peace," that the Civil Rights
Movement was dead, and asked, since it was dead, what she
thought about it. The old lady replied, hobbling out of his
presence on her cane, that the Civil Rights Movement was
like herself, "if it's dead it shore ain't ready to lay down."
　　This old lady is a legendary freedom fighter in her
small town in the Delta. She has been severely mistreated
for insisting on her rights as an American citizen. She has
been beaten for singing Movement songs, placed in solitary
confinement in prisons for talking about freedom, and
placed on bread and water for praying aloud to God for

her jailers' deliverance. For such a woman the Civil Rights Movement will never be over as long as her skin is black. It also will never be over for twenty million others with the same "affliction," for whom the movement can never "lay down," no matter how it is killed by the press and made dead and buried by the white American public.
(Alice Walker, "The Civil Rights Movement: What Good Was It?," 170)

೧೨ Rely on the reliable What? When? Where? Why? Who? Look in a volume of *The Best American Short Stories*. Note how many stories have an actual date, an actual place name in the first sentence:

The year was 1962; the city, New York. I was fleeing from the protracted aftermath of a love affair that had run afoul of a false pregnancy or a miscarriage or a chemically induced abortion, I was never able to determine which, but in any case an unhappy mess for the girl, and painful for me too, since her mother's grief had elicited what all the inveiglements of her father confessor hadn't: penitence and a sincere vow of chastity. No crueler joke could be imagined....
(Joel Agee, "Eros at Sea," 27)

On the twenty-ninth of July in 1943, my father died. On the same day, a few hours later, his last child was born. Over a month before this, while all our energies were concentrated in waiting for these events, there had been, in Detroit, one of the bloodiest race riots of the century.
(James Baldwin, "Notes of a Native Son," 587)

Back in the sixties, I was in my twenties.
(John Olson, "The Bell of Madness," 19)

I left India in 1964 with a certificate in commerce and the
equivalent, in those days, of ten dollars to my name.
(Jhumpa Lahiri, "The Third and Final Continent," 248)

In 1975, fresh out of college, I moved to Savannah, Georgia,
to work as a client advocate in a legal aid office. It was an
old brick storefront and may once have been a shoe store,
but under the tenure of Legal Services it had become a
dreary, stained honeycomb of cheap cubicles, smelling of
disinfectant, insecticide, and burnt coffee. It sat among old
churches, luncheonettes, and pawnshops....
(Melissa Fay Greene, "On Writing Nonfiction," 229)

~ Begin with a good title. A good title says what the piece is about:

"How Did Hemingway Write?" (Allen Josephs)
"Learning to Work" (Virginia Valian)
"Objections to Objectivity" (Howard Zinn)
"The Kitchen" (Alfred Kazan)
"Nana" (Amiri Baraka)
"What Is Eros?" (Rollo May)
"The Education of a Poet" (Muriel Rukeyser)

These titles, and all of these beginnings, give readers an extremely
accurate idea of what's behind the door they are about to walk through.
They shun lyrical flourishes, obscure metaphors, and anecdotes with
delayed points. They are direct. They are plain and simple. They put the
reader in a time and place, or they say what the problem is ("I steal"), or
they flatly state what the piece is about. They make instantly clear what
the relationship of the *I* is to the matter at hand.

The temptation is to begin fancy. The practice is to condense what
is offered into its shortest, most accurate, most telling form. Often, in

the process of composing, beginnings do not clarify themselves until endings arrive. "Good leads often show up late," writes many-book author Ralph Keyes in *The Courage to Write*. "In my own writing and that of students, I generally find the best opening deep within the narrative. This opening only makes itself known as I read drafts, see what catches my eye, something that sets a tone, that gets the piece up and running. Knowing this I don't concern myself with beginnings till the end."*

HANDS ON: OPENINGS

As with all the exercises, do this one in relation to work you have in progress.

ᐁ Take five of your works that have yet to be published. Lay them out on the table or on the floor. Choose one type of opening, say Vollmann's "Death is ordinary." For each of your chosen five works, make an opening that is syntactically identical to Vollmann's opening, that is, it is an equation using the "to be" verb — X is Y. This sentence holds the essence of what you want to say in the piece.

ᐁ Take the piece that pleases you most or that you most want to finish. *Do not go into it and begin flailing about.* Rather, copy out into your writing-practice notebook or type out the present opening. This is your "before" paragraph. Now, below it, make your new opening, beginning with your new "X is Y" sentence. Work on the paragraph to make it fit the new opening and in any other way you see fit. Here is an example of a Before/After from a piece I wrote called "Solitude." This is the opening paragraph:

---

* Ralph Keyes, *The Courage to Write*, 154.

Before

> When I was five years old, we moved to a farm in Maryland
> called Ravenswood. We lived there for a year before moving
> to Comegy's Bight Farm a few miles down the road. At
> Ravenswood, I got a room of my own — an attic room
> with steep gables and a square casement window made of
> wood on the vertical end wall. To me at the time — I'm a
> twin and have a brother ten months older — it was pure
> happiness to possess this sunny, silent kingdom at the top of
> the house.

After

> Solitude is delicious. It can be delicious even to a five-year-
> old. The year we turned five — I have a twin sister and a
> brother ten months older — our family moved to a farm in
> Maryland called Ravenswood. At Ravenswood, I got a room
> of my own, an attic room with steep gables and a square
> wooden window that opened sideways like a book. This was
> my own silent kingdom at the top of the house.

That is a great improvement, or so it seems to me.

Do the Before/After exercise with each type of opening offered here.
You can do the Before/After exercise again and again. In the years of
assigning it and actually doing it myself, I cannot remember a case in
which the "after" paragraph did not turn out better; often it is much
better. The exercise works almost like magic, partly because you are
focusing on a single paragraph.

The act of removing the paragraph from your piece before starting
to work on it is essential. This makes the job finite, one you can entertain
yourself with for an hour or so before returning the paragraph to its
appointed place. Doing this exercise on the *first* paragraph of any given
piece will repay your efforts many times.

〜 Begin your own collection of virtuoso openings written by others. Write them in your sentence book. Collect these passages and study them. What can you learn from them?

The Art of the Sentence
and
The Art of the Paragraph

*As a beginning novelist long ago, I learned to write dialogue not in
a fiction workshop ruled by a sophisticated "mentor," but by reading
Graham Greene's* The Heart of the Matter *over and over again.... The
perfected work was the mentor.*

—Cynthia Ozick

II.

Sentence Craft

A good sentence alters the world.
—Jonathan Raban

SUPERB WRITERS WRITE SUPERB SENTENCES. Writers like Ernest Hemingway and Gertrude Stein and Colette and Cormac McCarthy and Eavan Boland and Joan Didion and Don DeLillo and Susan Sontag and James Baldwin and William Gass have taken on the sentence as its own project. The project is: How does this sentence structure carry this content? To begin with, superb writers have taught themselves the basic sentence structures and know how to use each one fluently. And why not? Is there such a thing as a good carpenter who does not know the types of woods and nails?

First-rate writers do not use sentence forms out of tired habit or conventional but mistaken notions of correctness. All really good writers use fragments. They repeat words and phrases as a saxophonist repeats notes and phrases. They use parallel structures to express parallel thoughts. They write very short sentences and they write very long sentences. They write list sentences, that is, sentences that contain a list:

> They haven't seen our gardens full of lemongrass, mint,
> cilantro, and basil.
> (Lê Thi Diem Thúy, "The Gangster We Are All Looking For," 197)

The most gratifying way to work with the sentence is to make the form of a sentence perform its own meaning. Make the sentence do what it says. A sentence about a long slow quietly flowing river can be a long slow quietly flowing sentence. A sentence about something sharp and hard-hitting can crack, bite, kick, or slap. Sentences describing soft pillowlike afternoons or persons should puff and billow with hazy, willowy, pillowlike words. A sentence that brings a car screeching to a halt should itself screech to a halt. A sentence describing something going on and on should itself go on and on. There might be a clean, empty sentence or again a sentence crowded as a shoe-clotted closet. A sentence about stepping should step:

> Each of the stone steps up to the heavy wooden doorway
> is worn in the middle into a smooth hollow. All those years
> of weight in the same place, like a promise kept and kept
> and kept.
> (Helen Humphreys, *The Lost Garden*, 15)

Virginia Tufte's eye-opening book on the sentence, *Artful Sentences: Syntax as Style*, offers this sentence written by Stewart Alsop to show

how diction (word choice) can intensify meaning. Of the American political system Alsop writes:

> That system, for all its elephantine cumbersomeness, is also, in the long run, adaptable and flexible.
>
> (Stewart Alsop, *The Center*, 352)

Here the diction is cumbersome just as the American system is cumbersome. The signifier (the sentence) enacts or performs that which it signifies (the American system).

Tufte's marvelous museum of sentences includes one from James Agee's *A Death in the Family*, about the death of a father in a car wreck, written from the point of view of the son, a small boy. After the death:

> They are not talking much, and the talk is quiet, of nothing in particular, of nothing at all in particular, of nothing at all.
>
> (James Agee, *A Death in the Family*, 14)

The talk is about nothing; the word *nothing* is chimed three times. The sentence about talking about nothing has nothing in it, no concrete word that refers to any visible concrete object (perceivable by eyes, ears, nose, skin, taste buds). The sentence talking about talking about nothing sounds like a child's perception of adults murmuring. Think of sound as an element to work with when you are making sentences that both say what they mean and do what they say.

Here is a sentence by Maya Sonenberg, in which the spread of a bird's wings spreads the sentence wider:

> Then out of the sky, a great white bird came sweeping, wings spread wide wide wide.
>
> (Maya Sonenberg, "Beyond Mecca," 133)

Can sentences express silence? What is silence? Is there such a thing as absolute silence? Or is silence, rather, a pause in human cacophony, a moment when the clock ticks, the rain rains, a branch taps the kitchen window:

> Camille did not answer. The clock ticked. Zackery turned from the cookstove to look at her. The rain grew louder. A branch was tap-tapping the kitchen window.

Whenever you write a physical action, a movement, try making the sentences move that same way in order to intensify the motion being described. Here, in Jean Toomer's *Cane,* a boxing match between dwarfs is rendered in short fragments, short sentences, short fast hits — like boxing:

> The gong rings. No fooling this time. The dwarfs set to.
> They clinch. The referee parts them. One swings a cruel
> upper-cut and knocks the other down. A huge head hits the
> floor. Pop! The house roars. The fighter, groggy, scrambles
> up. The referee whispers to the contenders not to fight so
> hard. They ignore him. They charge. Their heads jab like
> boxing gloves. They kick and spit and bite. They pound each
> other furiously. Muriel pounds. The house pounds. Cut
> lips. Bloody noses. The referee asks for the gong. Time!
> The house roars.
> (Jean Toomer, *Cane,* 67)

Toomer's words hit, jab, spit, and stab. They say what they mean and they also enact their meaning.

Here Sherwood Anderson writes about a pretty wife who wants to kiss her "old stick" of a professor husband:

And that sort of thing, of course, pitching him down off his mountain top of thought, thump.
(Sherwood Anderson, "The Flood," 250)

A sentence can accumulate. It can accumulate the disaster unfolding in a Wisconsin farmhouse inhabited by a father and his two small daughters whose "navigator" — their wife and mother — has been handcuffed and carted to jail:

> The sifter's handle was bent, the clocks didn't work, the wooden blocks were covered with scribbling, the Magic Markers were dried up, the sofa was filthy, the wing chair was ripped, the stereo was missing half the knobs, the books had been gnawed on, by children, or mice.
> (Jane Hamilton, *A Map of the World*, 252)

A sentence can *be* what it *says*. Look at this passage from Lars Eighner's memoir on living out of Dumpsters. The sentence, making like a Dumpster, contains a jumble of separate items:

> Except for jeans, all my clothes come from Dumpsters. Boom boxes, candles, bedding, toilet paper, medicine, books, a typewriter, a virgin male love doll, change sometimes amounting to many dollars: all come from Dumpsters.
> (Lars Eighner, "My Daily Dives in the Dumpster," 19)

A sentence can move the way its actor moves. Here is a fast scene from Jack Kerouac's *On the Road*. The sentence is long but it jerks forward in short bursts. It moves exactly as the parking-lot attendant does:

The most fantastic parking lot attendant in the world, he
can back a car forty miles an hour into a tight squeeze and
stop at the wall, jump out, race among fenders, leap into
another car, circle it fifty miles an hour in a narrow space,
back swiftly into a tight spot, *hump*, snap the car with the
emergency so that you see it bounce as he flies out; then
clear to the ticket shack, sprinting like a track star, hand
a ticket, leap into a newly arrived car before the owner's
half out, leap literally under him as he steps out, start the
car with the door flapping, and roar off to the next available
spot, arc, pop in, brake, out, run; working like that
without pause eight hours a night, evening rush hours
and after-theater rush hours, in greasy wino pants with a
frayed fur-lined jacket and beat shoes that flap.
(Jack Kerouac, *On the Road,* 6)

In contrast, Hemingway's sentences in a scene from *The Sun Also
Rises* set in a cathedral drift in tandem with the protagonist's mind. By
the time we get to the sentence printed below he has prayed for every pal
he can think of, he has prayed for bullfighters, all of them together and
individually for his favorites, he has prayed for some good fishing, and
on and on. The sentences meander as the mind meanders:

I wondered if there was anything else I might pray for, and
I thought I would like to have some money, so I prayed
that I would make a lot of money, and then I started to
think how I would make it, and thinking of making money
reminded me of the Count, and I started wondering about
where he was, and regretting I hadn't seen him since that
night in Montmartre, and about something funny Brett told
me about him, and as all the time I was kneeling with my
forehead on the wood in front of me, and was thinking of

myself as praying, I was a little ashamed, and regretted that
I was such a rotten Catholic, but realized there was nothing
I could do about it, at least for a while, and maybe never,
but that anyway it was a grand religion, and I only wished
I felt religious and maybe I would the next time; and then I
was out in the hot sun on the steps of the cathedral, and the
forefingers and the thumb of my right hand were still damp,
and I felt them dry in the sun.
(Ernest Hemingway, *The Sun Also Rises*, 97)*

Here is Anthony Doerr, new father of twins. He can't sleep for worry, and runs through his list of failed techniques for falling to sleep. One failed technique is repeating words over and over. The sentence, too, repeats words over and over.

I tried thinking the same word over and over, *blue, blue,*
blue, blue, blue, rain, rain, rain, rain, rain.
(Anthony Doerr, *Four Seasons in Rome*, 18)

Once you get the idea of forming sentences to perform what they are saying, you can begin experimenting with syntax to make it intensify its load of meaning.

HANDS ON: WORKING ON SENTENCING

How do you embark on the project of becoming more skilled at sentencing? First, obtain a nicely bound, rather commodious blank

---

*Reprinted with the permission of Scribner, a Division of Simon & Schuster, Inc. from *The Sun Also Rises* by Ernest Hemingway. Copyright 1926 by Charles Scribner's Sons. Copyright renewed 1954 by Ernest Hemingway.

book in which to collect exquisite sentences (and paragraphs, passages) written by others. This is the way to begin. I possess an ample and ever-growing treasury of beautiful sentences. The more I study them, the more they teach me.

Second, sentence work requires a decent reference work, a grammar-and-usage handbook. There are a number of how-to-write books that provide useful advice but that do not explicate the simple, compound, and complex sentence. You want a handbook that has a chapter or chapters on sentence forms. One such is *The Little, Brown Handbook*. Another, considerably less pricey, is Nancy M. Ackles, *The Grammar Guide*. Yet another: Karen Elizabeth Gordon, *The Deluxe Transitive Vampire*. And there are others. Without such a reference work, you will at some point get lost. We all do.

I suggest two initial moves. First, learn the prepositional phrase and learn it cold. (See Chapter 17, on the phrase.) Second, learn to distinguish a clause (which has a subject and a verb) from a phrase. Learning these two forms will save you years of trouble. Now proceed.

Experiment. Try writing a scene of constricted emotion with constricted sentences. Begin with diction — word choice. Pick sharp short words like tick, whack, or poke to express a tight, tense, tough situation. Pick words like voluminous, mellifluous, or mellow to express softer scenes, scenes that languish or meander or drift like smoke. Try writing a scene of lazy happiness with lazy happy sentences. Try making sentences that dream along, sentences that race along. Master the sentence forms: simple, compound, complex, compound-complex, even if these terms are somewhat reductive and do not reflect current linguistics theory. For us writers they are supremely useful. Take a look at the particular uses first-rate writers make of fragments. Now you begin using fragments.

There are great pleasures in sentencing. Don't set out trying to learn everything at once. Rather, take pleasure in copying down a sentence you like, word for word. Then, in your writer's notebook (different from your sentence book, which contains only sentences composed by other writers), try making your own sentence using that form. Make certain moves — the list sentence, the fragment — habitual. Take a paragraph and write it several ways. Note the effects. Savor your growing skill.

You will want at your fingertips all the forms of the sentence. First-rate writers, unlike the vast majority of writers, use them all. They are driving with a full tank of gas.

HANDS ON: IMITATING GREAT SENTENCES

This is an old exercise. Jack London did it. Other writers have done it. It is thought of as a beginner's exercise and certainly, beginners benefit from it. But I suggest that very experienced writers can learn from it as well. Imitation acts as an aid to close, writerly reading and can carry you into strategies, styles, and forms different from your accustomed ones. Imitation can help you expand your range.

First, copy out a piece of superlative writing done by someone else. It can be a sentence or a paragraph.

Don't skip the physical act of copying out the passage. Copying it out slows it down, puts you almost physically inside it. Always, when I am copying out a paragraph, whether by hand or on the keyboard, I see moves and turns that I entirely missed when I merely read it. Consider the passage to be your master-teacher for this moment. When an interviewer asked Gina Berriault how she taught herself to write, she responded:

> One thing I'd do was put a great writer's book beside the
> typewriter and then I'd type out a beautiful and moving
> paragraph or page and see these sentences rising up before
> my eyes from my own typewriter, and I would think,
> "Someday maybe I can write like that." ... The someone

whose words were rising from that typewriter became like a mentor for me. And when I went on with my own work, I'd strive to attain the same qualities I loved in that other person's work. Reading and writing are collaborations.*

Go to any great art museum and you will see artists copying paintings. Artists have always trained themselves by copying masterworks. And composers copy. Beethoven so admired Handel's work, the curator of an exhibition of his music manuscripts wrote, "that he wrote it out so as to get the 'feeling of its intricacies' and 'to unravel its complexities.'"**

After you've copied out your model paragraph, imitate it by making a sentence or sentences of your own, using different words, but the same syntax, the same level of diction, the same parts of speech, the same sound strategies (if two words alliterate, make your own two words alliterate). In doing this exercise it is of paramount importance to use your own material. It is fairly easy — and quite useless — to make up nonsensical or irrelevant sentences. The sentence achieved through the imitation must be a good sentence and it must mean what it says. We find that this exercise, done properly, is quite time consuming. As you are working, consider the following strategies.

෴ Pay attention to diction (word choice). Replace low diction (*Shit!*) with low diction (*Drat!*) not *Goodness me!* Replace Latinate words with Latinate words, body parts with body parts, colors with colors, verbs with verbs, nouns with nouns. Repeat your substitute word for any repeated word in the model.

---

* Gina Berriault: "Don't I Know You?" in *Passion and Craft*, 62–63.
** Karpeles Manuscript Museum website accessed November 28, 2003 (http://www.rain.org/~karpeles/taqfrm.html).

∾ Pay attention to concrete words (*salmon, coal, sweat, salt*) versus abstract words (*anxious, love, dream, notorious, silly, bad, gentle*). Keep in mind that there are degrees of concretion: soft is concrete but feather-soft and mud-soft are more concrete.

∾ Replace verbs with similar kinds of verbs. Example: "Her eyes rent the air and left phosphorescent streaks" (Anaïs Nin, *Ladders to Fire,* 9). Replace *rent* with *cut* or *slash*, not *decompose*.

∾ Look at the sentences in a piece you admire, and repeat that structure in what you write. Choose a passage written by a superb writer that carries the very emotion — the joy or misery or boredom or fear — of the piece you are writing. How does the sentence structure carry the emotion?

12.

Fragments

Indian summer. Montana. Rivers. You get the picture.
—Annick Smith, "Sink or Swim"

WE BEGIN WITH A FORM THAT IS A NON-SENTENCE. Most great writers use fragments. Why then, have so many of us been taught that a fragment is an error? (What *is* an error is writing a fragment when you mean to write a sentence.)

Once you begin to appreciate fragments in your reading, and once you decide to use them in your own writing, the question becomes, What makes a good fragment? A fragment, stripped as it is of connectors, can hold a pure image, a critical moment, the point, or the pivot. Because it is isolated, it is emphatic.

A fragment can put a setting on the page fast:

> **A purple sea.** We wade in, but the going is slow.
> (Judith Kitchen, "North Yorkshire," 81)

Judith Kitchen is a master of the fragment. It is tempting to think that for her it stands for memory, for the way memory can arrive in bits and scraps.

> This is where Scotland's dream was dashed. **Windswept**
> **moor, purple with blooming heather. Bog land.**
> (Judith Kitchen, "Culloden," 27)

Shocking, traumatic moments can be created or re-created in shattered language — fragments. Here soldiers are breaking into a home. The narrator remembering this episode was at the time a boy hiding in the closet.

> **The burst door. Wood ripped from hinges, cracking like ice**
> **under the shouts. Noises never heard before, torn from my**
> **father's throat. Then silence.** My mother had been sewing
> a button on my shirt. She kept her buttons in a chipped
> saucer. I heard the rim of the saucer in circles on the floor.
> I heard the spray of buttons, little white teeth.
> (Anne Michaels, *Fugitive Pieces*, 7)

And here is the devastating moment in *Ordinary People* when the parents are informed that their son has drowned:

> They had neither of them cried that night on the dock.
> **Too awesome, too catastrophic for tears. That murderous,**
> **lead-colored moon. The sky, wispy with cloud-strings. The**
> **black water all around them, indistinguishable from the**
> **black sky. The people who didn't know who they were, only**
> **that something terrible had happened.**
> (Judith Guest, *Ordinary People*, 205)

Very commonly, too, fragments serve a more sunny purpose. Writers use them to put down sensory evidence following a question or a generalization:

> The house is infinitely grander than our quarters. **Crystal chandeliers. Polished mahogany.**
> (Helen Humphreys, *The Lost Garden*, 41)

> Why they released Ava was never clear. **Crowded wards. Her age, her edges turning soft and blurred.**
> (Kiana Davenport, "Bones of the Inner Ear," 85)

Use fragments to saturate the prose with sensory detail. Fragments made of concrete words like *red* or *ice* are vivid and immediate. Here is Tobias Wolff:

> We drove farther into the mountains. It was late afternoon. **Pale cold light.** The river flashed green through the trees beside the road, then turned gray as pewter when the sun dropped. The mountains darkened. Night came on.
> (Tobias Wolff, *This Boy's Life*, 88)

And in this passage, Lauren Slater's narrator, a child, has been placed in some sort of custody. The custodian, nurse, social worker, whoever she may be, leaves the room:

> She left the room. A long time passed, and the day grew dark. The taillights of cars burned in the blue darkness and the horns honked. **Rush hour. Winter dark. A time of black cats and sad poems.** I started to cry.
> (Lauren Slater, *Lying*, 44)

Fragments can bring the person on the page to life:

Young Lily is eight now. **Brown-skinned, lovely. Very bright.**
Books and toys, a star chart on her ceiling.
(Kiana Davenport, "Bones of the Inner Ear," 88)

HANDS ON: WORKING WITH FRAGMENTS

If you've never used fragments before, begin by studying the models to
determine what makes a good fragment. I urge you to bypass a common
move made by writers who've just discovered to their joy that fragments
are "legal" and begin lopping off the subjects of rather long sentences.
Keep in mind that most fragments are quite short and that they hold the
vivid and the crucial. Gray ordinary language, non-critical moments —
these do not belong in fragments.

Take a passage from something you are working on. Can you use
a fragment or two in imitation of one of the models? Try it. Then read
it aloud. This way you will develop your ear. Keep trying a fragment or
two in various passages and see how they sound to you. You will soon
develop a knack for it.

13.

The Simple Sentence

I write three hours every morning.
—Walter Mosley

THE SIMPLE SENTENCE — A SENTENCE WITH ONE SUBJECT and
one predicate (the verb and words connected with the verb) — can be
made quite long by piling on phrases. (But add a clause and you've made
a compound or a complex sentence.) Simple sentences can be long but
often they are short. A short simple sentence can deliver a good punch:

> I have begun my own quiet war.
> (Sandra Cisneros, *The House on Mango Street*, 89)

> Memory is treacherous.
> (Eavan Boland, *Object Lessons*, 125)

Rot is one of the works of death.
(Mary Gordon, "My Mother's Body," 67)

The sun is moving toward the sea.
(Alistair MacLeod, "The Road to Rankin's Point," 174)

My kisses did not appear in my poems.
(Eavan Boland, *Object Lessons*, 107)

All sorrow feels ancient.
(Anne Michaels, *Fugitive Pieces*, 60)

My interest in biology began with an interest in birds.
(John Tyler Bonner, *Life Cycles*, 5)

Meaning is never monogamous.
(Susan Sontag, "Writing Itself: On Roland Barthes," 76)

A simple sentence has one clause. It is an independent clause. A clause must have a subject and it must have a verb. A simple sentence with one subject can have multiple verbs. A simple sentence with one verb can have multiple subjects. But as soon as you add a second *clause*, which has *both* a subject and a verb, you have either a compound sentence (two or more linked independent clauses) or a complex sentence (one independent clause and one or more dependent clauses).

Here are two simple sentences with multiple verbs:

I put on the kettle for tea, set out a plate, and cut some bread.
(John Haines, "Three Days," 69)

The guy had pushed him during a pool game and called him
a goddamn dirty Indian.
(Philip H. Red Eagle, *Red Earth*, 46)

Here are two simple sentences with multiple subjects:

Poetry and psychoanalysis strain words to their limits.
(Robert L. Bergman, "Blue Notes," 185)

Language and song are mingled in human history.
(Walter Mosley, *This Year Write Your Novel*, 93)

A simple sentence can be long, short, or somewhere in between. A
very short sentence (or a short fragment) within a paragraph of longer
sentences can focus the matter, punctuate it, drive the point home:

All writers create. I am always annoyed to hear fiction and
poetry called "creative" writing as if writing that explains,
describes, and narrates — nonfiction — should somehow be
relegated to the basement of the writing enterprise to dwell
with the pails and the pipes.
(Richard Marius, *The Writer's Companion*, 15)

A series of short simple sentences can carry a series of discrete
events:

Tiny sounds from the city drift through the room. A milk
bottle clinks on a stone. An awning is cranked in a shop
on Marktgasse. A vegetable cart moves slowly through
a street. A man and woman talk in hushed tones in an
apartment nearby.
(Alan Lightman, *Einstein's Dreams*, 4)

HANDS ON: WORKING THE SIMPLE SENTENCE

Again, take out a piece you are working on. Using it and its subject matter, practice making simple sentences that mimic and attain the weight and effectiveness of the models offered here. Each model offered, and certainly each *type* of model offered, will repay a work session or two to integrate into your skills. Do not rush. Keep reading your new sentences out loud to develop your ear.

- Take one of your pieces to work on. Does it have any sentence that resembles "Memory is treacherous" or "All sorrow feels ancient"? These are huge statements compressed into tiny truth-nuggets. Try a few. These sorts of sentences invariably give you clichés at first. Be aware and revise against. Strive for extreme accuracy.

- Try making a simple sentence with multiple verbs.

- Try forcing the main point of a paragraph into a very short simple sentence (or into a fragment).

- Try writing a Very Long simple sentence by multiplying a prepositional phrase. (See pages 225–227.)

- Take a paragraph you've written — this is your "before" paragraph. Now make one of the sentences extremely short. Make the short sentence capture the main point or the most burning moment.

14.

The Compound Sentence

Writing is not a matter of obeying rules;
it is a matter of observation and imagination.
—Richard Marius

THINK EQUALITY. Think of two racehorses, neck on neck. Think an eye for an eye. Think seesaw, one end balanced against the other end.

> I can understand pessimism, but I don't believe in it.
> (Howard Zinn, "Failure to Quit," 157)

> I don't mind deceiving, but I don't want to be deceived.
> (Mary Gordon, "My Mother's Body," 71)

It is 6 a.m. and I am working.
(Mary Oliver, "Of Power and Time," 7)

Riotous living racked the town and shooting frays made
life precarious.
(Charles A. Beard and Mary R. Beard, *The Rise of American
Civilization*, 613)

Beauty spins and the mind moves.
(Anne Carson, *Eros the Bittersweet*, xi)

He was nobody out here and he liked it that way.
(Philip H. Red Eagle, *Red Earth*, 124)

The compound sentence has two or more independent clauses
connected by a coordinating conjunction, or by a colon or a semicolon.
A clause has both a subject and a verb. This sentence — *I got up and
washed my face and poured coffee and sat down to write* — is a simple
sentence with multiple verbs. Why? Because there is only one subject,
the *I*. To make it compound you would write: *I got up and I washed
my face.* A compound sentence has two or more independent clauses. A
clause has a subject and a verb, so any compound sentence must have at
least two subjects.

The independent clauses in a compound sentence can stand alone
and still make perfect sense.

> I can understand pessimism.
> I don't believe in it.
> (I can understand pessimism, but I don't believe in it.)
> It is 6 a.m.
> I am working.
> (It is 6 a.m. and I am working.)

Beauty spins.

The mind moves.

(Beauty spins and the mind moves.)

Conjunctions are connectors. Coordinating conjunctions connect sentence elements of equal grammatical rank. Use them to hook together two independent clauses to make a compound sentence.

for	and	nor	but
or	yet	so	

The parts are parallel or they are begging to be parallel. Speaking of lovers, Anne Carson writes:

They hate to wait; they love to wait.

(Anne Carson, *Eros the Bittersweet*, 117)

And speaking of herself as a 20-year-old in New York for the first time, Joan Didion writes:

Nothing was irrevocable; everything was within reach.

(Joan Didion, "Goodbye to All That," 683)

Think of lifting dumbbells, one in each hand, high over your head. That image of strength — equally distributed weight — is the image of the compound sentence. No part hangs off any other part.

They took their turns speaking, and permission to talk was neither sought nor given.

(Charles Frazier, *Cold Mountain*, 128)

I pointed out the injustice of the charge, and we had a
refreshing little discussion.
(Elizabeth Peters, *The Mummy Case*, 10)

A compound sentence can have two clauses, three clauses, four
clauses or many clauses. Still, the clauses are equal to one another. Each
independent clause has its subject and verb, and they are connected with
a conjunction, or with a colon or a comma or semicolon. Don't confuse
a phrase with a clause. Don't confuse a dependent clause (*When you
come...*) with an independent clause that makes sense all by itself.

The table is round and drab; the worn linen stays on the
armrests; the sky is full of the light and danger of spring.
(Eavan Boland, *Object Lessons*, 79)

The philosopher O. K. Bouwsma, in "The Mystery of Time," writes
a compound sentence using twenty-eight clauses, all independent, all
parallel in form. The sentence is about time itself, what we do with it:

We give, we fill, we take out, we steal, we shorten, we
squeeze out, we spare, we stretch, we lengthen, we cut,
we halve, we keep, we hoard, we get, we take, we seize, we
use, we watch, we pick up, we lack, we find, we need, we
divide, we lose, we fritter away, we kill, we beat, we invest.
What? Time.
(O. K. Bouwsma, "The Mystery of Time," 110)

Non-virtuoso writers seldom if ever use a compound sentence. I don't
know why. I've often wondered if it's because compound sentences — *I
patted the goat's nose and the goat bleated* — seem like baby sentences. But
why not express equal actions or equal conditions in equal independent
clauses — in a compound sentence?

The music stops and the sun moves westward.
(Alistair MacLeod, "The Road to Rankin's Point," 172)

He was dependent on alcohol and he was dependent
on work.
(Louis Menand, "Saved from Drowning," 68)

To write such elegant sentences requires a technical grasp of the simple, compound, and complex sentence. These sorts of sentences do not flow out the pens of writers oblivious to the differences among them. It has never happened. At least I have never been witness to a lovely compound sentence extruded from the pen of a writer who can't tell compound from complex.

First-rate writers use compound sentences all the time. Hemingway gets a kind of stunned, traumatized voice out of them. Here, the shell-shocked narrator relates his story using *only* compound sentences.

In the fall the war was always there, but we did not go to
it any more. It was cold in the fall in Milan and the dark
came very early. Then the electric lights came on, and it was
pleasant along the streets looking in the windows. There
was much game hanging outside the shops, and the snow
powdered in the fur of the foxes and the wind blew their
tails. The deer hung stiff and heavy and empty, and
small birds blew in the wind and the wind turned their
feathers. It was a cold fall and the wind came down from
the mountains.
(Ernest Hemingway, "In Another Country," 267)*

*From "In Another Country." Reprinted with the permission of Scribner, a Division of Simon & Schuster, Inc., from *The Short Stories of Ernest Hemingway*. Copyright 1927 by Charles Scribner's Sons. Copyright renewed 1955 by Ernest Hemingway.

A compound sentence can express an **action-reaction sequence:**

> He meets their eyes, and the trysts are settled.
> (Pauline Kael, "Vulgarians and Ascetics," 126)

> The horse buries his nose in her hair and she reaches up to
> stroke the side of his face.
> (Helen Humphreys, *The Lost Garden*, 49)

> He flipped his wrist, and the hat skimmed out the window
> and caught an updraft and soared.
> (Charles Frazier, *Cold Mountain*, 5)

Note how Frazier's sentence moves as the hat moves, smoothly without hitch or pause (no commas). He forms the sentence to perform its meaning. In contrast, a less skilled writer might write: *He flipped his wrist and the hat skimmed out the window, catching an updraft and soaring.*

A compound sentence can **state a situation and something that arises from the situation:**

> The man had a big paddleboard with holes augered in it, and
> he liked to use it.
> (Charles Frazier, *Cold Mountain*, 5)

> I had reached the forest and you cannot mistake the forest.
> (Jean Rhys, *Wide Sargasso Sea*, 106)

A compound sentence can express **two or more sequential actions that have equal weight or value:**

> Zackery set down the clock oil and he stood up and he
> greeted the old man standing in the doorway.

A compound sentence can **shift equal small actions from one person to another:**

> Camille had bought the mochas and she set them on the
> table and he pulled out her chair and took her coat and went
> to get napkins and spoons.

The compound sentence can exude authority, even grandeur, and we often find it in sacred texts. Its steady feel has to do with its structurally equal clauses. No clause is hanging dippy-dependent off another clause. It is a steady marching thing, one foot after the other. Solid on the ground, nothing dragging.

Consider these passages from the Book of Job and from the *Rig Veda*:

> My flesh is clothed with worms and my body with dust;
> my skin is shrunk, and falls apart.
> (Job 7:5)

> The blind man sees; the lame man steps forth.
> ("This Restless Soma," *Rig Veda*, 121)

> King Soma, do not enrage us; do not terrify us; do not
> wound our heart with dazzling light.
> ("This Restless Soma," *Rig Veda*, 121)

HANDS ON: WORKING THE COMPOUND SENTENCE

I have taught the compound sentence over and over, to classes consisting mostly of advanced writers. Still, I've yet to teach a class in which some of these advanced writers did not confuse the compound sentence with the complex sentence, even after we've devoted an entire class to the compound sentence. (Don't despair: Mastering syntax requires time, attention, practice, and a good reference work. Be patient with yourself.) The compound sentence delivers its own feel, which differs within different contexts and for different writers. The idea is to master the form and then begin experimenting. If you mistakenly include complex sentences in your compound-sentence experiments, you will become confused and learn nothing, because complex sentences deliver a very different feel.

A compound sentence has no *dependent* clause. As soon as you put a dependent clause in a sentence, what you have is a complex sentence. (Mastering the compound sentence requires mastering the complex sentence.)

∾ To get a feel for the form, sit with yourself or with your writing buddies with your notebook and a timer. Set the timer for a full fifteen minutes. Describe your day in minute detail up to the present moment. Make every sentence a compound sentence. Now read this out loud to get the rhythm of this form into your ear.

∾ Again, take out a piece of your writing. Using the material of the piece, make a list of ten *really good* compound sentences. Use the equal-weightedness of the form to express two or more things that have equal weight. Then integrate this work back into the piece.

∾ Try a paragraph using only compound sentences. Make a compound sentence with three clauses, four clauses. Keep experimenting. Ingest the form, masticate it, make it your own.

15.

The Complex (and Compound-Complex) Sentence

I want to touch my blameless dreams,
even if to date it is all paper and mistakes.
—C. D. Wright

THE COMPLEX SENTENCE, WHICH HAS AN INDEPENDENT clause
and at least one dependent clause, can be a comely thing. But, alas,
it can easily overrun a writer's skill level and become chaotic, tangled,
and terribly untidy. There are two ways out of this unfortunate situation.
The first is to practice making very short complex sentences: *Wherever*
you go, there you are. The second is to practice multiplying one and only
one type of dependent clause in a long complex sentence:

He's the musician **who can always move you, who's a relentless bastard, who beats up on his piano player, who drinks himself sick.**
(Ira Sadoff, "Ben Webster," 255)

In the complex sentence, the dependent clause is hitched to the main clause with a subordinating conjunction — which, because, when, etcetera. Now let's step through the types of dependent clauses. Remember that a clause has both a subject and a verb. The types are:

> *what, why,* and *how* clauses
> *who* clauses (or *whoever, whomever*)
> *that* and *which* clauses
> adverbial clauses (nine types, see ahead)

Here are complex sentences with *what* and *why* clauses:

> **What frightens me** is the otherness of vultures.
> (Lee Zacharias, "Buzzards," 261)

> She couldn't explain **why she didn't take off her shoes.**
> (Mary Gordon, "My Mother's Body," 67)

> Janie learned **what it felt like to be jealous.**
> (Zora Neale Hurston, *Their Eyes Were Watching God*, 130)

Here are complex sentences with *who* clauses:

> Any critic **who attacks Corot** does so at his own risk.
> (John Berger, "Thicker than Water [Corot]," 206)

They are the only ones **who understand me.**
(Sandra Cisneros, *The House on Mango Street*, 74)

Here are complex sentences with *that* clauses. Note that in the Floyd Skloot sentence the word *that* is omitted. Although the subordinating conjunction *that* is implied rather than articulated, the sentence remains complex.

I know, for instance, **that my grandfather got lost in a certain wood.**
(Gaston Bachelard, *The Poetics of Space*, 188)

This is not the way **I used to be.**
(Floyd Skloot, "Gray Area: Thinking with a Damaged Brain," 149)

Here are complex sentences with *which* clauses:

I wore a school uniform, **which was dark green**, with a flannel shirt and a heavy sweater.
(Eavan Boland, *Object Lessons*, 78)

I suggest the old word "witness," **which includes the act of seeing or knowing by personal experience, as well as the act of giving evidence.**
(Muriel Rukeyser, *The Life of Poetry*, 175)

Thus I became one with those skulls **which no longer knew their death.**
(William T. Vollmann, "Three Meditations on Death," 10)

Now we come to the adverbial clauses. Most of us use adverbial clauses without much thinking about it, and a common writing fault is to write rangy loose sentences that unconsciously employ several different types of adverbial clauses. Using them consciously is a different matter entirely. We begin by mastering the nine types. Does this require struggling to memorize them as if we were miserable eighth-graders facing an English test? Not at all. Instead, we study them, we play with them, we try them. Remember that the dependent clause is hitched to the independent clause with a subordinating conjunction.

1. The adverbial clause of manner. Modifies the independent clause by answering the question how. The subordinating conjunctions are *as if* and *as though*. Adverbial clauses of manner are not overused. When apt, they work in any kind of writing, but are most often found in literary writing.

> The Ethiopians and the Indians joined in the meal **as if they were all of a color and equals.**
> (Charles Frazier, *Cold Mountain*, 128*)*

> My own body shuddered and pitched, **as if it wanted to shake me off.**
> (Joan Silber, "Gaspara Stampa," 83)

> "I think sixty or seventy people died," he said, taking off his glasses, **as though clear vision was a burden.**
> (Tim Gautreaux, "Misuse of Light," 30)

Note: *Fowler* instructs: "In the great majority of *as if* clauses, when the choice of verb is between were or was, the subjunctive form *were* is preferred. It indicates that something is hypothetical, uncertain, or not factually true."* However, in excellent writing you see *was* used all

---

* *The New Fowler's Modern English Usage*, 3rd Edition edited by R. W. Burchfield, 70.

the time too, even when uncertainty rules, perhaps because in our own times *were* is beginning to sound a bit formal. So let the writer decide.

2. The adverbial clause of comparison. Compares one action to a different action. The subordinating conjunction is *as*.

> The first day I had to go to the convent, I clung to Aunt Cora **as you would cling to life if you loved it.**
> (Jean Rhys, *Wide Sargasso Sea*, 49)

> Erotically enjambed in our loft bed, Clea patrolled my utterances for subject, verb, predicate, **as a chef in a five-star kitchen would minister to a recipe, insuring that a soufflé or sourdough would rise.**
> (Jonathan Lethem, "The King of Sentences," 135)

3. The adverbial clause of place. Modifies the independent clause by answering the question where. The subordinating conjunctions are *where* and *wherever*.

> Another cold blast of wind brings me back to our world, **where one human and a troop of baboons shiver together on a rock high above the sea.**
> (Peter D. Ward, *Rivers in Time*, 14)

> I want a house on a hill like the ones with the gardens **where Papa works.**
> (Sandra Cisneros, *The House on Mango Street*, 86)

> Frost crystals glitter in the still air **wherever a shaft of sunlight pierces the forest.**
> (John Haines, "Three Days," 63)

4. The adverbial clause of time. Places the independent clause into a framework of time. Subordinating conjunctions are *when, as, after, as soon as, before, since, till, until, whenever,* and *while.*

Collaltino didn't like it **when I bothered him about my fears.**
(Joan Silber, "Gaspara Stampa," 79)

Once, **when the woman lit up a smoke,** her lover pushed back her sleeve and pressed his cheek to the inside of her forearm.
(Francine Prose, "Cauliflower Heads," 27)

Long before I wrote stories, I listened for stories.
(Eudora Welty, *One Writer's Beginnings,* 16)

Tires squealed **as he roamed from one side of the road to the other.**
(Philip H. Red Eagle, *Red Earth,* 95)

Whenever I want I can open the perfume.
(Mary Gordon, "My Mother's Body," 76)

Here is a paragraph I wrote to illustrate how you can multiply a single type of adverbial clause to make a coherent, Very Long sentence:

And this person is going to write a novel. She's going to write this novel after she retires, after she marries off her daughters if it kills her, after she gets her boy off drugs, after she sorts her mother's papers and determines what to do with them, after she gets her photo albums organized for once and for all, after she retiles the bathroom, after she cleans out the closets, after she goes through the socks and

puts every non-paired sock in the ragbag, after she weeds
the garden, after she cleans the basement, after she sees a
little more of her friends or she won't have any friends, after
she gets the finances on a spreadsheet, after she hunts down
the lost aunt who raised her father, after she memorizes her
first poem, after she writes to Madeleine, after she does the
laundry and airs the beds, after she gets through this messy
divorce, after she quits her horrible job, after she rethinks
her wardrobe, after she completes the course in how to get
organized, after she makes a business plan, after she does
get organized, after she cleans up her study, after she checks
her email and deletes several hundred messages, after she
decides which diet to go on, after she buys groceries, after
she loses twenty pounds, after she looks at her finances to see
where she can economize, after she re-organizes the kitchen
because you really can't start a new diet when your kitchen
is in chaos, after she washes the windows, after she puts up
apples for the winter. This person has a novel she wants to
write and she will write it. She will write it after she retires.

5. **The adverbial clause of cause.** Modifies the independent clause
by explaining why it happened. The subordinating conjunctions are
because, for, since, now that, that.

> We believe some people **because they exude an aura
> of authority.**
> (Richard Marius, *The Writer's Companion*, 170)

> **Because Athos's love was paleobotany, because his heroes
> were rock and wood as well as humans,** I learned not only
> the history of men but the history of earth.
> (Anne Michaels, *Fugitive Pieces*, 32)

6. **The adverbial clause of condition.** Begins with the following subordinating conjunctions: *if, even if, provided that, unless,* and *in case.*

> **If my father was unstable,** I would be a rock. **If he squandered money on drink,** I would pinch every penny. **If he wept when drunk** — and only when drunk — I would not let myself weep at all. **If he roared at the Little League umpire for calling my pitches balls,** I would throw nothing but strikes.
> (Scott Russell Sanders, "Under the Influence," 743)

7. **The adverbial clause of concession.** Presents a fact that is in contrast to the fact presented in the independent clause. The conjunctions are *although* and *though.*

> And **though his tone darkens over his forty-year career, though he chooses gruffness over grace,** the tunes change only in minor ways.
> (Ira Sadoff, "Ben Webster," 256)

> Quite simply, determining the cause of death is the prerequisite for some kind of justice, **although justice, like other sonorous concepts, can produce anything from healing to acceptance to compensation to revenge to hypocritical clichés.**
> (William T. Vollmann, "Three Meditations on Death," 11)

8. **The adverbial clause of purpose.** Tells the intention, the reason why. Subordinating conjunctions are *in order that, so that, that.*

> Mondrian moved to New York **so that he could escape the war.**

9. The adverbial clause of result. Explains what happens as a result of something else. The subordinating conjunctions are *so* and *that*.

> **So deep is my sense of ignorance,** in fact, **that** I make certain to do my best to pass this character trait on to my writing students, both fiction and creative nonfiction, making them repeat after me each class session my motto: I know nothing.
> (Bret Lott, "Against Technique," 98–99)

> Everything is on top of everything else **so the whole store has skinny aisles to walk through.**
> (Sandra Cisneros, *The House on Mango Street*, 19)

COMPOUND-COMPLEX SENTENCES

Finally, of course, there is the compound-complex sentence. These too can be beautiful sentences. Now you should be able to see what makes them compound and what makes them complex.

> I said then, and I say now, that while there is a lower class, I am in it, and while there is a criminal element, I am of it, and while there is a soul in prison, I am not free.
> (Eugene Debs, "Statement to the Court," 297)

> I did not need to be convinced that slime molds were the ideal organism for the study of development, for I felt it in my bones.
> (John Tyler Bonner, *Life Cycles*, 13)

One day I'll own my own house, but I won't forget who I am
or where I came from.
(Sandra Cisneros, *The House on Mango Street*, 87)

When I desire you a part of me is gone; your lack is my lack.
(Anne Carson, *Eros the Bittersweet*, 32)

Trickster goes where the action is, and the action is in the
borders between things.
(Michael Chabon, "Trickster in a Suit of Lights," 12)

HANDS ON: WORKING THE COMPLEX SENTENCE

As you have discerned, there is a method to this madness, which is to
first separate sentences from their paragraphs and make a list of beautiful
ones. I suggest foregoing for the moment complex sentences that use two
or more *types* of dependent clauses. This will bring to a halt any tendency
to write those rangy, out-of-control, chaotic complex sentences.

∼ Make a list of ten very short complex sentences. Use one and only
   one kind of dependent clause.

∼ Make a complex sentence that is a page long and that repeats one
   and only one type of dependent clause.

∼ Using a piece of writing you are working on, make two stunning
   complex sentences of each of the nine types.

∼ Make sentences using the adverbial clause of manner (as if...) and
   work on them until the metaphor seems apt and natural.

∿ Take one of the compound-complex sentences and imitate it with a new sentence of your own.

∿ Always, after you've worked on individual sentences, reintegrate them back into your paragraphs.

16.

The List Sentence

He [Barthes] *speaks of the quiver, thrill, or shudder of meaning, of meanings that themselves vibrate, gather, loosen, disperse, quicken, shine, fold, mutate, delay, slide, separate, that exert pressure, crack, rupture, fissure, are pulverized.*

—Susan Sontag

A SENTENCE CONTAINING A LIST IS A LIST SENTENCE. It is a compression technique, like a well-packed suitcase. At some point many years into my apprenticeship, I began to notice list sentences in the work of superb, first-rate, virtuoso writers. And, really, I saw them nowhere else. Certainly not in my own work. So I began to fiddle with them and compose them. I began to love lists for their sounds and rhythms. Here is a specific craft technique that will repay the writer in pleasurable hours of wordplay and in striking effects.

Listen to the sounds in Susan Sontag's sentence on the French philosopher Roland Barthes:

His vocabulary is large, fastidious, fearlessly Mandarin.
(Susan Sontag, "Writing Itself: On Roland Barthes," 65)

Especially good are lists of nouns. Note how we are here looking at items of only one or at most two words. Of the ancient Greeks, Anne Carson writes:

They wrote on stone, wood, metal, leather, ceramics, waxed tablets and papyrus.
(Anne Carson, *Eros the Bittersweet*, 60)

A list can put a person on the page quickly and cogently. Speaking of Gertrude Stein, William Gass writes:

Her father was a nuisance: stocky, determined, uneducated, domineering, quarrelsome, ambitious, notional, stern.
(William Gass, "Gertrude Stein and the Geography of the Sentence," 67)

Laura Kalpakian's character Max is in a bad mood:

Max was saddlesore, hot, cross, thirsty, and bored.
(Laura Kalpakian, "How Maxwell Perkins Learned to Edit," 73)

And here is Ursula K. Le Guin's summation of her mother, the writer Theodora Kroeber:

She was also, to her daughter, a demanding, approving, nurturing, good-natured, loving, lively mother — a first-rate mother.
(Ursula K. Le Guin, "The Fisherwoman's Daughter," 232)

Another type of list is a list of verbs. Again note how the individual items in the list are one or at most two words. A good trick is to count the number of items in someone else's list, and put that same number — or more — in your own. Here that master essayist E. B. White evokes his dog:

> He never just lay and rested. Within the range of his
> tether, he continued to explore, dissect, botonize, conduct
> post-mortems, excavate, experiment, expropriate, savor,
> masticate, regurgitate.
> (E. B. White, "Bedfellows," 83)

Tim O'Brien's classic Vietnam story, "The Things They Carried," gets an entire war and its soldiers on the page with list sentence following list sentence:

> The things they carried were largely determined by
> necessity. Among the necessities or near-necessities were
> P-38 can openers, heat tabs, wristwatches, dog tags,
> mosquito repellent, chewing gum, candy, cigarettes, salt
> tablets, packets of Kool-Aid, lighters, matches, sewing kits,
> Military Payment Certificates, C rations, and two or three
> canteens of water.
> (Tim O'Brien, *The Things They Carried*, 2)

Lê Thi Diem Thúy employs list sentences frequently in her memoir "The Gangster We Are All Looking For":

> Ma is in the kitchen. She has torn the screen off the
> windows. She is punctuating the pavement with dishes,
> plates, cups, rice bowls.
> (Lê Thi Diem Thúy, "The Gangster We Are All Looking For," 198)

Everywhere you look among first-rate writing you find the list sentence. Here is Mary Oliver writing about the great horned owl:

> They are swift and merciless upon the backs of rabbits, mice, voles, snakes, even skunks, even cats sitting in dusky yards, thinking peaceful thoughts.
> (Mary Oliver, "Owls," 20)

A. S. Byatt, in her witty and perceptive short story "Art Work," uses a list to create the household of a stressed-out London family. The list holds not only the contents of the room but also the discontents of this disorganized family:

> Apart from the inevitable mess, splashed palettes, drying canvases, jars of water, there are other heaps and dumps. Magazines, opened and closed, wine glasses, beer glasses, bottles, constellations of crayons and pencils, unopened messages from the Income Tax, saucers of clips and pins.
> (A. S. Byatt, "Art Work," 46)

Finally, John McPhee, rising to the defense of his ancient mother:

> We have now covered everything even faintly unsavory that has been reported about this person in ninety-nine years, and even those items are a collection of rumors, half-truths, prevarications, false allegations, inaccuracies, innuendos, and canards.
> (John McPhee, "Silk Parachute," 177)

The list sentence is a prime place to work sound. Look at how Joan Silber echoes long *o*'s, and alliterates *p*'s and *b*'s:

He called me an oaf, a potato, a slob, a blight,
a hippopotamus.
(Joan Silber, "My Shape," 25)

And here is William Boyd putting the painter Michael Andrews on the page:

His achievement stands there — inspiring, incontrovertible, immutable.
(William Boyd, "Michael Andrews," 348)

HANDS ON: MAKING LIST SENTENCES

Use lists to convey the most important things you have to say. No digressions. No decorative moves. Use a list to convey the essence of the dramatic action, the main point. And work to make the items in the list one- or two-word items — uncomplicated.

⟡ Begin making lists in your writer's notebook. Begin putting lists in sentences. Put words together that sound good together.

⟡ Make a list to make a setting.

⟡ Make a list to put a person on the page.

⟡ Make a list to make a philosophical statement.

Use single words or very short phrases in your lists. Begin with a simple list of nouns. Or a simple list of verbs. Don't get tangled up in one complicated phrase following another. Stretch those lists out. Can you make a five-item list? A ten-item list?

17.

The Phrase

To paint is to love again.
—Henry Miller

PHRASES ARE NOT CLAUSES and do not a complex sentence make. It's handy to be able to easily recognize the types of phrases. The chief types are infinitive phrases, participial phrases (verbs used as adjectives), gerunds (verbs used as nouns), and the prepositional phrase.

Here are two sentences based on the infinitive phrase:

To see a turkey vulture up close is to know what loneliness looks like.

(Lee Zacharias, "Buzzards," 272)

To learn to speak is to learn to tell a story.
(Ursula K. Le Guin, "Some Thoughts on Narration," 39)

This simple sentence by Alice Walker includes a participial phrase (present participle):

And I stand still a few seconds, **looking at the weeds.**
(Alice Walker, "Looking for Zora," 4)

This simple sentence by Ursula K. Le Guin has one subject, two verbs, and one participial phrase (present participle):

Dreams tend to flout Aristotle's rules of plausibility and muddle up his instructions **concerning plot.**
(Ursula K. Le Guin, "Some Thoughts on Narration," 42)

Here is a simple sentence containing a participial phrase (past participle):

I have always cherished old things, used things, things **marked by the passage of time and human events.**
(Henry Miller, *To Paint Is to Love Again,* 18)

Here are two simple sentences with a gerund — a verb acting as a noun:

Watching children sleep makes me feel devout, part of a spiritual system.
(Don DeLillo, *White Noise,* 147)

Learning stamps you with its moments.
(Eudora Welty, *One Writer's Beginnings,* 10)

It is clarifying to grasp that gerunds and participles do not function as verbs. Therefore they cannot make a clause. They make phrases. For this reason, the model sentences we've just read are simple sentences.

THE PREPOSITIONAL PHRASE

The prepositional phrase is common as bugs and dust. Learning it cold clarifies so many things about sentences. Sentences, you come to see, are not about individual words prancing and mincing along; instead they are constructed of units, rather like a freight train. The units consist of various types of clauses and phrases. Once you easily recognize the prepositional phrase you begin to see it everywhere.

It is ubiquitous and also highly mobile. Mastering it enables the writer to start moving it around as a unit, with varying effects. Writers who haven't mastered the prepositional phrase frequently divorce the preposition from its complement, creating misery all around. Writers who haven't locked onto the notion that the end of the sentence is the most conspicuous location are constantly putting this prime location to use as a prepositional-phrase dump as if the prepositional phrase was the most important thing. Sometimes, of course, the prepositional phrase is the most important thing:

She won the race — despite everything.

A preposition expresses the relation between two entities. The entity that resides within the prepositional phrase is the prepositional complement. Often, but not always, the relationship will be one of time or space: where something is, or when it happens.

I see a wall of skulls **in the Paris Catacombs.**
(William T. Vollmann, "Three Meditations on Death," 20)

In Vollmann's sentence, *in* is the preposition and *the Paris Catacombs* is the complement of the preposition. The two entities being connected by the preposition *in* are the wall of skulls and the Paris Catacombs.

A preposition and its complement make a prepositional phrase. A prepositional phrase often acts as a transition and thus may sit happily at the beginning of the sentence:

> **In those other summertimes** all motors were inboard; and
> when they were at a little distance, the noise they made was
> a sedative, an ingredient of summer sleep.
> (E. B. White, "Once More to the Lake," 200)

You can make an elegant sentence by multiplying one kind of prepositional phrase. Here is Violette Leduc. Subtract the proliferating prepositional phrase and the sentence is *To be separated from my mother gave me a fever.* The subject is *To be separated,* an infinitive phrase. I like the way this sentence keeps growing longer, performing its meaning by clinging to all that is longed for. And then "I learned nothing" also performs its meaning by being small, a little nothing:

> I missed the private jargon of our street and was homesick
> for it. To be separated **from my mother, from our big bed,
> from my basket, from the gardens I plundered, from the
> sawdust in the bar, from the tobacco juice, from Caramel's
> spitting, from the love songs, from the red heat of our iron
> stove, from the stew spread on bread, from the nocturnal
> visits of our smuggler** gave me a fever. I learned nothing.
> (Violette Leduc, *La Bâtarde,* 26)

Here are common prepositions shown with complements:

for your efforts

at the store
during the summer
in 1874
after the deluge
before the deluge
under the bridge
between a rock and a hard place
until tomorrow
over the river and through the woods
despite the cold
out of the frying pan
into the fire

Prepositions can consist of more than one word:

According to my mother, beggars can't be choosers.
Because of your kindness, we have survived.
In addition to the plum pudding, we served plum ice cream.
Thanks to the dry weather, the garden withered.

When a prepositional phrase does occur at the end of a sentence, it can be made even more conspicuous by being set off with a dash:

According to recent biographers, Freud took many
of his ideas from the work of colleagues — without
acknowledgment.

Learn the prepositional phrase cold. Then you will never separate a preposition from its complement. You will have fun moving it around as a unit. You will be the happiest writer in the world. Never again will you wander from the path of righteousness into the pit of confusion and darkness.

HANDS ON: WORKING WITH PHRASES

∼ Take a page of your writing and circle all the prepositional phrases. Make "before" and "after" sentences in your notebook to gauge the effects of moving them around.

∼ Write a Very Long sentence by multiplying one type of prepositional phrase.

∼ Take something you are working on and make five sentences using the infinitive phrase. If you haven't done so already, incorporate this type of phrase into your repertoire.

18.

Passive Voice

Art is made by ordinary people.
—David Bayles and Ted Orland

THE PASSIVE VOICE TURNS SENTENCES WORDY, FLABBY, and flatulent. Except when it turns them forceful and eloquent.

Art is practiced by both artist and audience.
(Muriel Rukeyser, *The Life of Poetry*, 25)

In the end, it was necessary that all intellectual gadgetry be discarded.
(Susan Sontag, "Writing Itself: On Roland Barthes," 83)

In the active voice, the actor — the he, she, or it that performs the action — forms the subject of the sentence. (The girl throws the ball.) In the passive voice, the thing acted *upon* — the *receiver* of the action — forms the subject of the sentence. (The ball is thrown.) In the passive voice, the actor, the one who did it, is omitted or is tacked on following the word *by*. (The ball is thrown *by the girl*.) Here are some sentences in the passive voice:

> Mistakes were made. (by?)
> She was raped. (by?)
> Dinner was prepared. (by?)

A sentence in the active voice of necessity supplies the actor:

> Jonathan made mistakes.
> The guard raped her.
> The grandfather prepared dinner.

The following sentences are *not* in the passive voice:

> There is no intimacy without attention.
> (Ralph Angel, "The Poem, As and Of Address," 321)

> There were always fresh surprises in store.
> (Henry Miller, *To Paint Is to Love Again*, 35)

Some English-usage experts call the *there* a dummy subject, delaying the real subject. Here, *there* is a pronoun. *There* can also serve as an adverb indicating place: *There I found my keys.*

The following sentences *are* in the passive voice:

A familiar tune, a tribal tune, really, is given
an interpretation.
(Ira Sadoff, "Ben Webster," 255)

Such bound children were often enough cruelly treated.
(Sherwood Anderson, "Death in the Woods," 7)

Use passive voice consciously. Awareness is the key. When we fall
into the passive voice all unawares (because, usually, we are focusing on
the thing acted upon), it often begs to be converted. Editors of nuts-and-
bolts writing spend a good deal of their time converting passive voice
constructions to active voice, and rightly so.

Still, there are no hard rules. Only strategies toward effects.

HANDS ON: EMPLOYING PASSIVE VOICE ACTIVELY

ᕼ Take a piece you are working on. Look through it and identify
any passive voice constructions. Would the sentence read better
in active voice?

ᕼ Using one of your current projects, make a list of ten passive-
voiced sentences. Make them earn the passive voice. Make
them sentences you would not, on second thought, revise to
active voice.

19.

The Art of the Paragraph

Every paragraph should develop a central idea.
—Richard Marius

NO ONE HAS READ ALL THE WORLD'S PARAGRAPHS. Whatever the qualities of many paragraphs, there may be other paragraphs with different qualities. Principles commonly taught such as "a paragraph is about one thing" may not be true of some paragraphs. But, often a paragraph *is* about one thing, and often the topic sentence says what that thing is.

Let's consider four different types of paragraphs.

TYPE 1: THE DIRECT PARAGRAPH

The direct paragraph begins with a topic sentence that says what the paragraph is about. It is a generalization, a statement of the paragraph's controlling idea. Following the topic sentence comes a list of *at least three* specific examples illustrating the general statement. First-rate writers give many examples (three, four, five, even ten). Average writers skim. They tend to illustrate a topic statement with only one example or maybe two before moving on. Writing is partly about taking the time to thoroughly articulate a thing, to think it through. Spelling out specific concrete examples to illustrate your controlling idea is one way to do this.

> Father's drinking became the family secret. While growing up, we children never breathed a word of it beyond the four walls of our house. To this day, my brother and sister rarely mention it, and then only when I press them. I did not confess the ugly, bewildering fact to my wife until his wavering walk and slurred speech forced me to. Recently, on the seventh anniversary of my father's death, I asked my mother if she ever spoke of his drinking to friends. "No, no, never," she replied hastily. "I couldn't bear for anyone to know."
> (Scott Russell Sanders, "Under the Influence," 735)

The controlling idea is that the father's drinking was the family secret. Then Sanders gives four specific instances of keeping it a secret (children growing up, brother and sister now, wife, mother).

In "The Work of Mourning," Francine du Plessix Gray's controlling idea is that the family is lousy at mourning:

> Mind you, until recently my own family has never been much good at mourning. There is the case of my stepfather,

who bade me get rid of my mother's clothes within a week of
her death, sold the house they'd lived in for forty-nine years
within the month, and promptly had his second, near-fatal
heart attack. There is the case of my husband's aunt, eighty-
six-year-old Rosalind, who, after the death of her second
husband, committed suicide while staying at a summer hotel
with her baby sister, my eighty-four-year-old mother-in-
law. "Just send her ashes parcel post!" her sons bellowed on
the telephone from New York when queried about funeral
arrangements. And there is the case of my own father,
the love of my early life, whose only daughter is as late a
mourner as can be found.
(Francine du Plessix Gray, "The Work of Mourning," 64)

She gives four instances: stepfather, husband's aunt, husband's
aunt's sons, and herself.

TYPE 2: THE CLIMACTIC PARAGRAPH

The climactic paragraph is the exact reverse of the direct paragraph. It
begins with a list of specific illustrations that build to the controlling
idea at the end.

Here's a climactic paragraph I wrote for a class I was teaching on
the paragraph:

It began with my first journal, a black-and-white
composition book into which I entered grievously misspelled
adolescent pronouncements. And it began with bad poems,
one of which contained the line, "Great balls of fire!" It
continued for a long time as nothing more than a rather
badly written journal. In this journal I recorded important

thoughts such as "Nature is so beautiful I just can't describe it!" I commemorated seminal national events — the Cuban Missile Crisis, the Kennedy assassination — with special journal pages left blank. After college, I commenced a yearlong effort to write and rewrite a short personal essay for a woman's magazine. It was accepted in 1969, my first published piece. In their transcendent wisdom the editors edited out everything I liked about it, and it stands on the record as a total embarrassment. This was a setback, but it did not prevent me from continuing to write bad poetry.

I became a printer rather than a writer. For what must have amounted to three years, I spent hours after work every day writing and rewriting a 100-page booklet on how to set up a job for offset printing. It was here that I began to understand the paragraph, how it was structured, how it could work.

And so it was that my road to becoming a writer was a rocky one, full of ruts, potholes, and storm-dropped trees.

Since the beginning of a climactic paragraph doesn't summarize or generalize anything or make a broader point (which comes at the end), it can begin rather dully. Don't let it.

TYPE 3: THE TURNABOUT PARAGRAPH

The turnabout starts in one place and ends up in the opposite place. It begins with an observation or suggestion, not a controlling idea. It begins with an idea that opposes an idea you are going to argue for: *Some people think...* It has a turn in the middle that reverses the direction — signaled by words like *And yet* or *But* or *Nevertheless*. Turnabouts are especially fitting when you want to argue for something or when you are of two minds about something. Here is Scott Russell Sanders:

I no longer fancied I could reason with the men whose
names I found on the bottles — Jim Beam, Jack Daniels —
nor did I hope to save my father by burning down a store.
I was now able to press the cold statistics about alcoholism
against the ache of memory: ten million victims, fifteen
million, twenty. **And yet,** in spite of my age, I reacted in
the same blind way as I had in childhood, ignoring biology,
forgetting numbers, vainly seeking to erase through my
efforts whatever drove him to drink. I worked on their place
twelve and sixteen hours a day, in the swelter of Mississippi
summers, digging ditches, running electrical wires, planting
trees, mowing grass, building sheds, as though what nagged
him was some list of chores, as though by taking his worries
on my shoulders I could redeem him. I was flung back
into boyhood, acting as though my father would not drink
himself to death if only I were perfect.
(Scott Russell Sanders, "Under the Influence," 743)

And here is Ralph Keyes, in a passage from *The Courage to Write*:

After spending more than half my life as a writer, I
sometimes wonder why I am still at it. The pay is usually
Spartan. Although flexible, writers' hours tend to be long.
The stress level is high. Some days I have to fight pitched
battles with my resolve just to get to my desk. **But** I've
continued to write and am glad that I have. I can't think
of any work I'd rather do. Some of the lowest lows of my
life have come while I was writing, and some of the highest
highs. Perhaps one couldn't happen without the other.
(Ralph Keyes, *The Courage to Write*, 187)

Here is a turnabout paragraph I wrote for another class I was teaching. The exercise reminded me how writing works as an aid to thinking. Often the turnabout paragraph requires you to express, in the sentences before the turn, a point of view opposite your own. A good writer will express this opposing viewpoint as fully and fairly as possible.

Some writers believe that writing every day is a bad idea. The poet Louise Glück writes only when inspired, believing it a mistake to write as if forced. And Glück is a fine poet. There's a how-to-write book, *A Writer's Time* by Kenneth Atchity, which suggests sitting on a park bench *not* writing until you have something definite to say. The brilliant novelist Robert Olen Butler has devised an elaborate system of dreaming scenes on 3 x 5 cards for ten or twelve weeks before actually beginning to write a novel. Believers in not writing wonder, What is the good of bad writing, aimless writing, writing going nowhere? **But** I've found writing every day to be a benison. Writing every day, even if only for fifteen minutes, makes you a writer. It renders moot the whole aimless discussion of "writer's block." It terminates any question of whether or not you are really a writer. You write to find out what you have to say and that in turn opens out the next thing you have to say. You write to observe, to record your day, to work on stories or essays or poems. You write to think and you write to play. Writers who write every day have the chance to improve, to become good writers and even great writers. Writers who write every day can open out all that is given to them to write. They always have material to work on, to shape, to craft. They forever subtract themselves from that huge population of would-be writers who "want to write," who "would write if they had time," who "will write a novel once they retire," who "could write a really great memoir."

I must admit that here I failed in my goal — in what should be our goal — to make both sides of the argument equal in length.

TYPE 4: THE OTHER ONE

We began this chapter by stating that there are four types of paragraphs. What is the fourth type? Simply a paragraph that begins with a statement, not a topic sentence but just a statement, followed by a sentence that closely follows the first sentence, followed by a third that elaborates the second, and so on. This paragraph doesn't have a topic sentence but it does have a controlling idea. Here is one such paragraph from *The Rise of American Civilization* by Charles A. Beard and Mary R. Beard. The controlling idea is something like "George Washington takes leave."

> Nearly nine years after the battle of Lexington, to be exact, on December 4, 1783, General Washington bade farewell to his officers in the great room of Fraunces' Tavern in New York City. When the simple but moving ceremony was over, the Commander marched down the streets through files of soldiers and throngs of civilians to the barge at Whitehall Ferry that was to bear him across the Hudson on his way to Mount Vernon. Cannons boomed, bells in the church steeples clashed, crowds cheered as the tall Virginia gentleman stood in the boat, bared his gray head, and bowed his final acknowledgments.
> (Charles A. Beard and Mary R. Beard, *The Rise of American Civilization*, 297)

HANDS ON: COMPOSING PARAGRAPHS

As always, do your assignments using your own real works-in-progress.

〜 Write out a "before" paragraph from something you are working on. For your "after" paragraph, make a strict and lovely direct paragraph. This paragraph is about one thing. It has a general statement about that thing at the top (or right after the transition). It provides three or more specific concrete instances of the generalization expressed in the topic sentence. In doing this exercise, I often find that my "before" paragraph contains only two concrete examples, whereas it ought to have three or six. Often, too, I must purge a digression. As usual, the writing exercise is also a thinking exercise, forcing you to articulate the thought more thoroughly.

〜 Write a classic turnabout paragraph either from scratch or as an "after" paragraph. Once you have mastered this lovely form, look around among your pieces. Where would such a paragraph fit? Make the turnabout paragraph one of your specialties.

〜 Write a classic climactic paragraph. Work especially on the beginning of the paragraph.

〜 Plan out a new piece by making a list of eight or ten topic sentences. This is, essentially, your list of paragraphs. Work on your list, making sure it captures all you want this piece to include. Now write the ten paragraphs. You will have a piece of about 1,000 words. After all, what is prose but a series of paragraphs?

20.

Transitions

Meaning is not in things but in between; in the iridescence,
the interplay; in the interconnections; at the intersections, at the
crossroads. Meaning is transitional as it is transitory; in the puns
or bridges, the correspondence.
—Norman O. Brown

MEANINGS MOVE from one paragraph to the next. Transitions are the bridges. They are the way across. They get you from here to there. They connect what was not before connected. They hold two things together: what has been said and what is to come. Transitions are two-faced, like Janus, the Roman god of gates and doorways. They look backward and forward at the same time.

Consider a few simple transitions:

The next afternoon, …
Also, …
After that, …
Besides which, …

As a young writer I had a terrible time with transitions. I blame my utter lack of mobility in getting from one paragraph to the next on the fact that I had no teacher — and neither did I seek one out. (I don't think I realized that there were teachers who could teach you to write.) Relief arrived in the form of three lucid pages on transitions in the late Richard Marius's lovely little book, *A Writer's Companion*. (That book *was* my companion for a few years, and I'm grateful for it.)

Marius allows that *however, moreover, furthermore,* and *therefore* make clunky transitions, to be avoided whenever possible. We seldom see such clinkers in first-rate writing found in such publications as *The New Yorker* or *The American Scholar* or *Time* or *The Smithsonian*.

Instead, try these transition techniques.

TRANSITION BY REPETITION

A transition is like a switch in a railroad track — it connects the track you're moving off to the track you're moving onto. An excellent switching devise is to repeat a word or phrase from the previous paragraph at the beginning of the new paragraph.

REPEATED VERB
May Sarton wrote of the visit of an old family friend:

At last we turned into the village green, past the church, and up to the front door. While I unloaded, she sat down on the sill, the door open behind her, a glass of milk in her hand...and the silence fell at last, the silence of Nelson. I saw her look up at the astonishing gold of the maples, and across the green to the brick schoolhouse and tiny library. **We had arrived.**

We had arrived through all the years, and the wars, and the deaths, through all the partings — when each time we thought we might never see each other again — through all the hopes and fears, to this moment of luminous quiet.

(May Sarton, *Plant Dreaming Deep,* 64)

Repeated Adjective

Stephen Mitchell wrote on the poet Rainer Maria Rilke:

It is possible to see him, for all these reasons, as the last symbolist. He takes a great deal from the eyes and the working methods of Rodin, but he takes it on his own terms. For all their objectivity, *Neue Gedichte* are profoundly **inward** poems.

Inward and almost savage.

(Stephen Mitchell, introduction to *The Selected Poems of Rainer Maria Rilke,* xxi)

And here is Richard Marius, following his own advice. In the second sentence, the repeated adjective *common* becomes the noun *commonality.*

You should show your audience that you and they have a **common** nature or a **common** interest or a **common** purpose.

Many speakers show **commonality** with their audience
by beginning with a joke.
(Richard Marius, *The Writer's Companion*, 157)

Repeated Noun

Here is Edward Abbey in his classic work on the Arches National
Monument near Moab, Utah:

This is the most beautiful **place** in the world.
There are many such **places**. Every man, every woman,
carries in heart and mind the image of the ideal **place**, the
right **place**, the one true home, known or unknown, actual
or visionary. A houseboat in Kashmir....
(Edward Abbey, *Desert Solitaire*, 1)

TRANSITION BY SYNONYM OR PRONOUN

He, she, they — pronouns always link to what has gone on before while
also propelling the action forward:

The store's electric bell rang, and **Mel DeSoto** saw **the young
woman** come in out of the heat with something under her
arm....
He realized that though **she** was tall and blond, and
wearing a very serious and knowing expression, **she** was only
about eighteen.
(Tim Gautreaux, "Misuse of Light," 21)

Like repeated words, synonyms link back to what has just transpired
while also carrying a thought forward. Here is a passage from Tobias
Wolff's *This Boy's Life*:

Sometimes I just sat on a railing somewhere and looked up
at the mountains. They were always in **shadow**. The sun
didn't make it up over the peaks before classes started in the
morning, and it was gone behind the western rim by the
time school let out. I lived in **perpetual dark**.

The **absence of light** became oppressive to me. It took
on the weight of **other absences** I could not admit to or even
define but still felt sharply, on my own in this new place. My
father and my brother. Friends. Most of all my mother....
(Tobias Wolff, *This Boy's Life*, 98–99)

FROM THIS TIME TO THE NEXT TIME

Grounding the reader in time by using phrases such as "The next day..."
or "That night..." at the beginning of a new paragraph or section is a
simple way to drive a story forward while keeping the reader oriented. In
most cases such phrases should go at the beginning of a sentence, not in
the middle, not at the end. In one (not overly long) short story, "Misuse
of Light," Tim Gautreaux makes this move ten times:

At lunchtime, he walked down the street...
One evening after his wife and daughter had gone to bed...
The next day, he sold three expensive press cameras...
That night, he went in to print the roll...
The next day, Mel spent two hours in the library...
Mel went through the next week trying not to think
about...
In the middle of the next week...
The next afternoon Mr. Weinstein came up to Mel's
counter...
That night, Mel had a dream...

FROM THIS PLACE TO THE NEXT PLACE

Moving the reader from place to place works the same way. These paragraph beginnings are from Barry Lopez's "Replacing Memory":

> Our train arrived at Grand Canyon Village...
> Near midnight we stopped for a few minutes in Needles...
> We turned around and headed north on Wilbur...

FROM FACT TO MEANING

Writing can march in regular fashion from one place to another or it can leap like the jump-cut in a film.

One type of leap is from the literal presentation of some process or object to what it stands for — to its cultural, historical, or emotional meanings. In "Building the House" Mary Oliver first details her literal process of building a shack in her back yard. Then she leaps to what *house* stands for in our emotions, dreams, imagination; she gives us house as metaphor. The essay is structured in numbered sections. The passage quoted begins in the middle of Section 2 in which she tells how she built the house physically, literally. She comes to a place where she does not have the physical strength to carry out the next task:

> Then I would have to wait, in frustration, for a friend or
> acquaintance or even a stranger — male, and stronger than
> I — to come along, and I would simply ask for help to get
> past that instant, that twist of the screw. Provincetown
> men, though they may seem rough to the unknowing, are
> as delicious and courteous as men are made. "Sure darling,"
> the plumber would say, or the neighbor passing by, or the

fisherman stepping over from his yard, and he would help me, and make a small thing of it.

3.

Whatever a house is to the heart and body of man — refuge, comfort, luxury — surely it is as much or more to the spirit. Think how often our dreams take place inside the houses of our imaginations!

(Mary Oliver, "Building the House," 182)

MOVING WITH THE MIND

Writing does not always proceed in logical order, as if words were soldiers and paragraphs were troops in an army. Some types of reflective writing can drift and dream just as the mind does. Addressing art students, the art-weaver Anni Albers said, "You can go anywhere from anywhere."* And so it is in narration. (Still, you need transitions.) Here, in "Stealing Glimpses," Molly McQuade's paragraphs follow the drift of her mind:

My last encounter with the poet A. K. Ramanujan took place as we were riding on a train headed for downtown Chicago. I remember the scene through the window as though I had invented it: tumbledown industrial outskirts, the quaintly gracious backyard stretches of a few museums, and the Zen hint of Lake Michigan in its pearly storehouse.

Smudgily speckled sunflowers usually flourished, during the right season, near the railroad tracks and in other agreeably neglected barrens. As I rode the train, I was picturing them, though they hadn't yet sprouted; it

---

* Anni Albers quoted in *The Woven and Graphic Art of Anni Albers*, 11.

would be July before the weight and conscience of a humid midwestern summer could force them to bloom.

Isn't it strange to be seduced by a flower that hasn't yet flowered? Perhaps, though, it's a morning state of mind. No one has had time, so far, to appraise you, and you owe nothing to them. You're only half present even to yourself, and the condition is a relief. You're susceptible — and serene.

In fact I didn't much want to be reminded of where I was or who I was, but when Ramon suddenly appeared in the aisle of the train, of course I asked him to sit beside me.
(Molly McQuade, "Stealing Glimpses," 23–24)

There is much to learn here. The first sentence is a classic topic sentence. It sets the scene and the ultimate subject, the meeting of the poet. This sentence orients the reader as to what and where, and it serves as ballast for the subsequent drift of the writer's mind. The passage then moves to the literal scene out the train window, then to the scene in the writer's mind's eye, then to a reflection on how the mind moves, which leads to the writer's state of mind when the poet (of the topic sentence) appears.

FROM REAL TO MAGIC OR MYTHIC REAL

To move from real to "magical realism" is often to follow an emotion (loneliness, confusion, the sense of abandonment) into a physical manifestation (cold snow, darkness, a barren landscape).

Sena Jeter Naslund's "Ice Skating at the North Pole" is the story of a husband's infidelity told from the wife's point of view. This passage occurs at the end, when the wife learns for a fact that her husband is off making love to their daughter's kindergarten teacher. The husband is away "on a business trip." The child comes home from kindergarten and informs her mother that the teacher was absent with a cold, which tells the mother-wife that it's a done deal, her husband has betrayed her. The child wants to go for a walk in the snow. Note: This is a perfectly non-Alaskan, non-Native story. There are no dogs or sleds, and though it is snowy out, they live nowhere near the North Pole.

> "Sure," I say, and smile at Rosetta [the child]. "Let's get our skates and wraps."
> We walk out into the snow and down the path away from the house. It is too cold to be out like this. The wind cuts through the black trees. When we can no longer see the house, I know that I am taking her north, all the way north by dog sled.
> We travel for many days. The feet of the dogs are bleeding.
> (Sena Jeter Naslund, "Ice Skating at the North Pole," 37)

AND, *BUT*, OR *SO* AT THE BEGINNING

I begin this section with a deep sigh. Only pity for my neighbors keeps me from wailing and pounding my chest and pulling out my hair. Writers! You can and often should begin a sentence with *And* or *But* or *So*. These make excellent transitions, and first-rate writers use them copiously.

So why is it that well-meaning teachers keep teaching that this is incorrect or at best, casual? Haven't these English teachers read first-rate writers? Haven't they read the entertaining and perceptive Fowler's *Modern English Usage*, the original one or any of its later (somewhat less entertaining) editions? The problem for writers shackled with the mistaken notion that beginning with *And, But,* or *So* is wrong is that they are forced back into the clunky However/Moreover/Furthermore/Therefore School of Transition.

The use of conjunctions at the beginning of a sentence is neither new, nor informal, nor slipshod, nor slang. Every stylebook, usage manual, and grammar on the shelf that treats the subject is utterly clear on this point. But don't take it from me. For your enjoyment I here present a few leading authorities on the topic. *The Chicago Manual of Style*:

> There is a widespread belief — one with no historical or
> grammatical foundation — that it is an error to begin a
> sentence with a conjunction such as *and*, *but*, or *so*. In fact,
> a substantial percentage (often as many as 10 percent) of
> the sentences in first-rate writing begin with conjunctions.
> It has been so for centuries, and even the most conservative
> grammarians have followed this practice.[*]

Garner's Modern American Usage:

> It is rank superstition that this coordinating conjunction
> cannot properly begin a sentence…. The very best writers
> find occasion to begin sentences with *and*….

> It is a gross canard that beginning a sentence with *but* is
> stylistically slipshod. In fact, doing so is highly desirable in
> any number of contexts, as many stylebooks have said (many
> correctly pointing out that *but* is more effective than *however*
> at the beginning of a sentence)….[**]

Charles Allen Lloyd, *We Who Speak English and Our Ignorance of Our Mother Tongue*:

---

[*] *The Chicago Manual of Style*, 15th Edition, 193.
[**] Bryan A. Garner, *Garner's Modern American Usage*, 44, 118.

Next to the groundless notion that it is incorrect to end an English sentence with a preposition, perhaps the most wide-spread of the many false beliefs about the use of our language is the equally groundless notion that it is incorrect to begin one with "but" or "and." As in the case of the superstition about the prepositional ending, no textbook supports it, but apparently about half of our teachers of English go out of their way to handicap their pupils by inculcating it. One cannot help wondering whether those who teach such a monstrous doctrine ever read any English themselves.[*]

The New Fowler's Modern English Usage:

There is a persistent belief that it is improper to begin a sentence with *And*, but this prohibition has been cheerfully ignored by standard authors from Anglo-Saxon times onward. An initial *And* is a useful aid to writers as the narrative continues. The *OED* provides examples from the 9c. to the 19c....

The widespread public belief that *But* should not be used at the beginning of a sentence seems to be unshakeable. Yet it has no foundation.[**]

Whew! Now we have that straight. If you've been burdened with this mistaken notion, you may now set that burden down. Begin your next sentence with *And*. And be happy.

---

[*] Quoted in *The Chicago Manual of Style*, 15th Edition, 193–194.
[**] *The New Fowler's Modern English Usage*, 3rd Edition edited by R. W. Burchfield, 52, 121.

HANDS ON: MAKING TRANSITIONS

But be forewarned. You have crossed the threshold into a new writing strategy. At first, any new strategy feels awkward. If you've never before begun a sentence with *And,* if you've never repeated a word to leapfrog from one thought to the next, it will take practice to learn to do so gracefully. Every new strategy involves comprehending it in principle and then practicing until it gets into your ear. To develop your ear, read your paragraphs out loud.

- Take a piece of writing that you are in the midst of and simply go through and work the transitions. Over the next few work sessions, review and make sure you've incorporated into your process every transition strategy explored in this chapter.

- Take a paragraph that narrates an event or occasion. Then write a following paragraph that reflects on its meaning.

- Venture from the real to the surreal, from the mundane to the magical or mythical. Set your timer for five minutes and write a scene in which an action takes place. Then decide what the emotion of the scene is. Then set the timer for another five minutes and using one sentence as a stem, generate similes. (She felt light as a feather, she felt light as a kite, she felt light as a piece of paper...) Choose a fitting one and turn it literal: She felt **light as a butterfly**. She lifted her wings, floated into bright air.

21.

Punctuation: Tricks and Ticks
of the Masters

*Why do I avoid, as much as possible, using the semi-colon? Let me
be plain: the semi-colon is ugly, ugly as a tick on a dog's belly.*
—Donald Barthelme

*Overseen by the semi-colon, the well-tended sentence can hold any
number of things: apples, prunes, persimmons; linen and lace; pheasant,
roast beef, goose; eggnog, brandy.*
—Barbara Mallonee

ARE YOUR PUNCTUATION SKILLS UP TO PAR? It's not about pleasing
your English teacher. It's not about wearing kid gloves or being proper or
obeying rules. It's about becoming entirely familiar with your medium
so that you can shape it the way a master potter shapes clay. Here's a
perfect beauty of a sentence. It would be entirely beyond the range of a
writer innocent of the structure of the compound sentence:

I had no friends I made no friends I didn't care.
(Lauren Slater, *Lying*, 141)

And here is a paragraph, written by a master. It is perfectly punctuated, considering that the speaker is drunk on rum.

I had a great wish to sleep. And why not? This is the time when everyone sleeps. I imagined the dogs the cats the cocks and hens all sleeping, even the water in the river running more slowly.
(Jean Rhys, *Wide Sargasso Sea*, 103)

In this chapter, you will not find a review of all the forms of punctuation; nor will you find a rant against the punctuation errors proliferating like rats in the attic as we speak. To brush up your skills, go to any standard usage manual, keeping in mind that American and British punctuation conventions differ radically.

Here we look at just a few moves that first-rate writers have under their belts and other writers don't.

COMMAS AND SEMICOLONS IN A LIST

Whether you adore or deplore the semicolon, know where it *should* go if you *should* want to use it. Knowing this, you can use it or refuse it without looking inept.

In a list, if a single item has a comma within it, then semicolons separate the different items:

Mondrian's loves were Paris, France; London; Amsterdam; and New York.

Even one comma within one item in a long list of items forces semicolons to separate the different items. Here is Don DeLillo:

> The roofs of the station wagons were loaded down with carefully secured suitcases full of light and heavy clothing; with boxes of blankets, boots and shoes, stationery and books, sheets, pillows, quilts; with rolled-up rugs and sleeping bags; with bicycles, skis, rucksacks, English and Western saddles, inflated rafts.
>
> (Don DeLillo, *White Noise*, 1)

PHRASAL ADJECTIVES

A phrasal adjective is an adjective made of two or more words: real estate broker, or better, real-estate broker. Except for *ly* words (nearly white walls) and proper nouns, phrasal adjectives should be hyphenated — to make reading easier and to avoid misreadings: small business owner (that tiny person). I like the way Bryan A. Garner puts it:

> **General Rule.** When a phrase functions as an adjective preceding the noun it modifies — an increasingly frequent phenomenon in 20th- and 21st-century English — the phrase should ordinarily be hyphenated. Hence *the soup is burning hot* becomes *the burning-hot soup; the child is six years old* becomes *the six-year-old child.* Most professional writers know this. Most nonprofessionals don't.*

Nuff said.

---

* Bryan A. Garner, *Garner's Modern American Usage*, 604.

COMMA, DASH, AND COLON

To the writer, small skills are endlessly useful. At one point during my long apprenticeship, I studied how to use the dash (technically, the em-dash). Ever since — I must admit — I've been addicted to them.

One use of the dash is to set off an appositive. Appositives clarify and expand the meaning of nouns, within the same sentence.

> The Chelsea seems to attract all the best people — the best painters, the best singers, the best killers.
> (Sarah Vowell, "Chelsea Girl," 83)

> Gauguin's life — poverty, disease, loneliness, disillusion, guilt — was wholly tragic.
> (John Berger, "Gauguin's Crime," 65)

> Along the docks, in the shops and hotels, at wayside taverns, in the stage coaches and canal-boat cabins, all conversation was devoted to the one absorbing theme — gold in California.
> (Charles A. Beard and Mary R. Beard, *The Rise of American Civilization*, 611)

There are three ways to punctuate an appositive, moving from least emphatic to most emphatic.

> Lou was the prize of Kent County, a sleek black racehorse.
> Lou was the prize of Kent County — a sleek black racehorse.
> Lou was the prize of Kent County: a sleek black racehorse.

INTERRUPTERS

Interrupters are a cool way to create emphasis or pack in information. An interrupter can be a phrase or an entire sentence interjected into another sentence.

> Words — I often imagine this — are little houses, each with its cellar and garret.
> (Gaston Bachelard, *The Poetics of Space,* 147)

> Otto fished up a magazine from the floor — one of the popular science magazines William always left lying around — and idly opened it.
> (Deborah Eisenberg, "Some Other, Better Otto," 49)

> After they got back from the ball field that night — it must have been after midnight — they went to sit on the front porch before her father's house.
> (Sherwood Anderson, "The Return," 32)

The interrupter *well* came into journalism at some point during the 1980s and was so effective that you started seeing it everywhere, to the point of annoyance.

> The market smelled of fresh fish and basil and, well, dog poop.

Yes, you do include the question mark or exclamation point in an interrupter sentence. And, no, you don't include the period.

Honing, Deepening, Stretching

Mauve takes offense at my having said "I am an artist" — which I do not take back, because that word of course, included the meaning: always seeking without absolutely finding. It is just the converse of saying, "I know it. I have found it." As far as I know it means, "I am seeking. I am striving. I am in it with all my heart."

—Vincent van Gogh to Theo, May 1882

22.

Metaphor and Simile

Is the bluing of the hills then a metaphor for distance?
—John Hollander

WE LOOK AT THE WORLD THROUGH METAPHORICAL GLASSES.
As George Lakoff and Mark Johnson explicate in *Metaphors We Live By*, we see good as up (we climb corporate ladders, get high, enter high society), and bad as down (we speak of an uncle's downfall, the pit of despair). Lakoff and Johnson's illuminating book (knowledge as light) is enlightening. It may be intrinsic to our *Homo sapiens* way of perceiving to look at A by comparing it to B. Consider the Milky Way (comparing the white light of our galaxy to milk); dead-end (comparing the end of a road to the end of life); a dog-eared book (comparing bent page-corners to a dog's ears).

But our concern as writers is to create metaphors that clarify and make vivid, metaphors we have never heard before. This last point is crucial, since many clichés are metaphors (to buy a house for a song, to cry over spilt milk, to run around like a chicken with its head cut off). And as Ben Yagoda observes in his excellent book *The Sound on the Page*, "Clichés are prominent features of *everyone's* first draft, whether we write it down or keep it to ourselves. How could they not be? We hear and read them all the time and our brains are filled with them. The key to avoiding them in the second and succeeding drafts is recognizing them and casting them out."*

A good metaphor is an original metaphor. It intensifies an emotion or clarifies a concept. It makes an abstract notion visual or visceral. It turns something unknown into something familiar.

Writers who make metaphors fluidly and aptly — and these are our best writers — practice making metaphors the way musicians practice scales. They practice making similes, which are a form of metaphor. Jonathan Raban, speaking of the notebooks he takes on his travels, writes of his "daily target-practice of a dozen or so experimental similes."**

AVOIDING LITERARY SHIPWRECKS

Good metaphors clarify. Rotten metaphors attempt to decorate, to be poetic. They distract and confuse. Be willing to freely try out metaphors and to freely discard the rotten ones. Watch out for "out" images. What is an out image? On a sweltering hot beach, don't make the sand snow-white: Snow doesn't belong on a hot beach. A metaphor should suck the reader further into the scene, rather than distract from it by introducing a foreign object.

---

* Ben Yagoda, *The Sound on the Page*, 233.
** Jonathan Raban, "Notes from the Road," 347.

Some subjects defy comparison. Pablo Neruda wrote, "Y por las calles la sangre de los niños / corria simplement, como sangre de niños." (And through the streets the blood of the children / ran simply, like blood of children.)* There's nothing to compare with the blood of children running in the streets, so don't try. Metaphors can weaken, trivialize, and falsify. As you set out to become more skilled at making metaphors, keep in mind that some things are beyond comparison. The practice of making metaphor ought to include the practice of eschewing metaphor.

How to avoid mixing metaphors? A metaphor compares two things. "Dora Maar became Picasso's doormat" compares a person to an object that is frequently stepped upon. A (Dora Maar) compares to B (door mat). A mixed metaphor compares A to two things. "Dora Maar became Picasso's doormat, never yapping or nipping his hand" is a mixed metaphor in that it compares Maar to both a doormat and a dog. Mixed metaphors confuse rather than clarify. They usually come about because the writer is unaware of using a metaphor. "The window gaped open, beckoning the thief to enter" is mixed because it compares the window to both a mouth (gaping) and a hand (beckoning).

DEFINITIONS AND PRINCIPLES

A metaphor compares two things. Often it characterizes something abstract (memory, childhood, temper, death) by comparing it to something concrete (violets, volleyball, firestorm, tombstone).

> His temper was like a red dog, and he always had it close
> to hand.
> (John Fowles, *The Magus*, 15)

---

* Quoted in Patricia Hills, *May Stevens*, 81.

Temper is abstract. You can't see it or hear it or touch it. But you can see red. You can see a dog. A dog, like a temper, may be held ready to leap out, fangs bared.

A simile compares two things (white as snow, black as a crow's wing) using the connector "like" or "as." Similes usually compare just one aspect of a thing with one aspect of something else.

> When you do find a match between the provisional words
> in your head and that shadowy, half-buried recollection of
> events, there's no mistaking it; it's **as plain as a pair of jacks
> on the table.**
> (Jonathan Raban, "Notes from the Road," 349)

> My story is not important but **odd like horses lying down.**
> (C. D. Wright, *Cooling Time*, 71)

It's a mistake to think of metaphors and similes as surprising gifts or as something only literary writers use. Certainly, an apt metaphor is a pleasing thing, but it also works as a conceptual tool. The best writing, whether memoir, science, history, or philosophy, uses metaphor to clarify ideas. The French philosopher Gaston Bachelard writes: "So, like a forgotten fire, a childhood can always flare up again within us."* The English historian E. P. Thompson, author of the monumental *The Making of the English Working Class*, writes: "The working class did not rise like the sun at an appointed time."**

The classics scholar, poet, and essayist Anne Carson describes love:

> Even now it is hard to admit how love knocked me over. I
> had lived a life protected from all surprise, now suddenly

---

* Gaston Bachelard, "Reveries Toward Childhood," in *The Poetics of Reverie*, 104.
** E. P. Thompson, *The Making of the English Working Class*, 9.

**I was a wheel running downhill, a light thrown against a
wall, paper blown flat in a ditch.**
(Anne Carson, "Very Narrow," 60)

Metaphor works not as ornament but to deepen, to clarify, and
to extend meaning. Metaphors make ideas more vivid. Here is the
opening passage of Faulkner's story "Dry September." To intensify the
terror of his story about a lynching, Faulkner compares the red of the
sunset to blood.

Through the bloody September twilight, aftermath of sixty-
two rainless days, it had gone like a fire in dry grass — the
rumor, the story, whatever it was. Something about Miss
Minnie Cooper and a Negro.
(William Faulkner, "Dry September," 169)

If Faulkner had made the evening light "rosy" or "flushed," that would
have set up a different story — perhaps an erotic story. For this story it
would have been inapt and certainly inept. If the rumor had run like a
dancing nymph...

Metonymy exists in the realm of metaphor. Metonymy names an
associated object to stand for the object, "the crown" to stand for the
king, "a uniform" to stand for a police officer. "The pen is mightier than
the sword."

Synecdoche also exists in the realm of metaphor. A synecdoche
names a part to stand for the whole. Do you have wheels? He worked as
a hired hand. She was the brain of the class.

265

FORMS OF METAPHOR

A good way to approach working with metaphor is to practice, not metaphor in general, but metaphor as it occurs in particular syntactical forms. That way you can practice one form at a time. Here are seven ways of making a metaphor.

1. **Adverbial clause of manner.** The adverbial clause of manner, beginning with "as if" or "as though," compares one action to another. It is inherently metaphorical. It is found ubiquitously in literary writing, but not so much elsewhere. One way to begin working with metaphor is to begin working with the adverbial clause of manner.

> He jerked at his tie **as if he were trying to hang himself.**
> (Tim Gautreaux, "The Pine Oil Writer's Conference," 107)

There is also such a thing as an adverbial *phrase* of manner. The Tim Gautreaux sentence above could be rendered using a participial phrase:

> He jerked at his tie **as if trying to hang himself.**

> "Hassan is going to be a doctor," he said, rubbing his hands together, looking down at them **as if expecting some visible result.**
> (Tobias Wolff, "Bible," 321)

2. **X does something the way (or as) Y does something else.**

> At this point a large hopeful-looking woman stepped into the conversation and **cut him off with her thick body the way a cowboy's horse cuts a calf out of a herd.**
> (Tim Gautreaux, "The Pine Oil Writer's Conference," 109)

Southern California lay before Mike **as Italy before Napoleon.**
(Alva Johnston, "The Education of a Prince," 262)

3. Appositive as metaphor. (An appositive defines a noun: Mr. Brown, the janitor...)

So we had it out in the room that night — anger, guilt, defensiveness, **and all of the other carrion birds.**
(Albert Goldbarth, "Everybody's Nickname," 73)

To see a turkey vulture close up is to know the bird's tragic beauty, for there is a majesty to the crimson head, bare save for a sparse black stubble; the bird looks less bald than vulnerable and shorn, **a Nazi collaborator exposed before a French village.**
(Lee Zacharias, "Buzzards," 271)

4. It was like... It would be like...

To keep Mike away from the Beaux-Arts Ball **was like barring a bishop from his own cathedral on Easter morning or locking up the toast of the waterfront on Fleet Day.**
(Alva Johnston, "The Education of a Prince," 261)

The turtle was about fourteen inches long and a shining horn-brown. The bright spots on its marginal scutes **were like light bulbs around a mirror.**
(John McPhee, "Travels in Georgia," 162)

5. X is Y.

But **comedy is rock and roll**, and Pryor had his share
of hits.
(Hilton Als, "A Pryor Love," 401)

To one who lives in the **snow** and watches it day by day, **it is
a book** to be read.
(John Haines, "Snow," 3)

[Speaking of her baby]: But **he was my first wonder of the
world, my Grand Canyon.**
(Patricia Brieschke, "Cracking Open," 3)

**Joe Morello, Dave Brubeck's drummer, and Max Roach
were the Homer and Virgil of my younger years.**
(Jeffrey Hammond, "Close Enough for Jazz," 20)

6. Word substitution: bringing in a word from a different world.

He sat at his little workbench and began to work with
Lilliputian brushes and screwdrivers.
(Tim Gautreaux, "Misuse of Light," 22)

I am desperate to learn more about the Lanvins, but the **well
of the Internet has run dry.**
(Mary Gordon, "My Mother's Body," 72)

Speed was not in the **vocabulary** of that engine.
(Colleen McElroy, *Over the Lip of the World*, 62)

In the following passage, John McPhee is climbing fences and crawling over barriers to catch a plane at Newark International Airport:

> Occasionally I lost direction and once I had to crawl under a **mastodonic** truck, but I did get through and I ran down the **cattle-pen corridors** of the airport and with a minute to go, up the steps and into the plane....
> (John McPhee, "Travels in Georgia," 175)

7. **Similes.** A simile compares by using *like* or *as*. Similes compare an *aspect* of one thing with an *aspect* of another thing. In the first example below, ghosts are compared to kites only in how they fly. In the second, the woods are compared to the inside of a box only in degree of light.

> The ghosts flew **like kites above his head.**
> (Rebecca Makkai, "The Worst You'll Every Feel," 157)

> I ran from the sound of the river into the woods, **dark as the inside of a box.**
> (Anne Michaels, *Fugitive Pieces*, 8)

HANDS ON: MAKING METAPHOR

I suggest a three-part program. First, study the concept. Read the warnings. Understand definitions and principles. Second, collect sentences that use metaphor. Collect the different forms and write them in your sentence book to use as models. Third, practice making metaphors using a specific syntax, working on one form at a time (rather than trying to think of metaphor in general).

Remember that you are comparing an unfamiliar thing to a familiar thing. She ate the chocolate cake (the reader doesn't yet know how) as if she were a starving person (something easily imagined). If you wrote: "She ate the chocolate cake as if she were cibophobic," that would compare something unfamiliar (how she was eating) to something equally unfamiliar except to an extreme minority of readers who know that cibophobia means fear of food.

~ Choose one of the forms to work, say, X is Y. *Love Is a Dog from Hell* (Charles Bukowski). Then take an abstraction that seems key to the piece you are working on. Set the timer for some excruciating amount of time — perhaps ten or twenty minutes. Write using the phrase over and over, spinning off comparisons using only your chosen form. For example, for a piece on the Human Genome Project, I might write: "The human genome project is a modern-day Lewis and Clark expedition. The human genome project is the twentieth century's search for the Northwest Passage. The human genome project is exploration in the outer space of the infinitesimal. The human genome project is a modern-day search for the philosopher's stone." And on and on. You keep going, never minding that some will be awful. While you are writing you are meditating on the thing you are writing about, sinking into the ambiance of it, the emotion of it. This is an exercise in association, so that, to use the Faulkner example again, if you were using a simile and a color (red as…) to describe the kind of evening on which a murder was to take place, your words might run to "red as gut, red as blood, red as hot lava."

~ When the time is up, look over the result and choose an appropriate one. This is not an arbitrary choice, but one that deepens meaning. ("She had leopard eyes, narrow and yellow at the rims" does not describe a sweet silly person.) Turn some of your similes into metaphors. Turn "twilight red as blood" into "the bloody September twilight."

✍ Over the course of several weeks, practice using all the forms of metaphor. Don't get stuck on just one. Take one at a time and make it your own.

✍ As you become more fluid, become more rigorous. Keep questioning your metaphorical language. Is this apt? Does the comparison make literal sense? A dog may run as fast as a train but can a dog run like a train? I don't think so. But perhaps a rumor can run through town fast as a grass fire.

A writer in one of my classes recently wrote an excellent piece on living on a cul de sac. In it she wrote that during the 1950s, in suburban developments, culs de sac spread like a virus. Well, actually, culs de sac and viruses spread in entirely different ways. But perhaps culs de sac became as popular as white bread. (Both are manufactured things, both are made by companies, both were seen in the 1950s as being superior to their previous forms — the grid, whole-grain bread. Both were later criticized as being inferior to their previous forms.)

You see how it works.

23.

Extending Connections, Deepening Insight

I love words but I love the world more.
—Scott Russell Sanders

I SOMETIMES ASK MYSELF: Why do the works that grab me grab me? What is it about the pieces I reread and pass around and quote from and teach from that hold me within the world they have created? Certainly, I love language. Certainly, I am drawn to writers who have a good ear, who play language as if it were a musical instrument. But beyond that, I am drawn to works that to me have significance, that offer insight. Alternatively, I shy away from works that seem slight, even if well-written.

In my own work I have been trying to extend my philosophical reach, to ask questions that matter to me but also to the world, to realize pieces that may be quite personal but that also weave connections to a wider circle. It is my desire, whether or not I succeed, to increase the philosophical weight of my work and to deepen any insight it can bring to bear. Does this strike a chord? Is insight something dispersed by the heavens or can a writer strive for it? Are such matters susceptible to intention and to conscious work? The answer I think is yes. Here are some approaches.

ASK QUESTIONS

One way to deepen and extend our work is to ask questions. Michael J. Gelb's *How to Think Like Leonardo da Vinci*, written not for writers but for anyone wishing to enrich his or her life, suggests writing out — in your writer's notebook in the writing-practice manner, continuously without stopping — one hundred questions. These can be personal questions, questions about the world, questions about science, about nature, about society, about your mother, your life, your spouse, your dog, your car engine. After writing out your questions freely and without censorship or even much contemplation, circle the ten that seem to you to be the most important. On a clean page, write down your ten most important questions.

How do these ten questions relate to your body of work as it is developing right now? Are your most important questions reflected in your work? Do your questions suggest areas into which you might extend your work?

There are no right or wrong questions. Each writer's concerns and core questions will be different and a writer's questions will shift over time. Questions do not necessarily have answers and the best questions — examples might be, How does a bird fly? or Why was my mother so silent? — do not have simple answers. Rather, they open doors into areas of inquiry. The question, Why was my mother so silent? might lead me to write a memoir, or an exploration of expressiveness and communication, or a mother-daughter story, or a piece on family dynamics.

It seems right that our work as creators should reflect our deepest questions, concerns, and values. It seems obvious. Yet if we've never articulated these concerns or if we are professionally oriented to completing assignments generated by someone else, this dream can get lost. Allowing your own values to shape a piece does not preclude balance. Balance means you represent both sides of a question fairly and with respect. David Foster Wallace's "Consider the Lobster" is balanced, in that he takes care to fully express the viewpoint of the Maine lobster industry. Yet he also introduces his own questions. The piece appeared in *Gourmet* — not an animal rights venue. In it, Wallace manages to insert and even bring to the fore his question of whether or not dropping a live lobster into boiling water causes the creature to die in terror and agonizing pain, and if so, do we want to do that?

Asking questions can help to shape our whole body of work and can extend and deepen individual pieces. An entire essay might articulate the essential questions facing some discipline or area of concern or interest. A piece titled "20 Questions on our Minds" by neuropsychiatrist Richard Restak, which appeared in *The American Scholar,* consists of nothing more (or less) than twenty questions on the human brain, taking into account the revolution in neuroscience currently under way.

Fiction writers ask questions through their characters. In Sherwood Anderson's story "I Want to Know Why," an adolescent boy is smitten with horses and with a horse trainer who proceeds to degrade himself before the boy's very eyes. The boy wants to know, "What did he do it for?" In Tillie Olsen's "I Stand Here Ironing," a teacher has asked an exhausted mother for a conference concerning her troubled teenage daughter. The mother, standing at her ironing, muses to herself:

Even if I came, what good would it do? You think because I
am her mother I have a key, or that in some way you could
use me as a key? She has lived for nineteen years. There is all
that life that has happened outside of me, beyond me.

And when is there time to remember, to sift, to weigh,
to estimate, to total?

(Tillie Olsen, "I Stand Here Ironing," 9)

Characters, like people, have conundrums, things they are seeking
to understand, things they find incomprehensible. They seek. They query
the universe, just as we ourselves do. Ask questions. Let your characters
ask their questions. They want to know why.

CONNECT WITH A WIDER WORLD

Another way to deepen your writing is to spin threads to connect
immediate personal experience with the big, wide, outside world. In an
essay on dressing, I might articulate the current chaos of my closet, but
also recall that Sappho was concerned with beauty, that there exists a
history of costume, that the silkworm is a worm, that cotton is a plant
requiring toil in a cotton field, that a fur garment was once a creature's
skin, that the detective in Raymond Chandler's *The Big Sleep* steps out
in a powder-blue suit.

We've seen how Diane Ackerman's "Mute Dancers: How to
Watch a Hummingbird" has only nine paragraphs. But my, what a
lot she fits into those nine paragraphs. At the core we find her own
experience — a walk in a rain forest with hummingbirds fluttering
about her braids probing her red ribbons for nectar. The essay includes
natural history, Aztec beliefs about the hummingbird, mating rituals
of the hummingbird (more natural history), her neighbor's experience
of attack by hummingbird, a friend's adventure saving a hummingbird

from her cat, the inability of explorers to the "New World" to grow the vanilla beans they brought back to the "Old World" not knowing that vanilla plants require hummingbirds for pollination, and the luminous colors of the hummingbird, "as if the northern lights had suddenly fallen to earth." Each and every paragraph is about the hummingbird, but in this tiny essay, how far we fly.

I am presently working on a piece called "Housekeeping." It is based on my childhood experience growing up in an unkempt household, which stood in contrast to my maternal grandmother's household, which was vacuumed and polished to the point of fanaticism. What does my personal housekeeping experience connect to, out there in the wide world? Well. There is Hercules's fifth labor — cleaning the Augean stables. There are writers who are hyper-kempt (May Sarton with her washed cups and cut flowers) and writers who are hyper-unkempt (the poet Auden with his white wine-splattered suit; Iris Murdoch and John Bayley with their dustballs and dirt-desecrated dinner plates). There is feng shui in which clutter clogs energy. There is "ethnic cleansing," God help us. There was my sister whose refrigerator full of rotting food revealed a life spiraling into mental illness. There are the ten random people I asked, "How do you keep your house (or your room) clean?" (My favorite answer came from my nephew Eric Messerschmidt: "This assumes I do keep my room clean.") There is Marilynne Robinson's brilliant novel *Housekeeping*. And no doubt there are other connections I haven't thought of yet.

Look at the piece you are working on. Where are its mirrors, out there in the world? Is there a way you can spin a thread to the moon? Back to the Middle Ages, to the black plague? Is your personal situation connected to a scientific or medical finding? (I am an identical twin. Twins are clones. Clones bring us to the first cloned mammal, Dolly, to the debate about cloning and stem cells, to the Human Genome Project...) You get the idea.

READING

"Reading is important," writes Yusef Komunyakaa. "I can't see how anyone can write and not read. I'm not just talking about only reading literature, but reading in the sciences, philosophy, mythology, history, about the arts, current events — everything that one can possibly read. This feeds the imagination."*

Reading is one of the absorbing pleasures of the writing life. Research is part of it. Say I have a character, an elderly photographer. How does her work fit into the history of photography? What does she herself know of this history? What were the influences on her? As a woman, was she an anomaly, a maverick? Or part of a long tradition? These questions may lead to happy hours in the library. And the Internet has become another library whose riches multiply as the years roll on.

Reading carries us into wider worlds, sparks ideas for our own work, lets us rest from our own work, and provides shelter for mind and spirit. Just as visual artists spend hours and years looking at contemporary and past art, so we writers read.

One immediate way to let your reading inform your writing is to collect epigraphs — a quotation taken from your reading, placed at the beginning of a work, setting forth the theme. Whenever I read a passage that strikes me, and that can stand alone, I copy it into a small blank book I call my epigraph book, carefully noting the author, and where I got the quote from. I do this with no preconceived notion of where to use it. It's remarkable how many of these quotations have found their way into something I'm working on. Here is a random list of epigraphs taken from a few consecutive pages of my epigraph book:

"I have two homelands, Cuba and night." (José Martí)

* Yusef Komunyakaa interview by Miller and Zoe Anglesey, *The Writer's Chronicle*, October/November 2000, 16.

"Houses that are lost forever continue to live in us."
 (Gaston Bachelard)
"Let us have a good fire and be beloved." (*Rig Veda*)
"It's all a matter of keeping my eyes open." (Annie Dillard)
"I am here to burn for you like a black candle."
 (Osip Mandelstam)
"I touched the stones and they had my own skin."
 (Theodore Roethke)
"I have often cursed my existence." (Beethoven)
"Stony limits cannot hold love out." (Shakespeare, *Romeo
 and Juliet*)
"Yellow light. Supreme good fortune." (*I Ching*)

Beginning a piece with an epigraph makes an immediate connection between what is to follow and something out there in the world that mirrors it.

INTENTION

After you've finished a draft of a piece, set your timer for ten minutes. In your writing-practice notebook, write the start line, "If I could bring 5 percent more insight to this matter, it would be that..." Write for ten minutes without stopping, letting anything that comes to mind go on the page.

You may be surprised at the further insights and understandings you can come to in this way.

24.

On Revision

Let's say it's a mess. But you have a chance to fix it. You try to be
clearer. Or deeper. Or more eloquent. Or more eccentric.
You try to be true to a world. You want the book to be more spacious,
more authoritative. You want to winch yourself up from yourself.
You want to winch the book out of your balky mind. You try to
liberate it. You try to get this wretched stuff on the page closer to what
you think your book ought to be — what you know, in your spasms
of elation, it can be. You read the sentences over and over. Is this
the book I'm writing? Is this all?

—Susan Sontag

REVISION IS ABOUT DEEPENING, EXTENDING, ELABORATING,
and only then burnishing and honing. Polishing a too-thin piece is to
do the right thing at the wrong time. And most unrealized works are,
basically, too thin. They don't extend far enough. Perhaps they lack
insight. Perhaps the language is thin as weak tea. Perhaps the structure

needs correcting for the piece is structured nonsensically or lacks a dramatic structure altogether. Perhaps the emotional ground is merely hinted at because the setting is not saturated with the emotion of the piece. Perhaps the character is engaged in some job or sport or activity that is scarcely on the page, no glimpse of the tools or smells of this trade. Perhaps someone comes on stage without portrayal. Or speaks but lacks body language. Perhaps the sentence forms bear no relationship to the meanings they are carrying.

For writers who make themselves students of the language — of words and word origins, of forms of the sentence and of the paragraph — revising becomes a pleasurable stage of composition. This is the time to play, to experiment, to enjoy the delicious sense of mastery that comes from growing skills.

As you revise, keep hold of the idea that you are working out your own thoughts in your own words. You're not trying to second-guess some teacher or mentor or reader. There's a time to focus on the demands posed by the work itself, the work in front of you. I've known writers who are so externally oriented, so concerned with whether anyone will ever like it or read it or publish it, that they've lost track of both what they want for the piece and what the work itself requires. There's a time to turn inward, to create an interior space in which the two forces interacting are the piece itself and the writer's imagination.

Here are some approaches and strategies.

⤳ You have a rough essay, with various blocks of type in place. Perhaps some of the segments are rather badly written, perhaps transitions are lacking. But, as far as you know, every piece is there. Do not, I repeat, *do not* go into the essay and begin hacking or thrashing about. Do not enter the premises with a wrecking bar. Instead, work on craft outside the essay itself. Work in your writing-practice notebook. Copy down a sentence or a paragraph that needs work, and work on it there, in the notebook.

Experiment with alternatives until you get one you like. Then type it back into the essay.

∾ There is no need to begin at the beginning, but when you do return to the beginning, remember to ground the reader in time and place, and in your connection to this material. Is there something surprising, or startling, or unusual that unfolds within the first few paragraphs? Try putting it in the first sentence. Can you make a first sentence that captures the core of the dramatic conflict?

> I've hit a lot of people in the face in my life.
> (Richard Ford, "In the Face," 51)

∾ Does the piece ask questions? Does it open up the key questions inherent in its subject matter? If it is fiction, what are the protagonist's questions?

∾ Structure: Look at complication/resolution (at least 85 percent of stories use this structure). Or look over the structures presented in this book or elsewhere, structures you've taken into your repertoire. Does the structure of the piece fit its content? If it is about baseball, could it have nine innings? If it is about twins, could it repeatedly double itself? If it is about the new social media Twitter, in which persons communicate using no more than 140 characters, could it progress in sections each employing no more than 140 characters?

∾ Verbs carry the piece. Circle every verb. Question every verb. Can you make a verb more active, more accurate? Does at least one sentence have multiple verbs?

↬ Go through and circle areas that are vacant of images (gray areas). Rewrite the sentence to expel the gray and the drab. Make general words more specific. Change *casual attire* to *tee-shirt and blue jeans*. Change *She packed her undergarments* to *She packed her black lace panties and matching bra*.

↬ Work on sentences. Make a sentence or paragraph enact its own meaning.

↬ Body parts ground writing and increase its visual and visceral impact. Merely increasing the number of body parts can improve a story. Not, *He leaned against the doorjamb* but *He leaned his shoulder against the doorjamb*. Not, *He touched her face*, but *He touched her face with his fingertips*.

↬ What is the emotion of the piece? Is the setting saturated with this emotion? Can you put in an object that holds a love or a pain or a recurring dream or memory?

↬ Work on coloration. Color is not arbitrary but resonates metaphorically. Thus, *blood-red nail polish* will deepen a sense of doom, whereas a *rose-silk gown* adds an erotic blush. It is important what you choose to color and what you choose to leave alone. Color what is significant to the story. Leave the rest alone. All this language work is about making a piece more visual and more sonorous. It is not about making it more flowery.

↬ Whenever a person comes onstage, he or she becomes visible and needs a portrait. Whenever a person speaks, he or she speaks from a body, moves the body or holds it still.

～ Voice: Do persons and characters each have their own voice, or do they sound generic?

～ Go through and take out every lie (Grace Paley).

～ Deepen insight, and deepen the connections of the piece with the outer world. What is the philosophy of a piece? How does it connect with the past, with history? What stories in mythology, fairy tale, or fable does this story carry? What are the icons, associations, archetypes? Do timed writes in your writing-practice notebook on each section, in which you ask yourself: What is the meaning of this? What further insight can I bring to this? Is there any story out there in the world that this is an instance of?

～ There is a constant tension between accuracy and authenticity on the one hand, and language as music, as vision, as a palpable aesthetic object on the other. We are not in the decorating business but we are working to deepen our contact with the language, to engage it fully. Constantly measure the one — truth — against the other — color, odor, sound, sight.

～ Finally, after each session, insert your new changes into the piece and print out a clean version. Always have at hand a clean version including all your most recent tweaks. Do not work for long periods with a scratched-up, emended mess.

WORK VS. TALENT

Here is a good place to question whether some people may just have more talent. Most people, when speaking of great artists — writers or painters or musicians — speak of talent (for the undeveloped) or genius

THE WRITER'S PORTABLE MENTOR

(for the well-developed). Art students and apprentice writers often ask themselves, "Do I have it?" When I was in graduate school, a fellow graduate student in creative writing announced his intention to ask his faculty advisor whether he had "it." If not, he planned to quit. Some accomplished writers believe fervently that talent is fundamental to their own and other people's artistic achievement.

Perhaps because I did not grow up hearing the word *talented,* I have always belonged to the opposite school of artistic development, the practice-makes-perfect school. Pablo Picasso — the artist to whom the word "genius" most often sticks — may also have been in the practice-makes-perfect school because he was a prodigious, indefatigable worker, outworking all his friends, outworking probably every other artist in France. So yes, he was a "genius," but he may have come by that "genius" through his fanatical work habits.

Indeed, neuroscience and cognitive psychology have landed with both feet in the practice-makes-perfect school. The emerging picture, writes Daniel J. Levitin in *This Is Your Brain on Music,* "is that ten thousand hours of practice is required to achieve the level of mastery associated with being a world-class expert — in anything. In study after study, of composers, basketball players, fiction writers, ice skaters, concert pianists, chess players, master criminals, and what have you, this number comes up again and again…. No one has yet found a case in which true world-class expertise was accomplished in less time. It seems that it takes the brain that long to assimilate all that it needs to know to achieve true mastery."*

Let's assume you have talent, whatever that means. If you want to write, why waste time wondering? We all have some abilities and propensities. We all have potential. Now we know that to realize that potential, all we have to do is — work for 10,000 hours.

---

* Daniel J. Levitin, *This Is Your Brain on Music,* 193.

Getting the Work into the World

All of them want to know if they have enough talent to become successful artists. This is always a difficult thing to advise a student about. There are so many other factors that determine the complete artist other than the possession of artistic talent. Who can tell whether or not the young artist can bear all the vicissitudes of all the artist's life, not only standing up under the blows, but turning them to his own advantage.

—Romare Bearden

25.

Literary vs. Commercial Writing

Anything that happens to me as a writer has been precipitated
by an action of my own.
—Joyce Carol Oates, note kept on her desk

I LIKE THE DISTINCTION MADE IN THE VISUAL ARTS between commercial artists and fine artists. Commercial artists, whether freelance or employed, are working to earn a living and their product belongs to their employers. In general, before they begin they have a commitment to receive compensation. Fine artists want to make money, and some keep an eye on viable markets for their work, but their work belongs to themselves and they do it without regard to compensation. The fine artist may have a day job and the day job may be doing commercial art.

We writers are the same. The commercial writer — whether reporter, freelance journalist, grants-writer, or publicist — writes to earn a living.

THE WRITER'S PORTABLE MENTOR

This writer would not write for free any more than a grill cook would flip hamburgers for free. It is a job. In contrast, the literary writer writes with no guarantee of compensation. But the reality is that many writers cross back and forth over this line. And the distinction is muddied by the fact that at least some "commercial" writers scrimp along making a rather inadequate income whereas some "literary" writers make good money, and any well-known novelist will get a contract for his or her next novel. Still, between the two, procedures and strategies differ.

Commercial freelance writers query editors for assignments, and write a piece only after they get an assignment. Commercial freelance writers write to a word count and they write to a deadline. They send the piece to the editor on the deadline. The editor works the piece in conjunction with the writer, and the piece sees the light of day shortly thereafter. These writers learn to write expeditiously and they learn to complete work.

All of these are reasons why any writer would benefit from doing this some of the time. Many of our finest writers are literary writers who work or once worked as commercial freelance writers. I think of Jonathan Raban, Annie Proulx, Donald Hall, and William Kennedy. On the other side, editors of commercial periodicals sometimes do a large amount of rewriting on pieces they buy from commercial freelance writers. Certainly they value their brilliant writers, but all of their writers are not brilliant. Anyone knows this who has ever worked on the editorial staff of a commercial magazine.

Literary writers send out completed works to literary journals with a note (including thanks and a short bio that mentions previous publications, if any) and a self-addressed stamped envelope (SASE). Or they submit online in the case of journals that have established online submission systems. They do not query the journals, but they do read them constantly. At the literary journals, it's the quality of writing that counts above all. A literary journal does not take a poorly written piece containing good information and rewrite it. The writing has to be superb upon arrival, although small edits may be made. Of course, different editors have different tastes, and there are various aesthetics afloat. Literary journals also publish regular features and theme issues.

Although the writing found in the literary journals is not of course uniformly brilliant, some of the best work being done today can be found in their pages. Out of a random sample of journals stacked on my living room rug right now — *The Ontario Review, Field, The American Scholar, North Dakota Quarterly, Creative Nonfiction, Brick, Alaska Quarterly Review* — I see the works of these nationally acclaimed writers: Mark Rudman, Linda Bierds, Frederick Busch, Diane Ackerman, Francine Prose, Joyce Carol Oates, John Edgar Wideman, Andrei Codrescu, and Mary Oliver.

So don't look down on the literary journals, and do read them, even if they pay little. Think of it as a different career path — you are aiming for collected works, that coveted National Endowment for the Arts (NEA) award, a Guggenheim. Many literary writers end up teaching, as do some journalists.

If you are a "literary" writer, you might consider also doing some commercial freelance writing. Why? To make some money, of course. But also to learn to write to a word count, to a deadline. To learn to complete a piece and let go of it and on to the next. If you are a "commercial" writer — an articles writer, newsletter writer, publicist, or the like — you might consider doing some literary writing. Why? You can write longer, more honestly, more deeply, and you can write on your own agenda. You can aspire to literature. Among my clients are successful commercial writers who are good at cranking out articles but have lost the knack for writing longer, more substantive pieces that have more depth than is required by an airline magazine. On the other hand, some amazing literary writers — Hemingway for example — learned at least some of their craft strategies as reporters.

Why not have it both ways? Why not cross back and forth over this line from the start?

26.

First Time Out: Writing Buddies and Critique Groups

Writers feed off each other when they're in close proximity. It's not competition. It's just that somebody will read his poem to you, and you'll say, "Oh, man, that's wonderful!" And then you'll get charged up. You'll want to write something that's that effective.

—Tommy Scott Young

WE ARE A COMMUNITY OF WRITERS. The better one of us does, the better the prospects for all the rest. This is not an idle thought or sentimental wish. Biographies and creativity studies too numerous to list reveal that master-creators from Renoir to Picasso to O'Keeffe had a knowledgeable support group, whose composition shifted over time, but from which they received lifelong support. The important point here is that they got not just support — "This is great, send it out!" — but *knowledgeable* support, including praise, challenges, questions, criticism, and the sustaining company of others who understood their ambitions, compulsions, and way of life.

You can see how this works in practical ways. Sharing resources, knowledge, and venues results in more resources, more knowledge, and more venues. If I get better at paragraphing and tell you what I learned and how you might improve this paragraph, then you might question what my antagonist really thinks and whether he would say what he thinks or lie or say nothing. Multiply this over years and you have an enormous helping force, *especially if your peer artists are skilled.* One of the challenges and tasks of a writer is to learn to be a skillful reader of another's work. This skill is similar to that of learning to read (as a writer) a published masterwork. It is the skill of looking at such a work and being able to unravel the technical means by which it achieves its effects.

WRITING BUDDIES

Many writers begin alone. They experience the clandestine pleasure of the blank page — often a journal or diary page — that seems to invite their words. Other writers begin within the shelter of parental praise or the encouragement of a teacher. But all of us are eventually out here on our own, more or less. (I include the many writers who start late.) We all grow up. We discover that one or another of our pals who also aspired to being a writer, who was at least as talented as we were, who had a lot more promise, who had everything going for him or her, even the support of a husband or a mother or a brother, has fallen by the wayside, has quit writing. We become aware that, although, to be sure, our dear relatives want us to be happy, they do not actually care whether or not we write. (Indeed, it may take entirely too much time, and for what?)

Of course, if we make a mountain of money then it has all worked out in the end (according to them). But most of us don't make a mountain of money. (Is there a struggling writer in existence who has not been asked, Why don't you write a *Harry Potter* novel?) "Most good writing," says Edward Hoagland, "is done against the resistance of others — first parents, then spouses or colleagues at jobs. It's a candle you protect with both cupped hands."*

Under such circumstances, a writing buddy or two is not a luxury. We need a friend to meet every week in a café to write with for an hour. Or we need a workshop. Or we need to take a writing class or go to a writing conference or even enter an MFA program if and when appropriate. Writers and other artists simply do not accomplish excellent works year in and year out in a social vacuum. Those who attempt it work at a disadvantage and risk producing a mountain of failed works due to the lack of stimulation, challenge, inspiration, and encouragement that artists get from peer artists.

Writing conferences, adult education programs such as the Cambridge Center for Adult Education in Cambridge, Massachusetts, the proliferating MFA programs whether residential or nonresidential, and writing centers such as Seattle's Richard Hugo House and Bainbridge Island's Field's End provide many resources for writers: classes, critique groups, forums, lectures, readings, and resources such as a library or a place to work or a tutor. They provide introductions to other writers, connections.

Writing teachers — and many of us turn to teaching — have advantages: No one learns better or more deeply or more thoroughly than the teacher does. But because we live so much of the time in the bubble of our own classroom, we writers who teach have a particularly urgent need for peer writers: a literary and literate buddy or two, a

---

* Edward Hoagland, "Journal Vermont, 2002–2004," *The American Scholar*, Autumn 2004, 151–155.

workshop of our peers, or a writing-practice session that we don't lead or "teach" but attend just in order to write. It is useful for teachers to take a class now and then. I often have one or more writing teachers in my classes and I try to occasionally take a class, taking care to avoid the situation in which I must critique the work of my fellow classmembers (don't ask the carpenter to pound nails on holiday). There is that tragic, often secret situation: the teacher of writing who does not write. He or she is "blocked" or teaching has usurped all his or her time, or... If you are in that hole, begin your fifteen-minute practice today. And find a buddy — one of your equals — to write with.

Whatever your situation as a writer, whether you teach or write grant proposals or newspaper articles, whether you are just beginning or have years of experience, it's a good idea to take the time now and again to evaluate the question of whether you have an excellent social context in which to grow and thrive as a writer. Give yourself a writing-practice session to think it through. Set your timer for five or ten minutes. First write: What is my present situation in terms of a social context that supports me as a writer? What is the reality? Then take ten minutes to answer the question: How might I improve this situation by 5 percent? Then do those one or two things.

CRITIQUE GROUPS

One way is to find and join a critique group, a workshop in which writers take turns sharing work, giving feedback on it, and getting feedback in return. There are two forms of this: workshops taught in writing programs led by teachers who are master-writers, and writing-critique groups composed of peers.

I admit that I am at odds with the workshop method utilized as the main way to teach and learn how to write. Too many hours are spent in scrutinizing unrealized work when we should be putting those hours into scrutinizing masterworks. "One learns nothing from others' bad work, only from one's own," writes Marvin Bell. "Would we attempt to learn to sing by listening to the tone-deaf? Do we imagine we could learn to fly by imitating the labors of a kangaroo?"*

And, although any feedback is useful, too often the blind are leading the blind. Hasty, and sometimes wrongheaded advice can be given, and worse, taken.

But working alone is not the answer either. And some workshops are superb. I've participated in my own once-a-month workshop for nearly twenty years, and I wouldn't do without it. It includes some very skilled writers, and we help each other get better all the time.

Whether we "workshop" a little or a lot, there are ways we can improve our skill at giving feedback and receiving it. Here are some guidelines.

THE WRITER'S RESPONSIBILITY

Be open to feedback. Listen, and think about it. Don't argue.

But do not accept advice if it doesn't feel right. I have seen writers flounder for years dutifully following the contradictory advice of their writing group, getting increasingly lost. This does not work.

The problem is that if you follow someone's advice, even a good teacher's advice, while not really "getting" it, then the captain has abandoned ship. The ship is tossing directionless at sea. This is the case even if the feedback is exactly right. (Sometimes we get advice that we don't really understand until later. Later then, is the time to put it to use in the piece. Other times, we get advice that is plain wrong.) When you are hearing something you don't agree with or don't really get, try to listen, try to understand, and again, don't argue. Sleep on it. Think

---

* Marvin Bell, "Three Propositions," in *Writers on Writing,* edited by Robert Pack and Jay Parini, 4.

about it. But be loyal to your process and to your work. Be loyal to your vision.

Sometimes we get a suggestion that we know instantly is exactly right. Other times a suggestion seems off, but it clues us that something is amiss and we get to work.

As readers for a writer who takes responsibility for his or her own work, we can be more free, less timid, less worried that we'll make a mistake and lead the writer astray. This writer follows only advice that feels right.

THE READER'S RESPONSIBILITY

How can you upgrade the quality of feedback you give to your peer writers? Your job is to try to help the writer fully realize this piece, which is a piece in process. Bring everything you know to bear.

Here are a few points to think about:

∼ Compare the work to masterworks. How can this piece be improved enough to get into *The Best American Essays* or *The Best American Short Stories* of the year? (This is not, by the way, how you would look at a young person's writing. You would never treat a child's writing or even a freshman college student's writing this way. This is for adult writers who are or aspire to be professional published writers.)

∼ Naturally we are not trashing pieces. Trashing is truly an amateur move — it takes far more skill to say, here is a good part (specified and why) and here's what could use some work (specified and why). Make a huge effort to understand what the writer is trying to achieve (the weaker the piece, the more important this is). Then help the writer get there.

∼ Kindness, always. Vague praise is not kindness; it's condescending laziness. Still, kindness is a crucial virtue in this interaction as in all others.

∾ Structure: Know what the structure of the piece is. Does the structure work?

∾ Beginnings: Is this a good beginning or is it a long windup? Can you find a better place to begin on page two?

∾ When someone comes onstage does he get a portrait? When someone speaks does she have body language, gesture? Are the characters dressed? Does the setting carry its share of the emotion?

∾ Take one paragraph and do a micro-analysis of the sentences. Are they sturdy muscular sentences or are they weak and flabby? Is the diction conventional received diction (they buy a "home"; she is "a blonde"; he is "dark and handsome")? Is the writer avoiding repetition or fragments or the compound sentence? Why? Is this a door that could be opened?

∾ Do the characters have voice? (To write: "My mother used to scold and nag all the time" is to talk about her without giving her voice. To write: "Every day my mother yelled, 'Why can't you get up and dress yourself and go to school! I'm a failure! I have a 20-year-old living at home doing nothing! What's the matter!? Talk to me! What have I done?'" is to give a character voice.)

∾ Can the insight be deepened? Could a memoirist reflect on a past event from the perspective of the present? Did a character have some past trauma that causes her to be so close-mouthed? Ask questions that will help the writer think more deeply about the matter at hand.

∾ Could the piece benefit from a story or reference from somewhere else — another person's parallel experience? A myth? A quote from a philosopher or from the grocer down the street?

Finally, it's not really useful to say, "This doesn't work for me." This implies that technical skill and literary mastery are a matter of personal taste: I like chocolate but you like vanilla. Not so, dear writers. Not so.

PRESENTING AND PERFORMING

Readings are proliferating in cities and towns around the country, and often they include an "open mic" where you can arrive a bit early and sign up to read for a short time, five or ten minutes. Many reading venues welcome not only poetry but also prose. And, in my experience, nothing is better for a piece, whether poetry or prose, than reading it out loud to an audience.

First, practice. Read your piece into a tape recorder and listen back. You will learn to slow down and to get comfortable with it. You will also see spots to improve, to work. Then go out and read it to an audience. Gradually you will get over any stage fright; you will get comfortable, and you will find that reading the piece out loud helps you to hear it.

You work on it as you are working up to reading it and afterward you work on it some more — especially the sounds. Then, another time, read it again. Reading to an audience allows you to *hear* the piece. Nothing could be better for your work. And the practice of sharing your work with an audience is one more way to connect to the community of writers.

Be courteous. Time your piece in your practice sessions so you know exactly how long it takes to read it. Don't hog the mic, don't go over your allotted time. And stay for the entire reading to listen while others read. Those who read only to promptly depart are noticed.

27.

Sending Your Work Out

My first novella was returned with the succinct note: "We found the heroine as boring as her husband had."
—prolific novelist Mary Higgins Clark

FOR THE WRITER OF STORIES OR POEMS OR LITERARY ESSAYS, sending work out becomes part of the creative working process. Why? Because getting a personal essay or a poem ready to send out is tantamount to completing it. Work never sent out is very likely never completed. The author never has to stand by it, for better or for worse. It is never exposed to a stranger's eye. It is never received with love, hate, indifference, or with interest. It has no audience, no public. As a result, the writer is never obliged to see it through a reader's eye.

A dynamic process percolates in the interval between doing the work and exposing the work. You do that crucial read-through before sending the piece out for the first time. Suddenly the eye is more acute, aware of the imminent exposure. Adjustments are made, a sentence tweaked, the list of nouns in a list sentence jimmied to ratchet up colors and notes.

Your hard-won work is about to be exposed, with all the shame and actual humiliation that exposure can bring up, especially to writers still wet about the ears. We've all been there.

A writer's embarrassment about his or her short story says nothing whatever about its quality. A critical eye, the ability to see faults, has nothing to do with embarrassment. Embarrassment speaks, rather, to how exposed the writer feels in the piece. I once wrote a short story called "Storm." I worked it and reworked it. I went to the setting (the granitic seacoast of Massachusetts) and wrote on the setting. I made an extensive family tree for each character. And on and on. When I finished the story, I polished and polished. Finally, there was nothing more I could do. The story practically finished me off, but it too was finished.

There it was, all typed up. It caused me intense embarrassment. I put it on the mantelpiece in the living room to remind myself that I was a writer and that writers must send their work out. Every time I glanced over at the typescript propped behind the snapshot of my Grandma Henry, my face burned with further embarrassment. Finally, to get it out of my sight, I sent it to *The Southern Review*. I sent it to *The Southern Review* because it is one of the three or four best literary magazines published in the United States. No doubt these erudite editors read and reject the work of fools all the time, so one more story from one more fool could not possibly make a bit of difference. In about three weeks I received a letter from *The Southern Review*. They wanted the story.

But often a story does come back. Big deal. (Okay, sometimes it is a big deal. Nevertheless...) You look at it again, perhaps rework the sentences or deepen the insight or extend a thought or recast the beginning. Study the rejection note for any hint of a specific response. But even if it's only that inscrutable printed note, you have your own fresh eyes and improving craft skills to bring to the task. Thus is the endeavor of creating a work served by the rather different endeavor of getting it published.

If you are immersed in a writers' community, you know writers who seldom if ever send out work. Some of these writers have been working for years. They don't feel ready, personally. They don't feel the work is ready. Or they send out a piece and it is rejected, so they go into a major funk. That's it — nothing more goes out for two more years. Then maybe they send something else out. Again they are full of high hopes mixed with trepidation. Again they get a rejection. Now what?

Nobody gets published this way.

When I first began to send out my poems, the idea of getting one published seemed to me virtually an impossible dream. I had loved poetry since childhood, since "Now we are six..." and "The Raggedy Man." Starting when I was 16, I began writing "poems." Very late in the day, it now seems to me, I finally took a poetry workshop, Harold Bond's ten-week poetry seminar at the Cambridge Center for Adult Education. I owe the late Harold Bond a tremendous debt of gratitude. He taught us to look at lines and to ask what made this line a line of poetry. He taught us what enjambment was, as well as many other strategies and moves, some of which I have since rejected and some of which are so completely incorporated into my practices and aesthetics that I no longer remember where they came from. Harold Bond also taught us to send out our poems, three to five poems per envelope.

After taking his workshop three times for a total of thirty weeks, I began sending out my poems, three to five poems in an envelope with a short cover letter. I would make up a set and send out two or three identical sets simultaneously, as Harold Bond taught us to do. Perhaps I had three or four different sets out at any one time.

My plan was this. I intended to send out 500 different envelopes before I would reconsider my strategy, much less quit. (By the time I started sending out, I had written a fairly large number of poems.) Notice that my goal essentially was to open myself to receiving 500 rejections. My goal was not: Get a Poem Published. Of course, Get a Poem Published *was* my goal. But that goal does not require any action, except the action of sending out one envelope, which is virtually a waste of time.

My goal was to energetically accumulate 500 rejections by sending out that many envelopes as intelligently as I could ("intelligent" means, read the journal before you send poems). I wanted the number to be a large number, because I wanted time and I wanted room and I didn't want to fail. With this setup, a rejection wasn't a failure; it was progress toward the goal.

So what happened? It took me several months, and 70 rejections before I received an acceptance. That acceptance was one of the thrilling moments of my life.

I have no idea what made me think of that strategy, but years later I am still impressed by it. It reduces the weight of any one rejection and it requires the writer to send out lots and lots of envelopes. For many years thereafter I simply kept probably ten or fifteen works, including prose and poetry, in circulation at all times. Whenever a piece was accepted for publication, this required me to put another piece on the list of works completed and circulating.

Two years ago I thought of a strategy more similar to my original one, a strategy which entertains me quite a bit. (Entertainment is important. Why be miserable?) It is to send out 300 envelopes a year. This is my version of an athletic competition (for one who could not be less athletic). It ups the ante. It pushes me to be more productive. I've even experienced a twinge of anxiety upon an acceptance because that meant I had to fling another piece into circulation. The result, though, is that more works get accepted sooner. The cause is a matter of mathematics. A certain percentage of work gets accepted: The more you send out, the more gets accepted.

The process of unloading (read publishing) can happen in several stages, and each one can further the process of finishing a work. First the writer readies a piece to send out. (If you never send your work out, you never get to this stage of the creative work process.) Let's call this "Quote Finished," because its rejection (no big tragedy) becomes an opportunity to look at it again, to see its faults with clear eyes (the fickle writer embroiled in the current work-in-progress has now gained distance from this old thing). The job is to read it out loud again, to finish it again, to send it out again. Even first publication is not the end of the road for many pieces. As poets, fiction writers, essayists, we always hope for the collection of poems or stories or essays. Therefore, we indulge ourselves in post-publication revisions.

And what if you just don't like it any more? It no longer interests you. It's stupid and you never want to see it again.

Here I want to quote at length from a perceptive essay on "Learning to Work" that psychologist Virginia Valian published some thirty years ago. It is a reminder that losing interest in a piece may be nothing more than a bad work habit.

> Attitudes toward finishing work most distinguish successful from unsuccessful workers. I discovered that I resisted working my ideas out to the end. Many times I caught myself putting something away once the end was in sight. This was true both of writing papers and doing more menial tasks. Sometimes, when I went back to a task, I would discover that I had as little as thirty minutes' work left. This resistance to the end product contrasts sharply with what I have seen of or read about successful workers, who always finish everything, even after they have lost interest in it. Successful workers are also always thinking about the next project, planning ahead, integrating their current work into a larger picture which is constantly being revised. I tended not to do this. One consequence of viewing work as a continuing process is that one wants to finish the

present project to get on to the next. Although one could conceivably just go on to the next without finishing the present piece of work, important learning occurs in putting the finishing touches on a paper or project, learning that may govern the direction of the next work. One is gratified by the feeling of closure that comes with finishing a project, but aside from this feeling, the finishing touches to make what one has done presentable, to make sure the idea is expressed, puts the project in perspective, aligns it with what one has done so far and what one is going to do next.

Unfinished projects also have a way of nagging at the back of the mind, even if one has decided that the enterprise was mistaken to begin with. In everything I have begun but not finished there was an idea I thought was interesting and still think is interesting, even if its context was wrong, even if it itself was wrong. It's hard to lay those ideas to rest until they've been worked out and either found hopeless or given formal expression.

It also becomes depressing to be unsure from the very beginning whether or not you're actually going to do something with a new idea. If it's just going to end up in a drawer along with a bunch of other half-alive ideas, it's hard to get committed to it. Lack of commitment creates another problem; if you're going to be committed to an idea, you'll examine it very carefully at the outset to make sure it's worth spending time on. Thus, you are quicker to get rid of an idea that's only superficially appealing. The uncommitted person ends up neither developing worthwhile ideas nor getting rid of worthless ones soon enough.

(Virginia Valian, "Learning to Work," 173)

It may be rarely true that some works should be abandoned. But mostly we should plan to finish what we've started, even if, upon occasion, it is a struggle to do so.

SIMULTANEOUS SUBMISSIONS?

Should you submit a single work to more than one journal at the same time? This is the question everyone asks. The answer is simple: Yes and No.

Every literary magazine in existence today is reading simultaneous submissions. The journals that forbid them are nevertheless reading them. More and more journals see fit to accept them, as long as they are informed immediately if a piece is accepted elsewhere. That does not answer the question, but it is an important fact of the matter.

Pose the question to all manner of writers, teachers, editors. You will get the same two answers.

Answer Number 1: Don't do it.

Answer Number 2: Do it.

So in the end, you decide. Here is what I do.

I simultaneously submit to the numerous and growing number of journals, such as *Ploughshares* and *The Missouri Review,* that accept simultaneous submissions.

I simultaneously submit to journals that take a year to turn a piece around, no matter what their policy is. Life is short! I do not have a year to find out if my story, one of fifty received every day by the average literary journal, is going to make it!

I single-submit to editors with whom I have a relationship. A relationship may begin with a kind word — *Sorry!* — written on a printed rejection slip. Some generous editors have written notes for years, and have yet to take a piece. I appreciate their attention and I single-submit to them. I single-submit to journals that have published my work. Sometimes I single-submit a piece because I think it's the best thing written to date in Western Civilization and therefore it will not be denied. After it comes back a few times I get over that. I work on it some more, and I may start sending out two or three simultaneously.

There are a few journals to which I have submitted for years, without a word of response, without a hint that there is a living, breathing human being at that address. I am one of the plebeians, one of the masses. They are too busy to toss me a kind nod, a *Sorry!* Or a *Thank you!* One advantage of being completely ignored is that you are then free to make up your own rules.

That's what I do.

Now you decide what you are going to do.

READ THE MARKET

Smart writers read the target journal or target magazine. Fools send out blind. Of course we're all fools some of the time, but we try to keep it to a minimum. I consider reading literary journals as an indispensable part of my life in a writers' community. I might read *Boulevard* edited by Richard Burgin, and think about writers and music (the theme of a recent issue). I might read *Conjunctions* or *The Gettysburg Review*. My quest is partly to know where my work is going, to know with whom I'm speaking. It's partly to read some of the world's best writing — Floyd Skloot or Brian Doyle or Heather McHugh or Francine du Plessix Gray or Robert Adamson or Cynthia Ozick.

Of course, some works found in literary journals aren't especially good. And some isn't to my taste, and some I don't get. Sometimes I read a journal and I feel compelled to rise from my chair in disgust and flip this dog of a rag into the recycle bin. But I also find models, assignments, challenges, inspirations. American literature, as it is being written today, may be found, to a very great extent, in literary journals, plus in a very few mass-circulation magazines such as *The New Yorker*.

I enjoy grazing aesthetics and literary points of view. I enjoy reading poems and stories written by the editors of literary journals and published in other literary journals (usually not in their own). I enjoy opening a journal and finding one or two things to read, then putting it away or giving it away.

Sometimes too many journals pile up. There's too much paper in the house. I give the big pile away, or I might dump the lot into the recycle bin. Then I begin again.

"IT'S WHO YOU KNOW"

It's human nature to pay more attention to the work of someone you've had coffee with or played tennis with or had a beer with. So yes, to some extent who you know could matter to your career as a writer.

What does that have to do with you and me?

Whoever we are, and wherever we live, it's important for us to connect on a regular basis with people in the publishing world. Begin by being connected to other writers in your community. Take your place at the table. Go to writing practice or present your work at an open mic.

Go further. Write a note to someone whose work you admire. Shake an author's hand and thank her for her work. Buy the book of your fellow writer from time to time. Read the book. Write a note thanking this writer for this good work.

To this I would add that it's important to keep to good values, to be honest, to respect yourself, to retain your dignity, to keep your head up, to be proud, to keep priorities straight, to shun sycophantism.

That's right, *shun sycophantism!* Sycophantism sucks. Who wants to be a toady, a lickspittle? Instead, respect the working person, the janitor, the working mother, the clerk, the soldier. Respect the person who may not be in the limelight, but whose struggle to survive contributes to the survival of our communities.

But back to the publishing world. You are a writer. You are part of the publishing world. It is never too soon to take your place in this world. Your work deserves your best effort to connect. Yes, hobnob. Gad about.

It's time to overcome shyness and social dread. It's time to get out there and look around, look for allies, be an ally to other deserving writers. It might even be fun.

I used to be terribly shy about introducing myself to anyone who could conceivably aid me in my career. In fact I was so paranoid about appearing to suck up to a person "higher up on the food chain" — an expression I detest — that I must admit to having upon occasion actually left the premises rather than shake hands with such a person or thank him or her for his or her work or God forbid, actually initiate a conversation, suggesting by this action that this person might be just another human being with his or her own life to live.

Mind you, I grew up on a dairy farm where we had our best conversations with the cows. If I can change, so can you. We all live in a community (not only in the sense of our neighborhood or town, but we live in a writers' community). We, each of us, have a place in this community. It is better to value ourselves highly, to respect ourselves completely, to help when we can, and to ask for help when appropriate.

Envy is natural. We all feel it at times. But kindness, generosity, getting out there, saying hello, saying thank you for this good work (if it is good work) goes a lot further a lot faster.

Then of course, we work on our work. We get better. We work on craft, on sentencing. We help each other whenever we can. Did I mention that we work on our work? We work on our work every day.

28.

The Practice of Productivity

*How much time you spend on your writing will depend on how serious
you are about it. For the serious writer, writing is not merely an
assignment. It is a way of life, an everyday habit.*
—Richard Marius

"**THE CREATIVE LIFE HAPPENS**," writes researcher Howard Gruber,
"in a being who can continue to work."* Continuing to work through
uncertainty, through lack of recognition, and yes, even through
success, is a core attribute of most high-achieving creators. As a writer,
you can decide to be productive. It is a decision that can open many
doors. As we know, high-achievers in the arts are more *productive* than

---

* Howard E. Gruber quoted in Vera John-Steiner, *Notebooks of the Mind*, 78.

average achievers. They achieve more masterworks but they also make more messes, create more duds.*

I like the story told in that essential book, *Art & Fear*, written by visual artists David Bayles and Ted Orland. A ceramics teacher divides the class in half. Potters on the right need only make one pot, but to get an A, it must be a perfect pot. Potters on the left will be graded by quantity alone. Their output will be weighed on a scale, and the heavier the output the higher the grade. And here is what happened:

> Well, came grading time and a curious fact emerged: the works of the highest quality were all being produced by the group being graded for quantity. It seems that while the "quantity" group was busily churning out piles of work — and learning from their mistakes — the "quality" group had sat theorizing about perfection, and in the end had little more to show for their efforts than grandiose theories and a pile of dead clay.**

In the end what matters to the ambitious dreamer is a steady and even rather plodding stream of work. Poems, stories, novels, creative nonfictions do not emerge as perfect art-objects. They emerge rough, awkward, contrived, and arguably awful. "Artists get better," write Bayles and Orland, "by sharpening their skills or by acquiring new ones; they get better by learning to work, and by learning *from* their work."

One strategy toward increased productivity is to set forth on a project whose success is to be gauged not by quality but by quantity. I am currently composing "one bad poem a day," an idea I got from my good friend, the poet Bethany Reid. Why a bad poem? Because, frankly, it is impossible, at least for me, to write a good poem every day or even

---

* D. K. Simonton, "Creativity from a Historiometric Perspective," 122.
** David Bayles and Ted Orland, *Art & Fear*, 28–29.

every week. But to write a "bad" poem every day is quite possible, even for such a busy and overbooked person as myself. What I am providing for myself is a new body of work to work on.

THE LIST OF WORKS

Record-keeping is another strategy toward increased productivity. I have long studied the lives and practices of high-level creators, including visual artists like Georgia O'Keeffe. These predecessor creators inspire me. Perhaps I thought, I could ratchet up my strategies and techniques — do whatever they did — to realize my own dreams as a writer. One rather odd thing I discovered is that they keep track of their works. They keep records and these records account for all their works — not just works sold or commissioned or published.

In contrast, average creators tend to forget works, abandon works, reject works, and lose works. Because of this trail of lost pieces (poems, stories, essays, paintings, or whatever), they have a weak sense of what actually constitutes their body of work, and each new piece is brand new. Their lost writing is essentially devalued writing. (And if the writer does not value his or her own work, who will value it?) This is not to say that every piece is a good piece, but that any piece whether poem or story might be worked on and eventually driven into the barn of finished work. Writers who work on their craft gain a bit of skill each year and that skill is available for honing past work. A lost poem loses its chance at art. It is lost to the possibility of revision. The creative energy expended on it, which may have been considerable, is also lost (or at least dissipated). In contrast, Yeats (for example) continued to revise his entire body of work, including his juvenilia, throughout his lifetime.

Considering all of the above, I've worked out a system for tracking the body of work I've created over the past four decades. It is remarkable how my creative inventory has helped me to deepen and extend my creative efforts. I now require all the writers in my classes to do the same, and they too find it a useful and even remarkable tool.

Each writer will devise his or her own system for keeping track of works. But for any system, a few principles should be kept in mind. The first is that the creative inventory should include all works brought to the point of first draft, not just works deemed worthy. This is a creator's tool, not a résumé.

The second is that the inventory should be organized chronologically, with the most recent at the top, so that you can see at a glance what you were doing ten years ago or twenty years ago, and so that you will have an ever-growing record of your output for the current year. Georgia O'Keeffe's system was to keep a page in a notebook for every painting she started, in which she included materials, notes, title, dimensions, where the work was located, and so on. Because she did this as she went, the notebooks, which are dated, proceed chronologically. For visual artists such a notebook will become the basis for an eventual catalogue raisonné. A visual artist will typically include a visual representation of the work as part of the inventory.

The List of Works forms the core of my own inventory system. When I first started making my list, I was astonished at how much work I was sitting on. This, it turns out, is a common astonishment for writers who undertake to make a chronological list of every piece of work that has reached the point of first draft or beyond. If you've been writing for a number of years, you'll find that it will take some time to complete your list (you open another drawer only to find one more forgotten poem, one more forgotten story). However, the minute you begin to construct your list, the benefits start accruing, and once the system is set up, it's simple to maintain.

I keep two Lists of Works, one for prose and one for poetry. (For me this double list came about for reasons of personal history: I had begun the Complete Inventory of Poems years earlier and it is, alas, ordered from early to late—a lot of work to reverse. Most writers should simply make one list for all works.) My two lists literally contain every piece I've ever brought to the point of first draft or beyond. Among the items on my "List of Works — Prose" are my published history book, the draft of a novel, and a rather dreadful story I wrote in 1964, more than forty years ago. On the "List of Works — Poetry," the earliest poem is dated summer 1970. (It's the first poem I typed out of my journal. May the untyped "poems" of the sixties rest in peace in their respective journals.) My two Lists of Works tell me that to date I've written 394 poems (some published, some in circulation, some in draft, some inept) and 138 prose works, including the history book and including thirty-eight short stories (some published, some in circulation, some in draft, some inept).

What is this, quantity over quality? Exactly. But the speed of work is not at issue. I for one am a slow writer. And I definitely resist the idea of churning out slight pieces. The actual numbers matter only to the poet or writer. This is your private working tool, and the numbers it reveals are nobody's business but your own.

The list allows you to see the work you've done and it signifies respect for work done. It allows you to track your yearly production. It allows you to find any given piece to take up again. The list gives you a practice that you now share with those high-achieving creators who do quantify their works. (Georgia O'Keeffe, 2,045 objects; Edouard Manet, 450 oil paintings among other works; the American painter Alice Neel, about 3,000 works; dare we mention Picasso? — 26,000 works; the remarkable short-story writer Edith Pearlman has published, according to her website, more than 250 works of short fiction and short nonfiction. That of course, does not tell us how many works Pearlman has *composed*.

How to Set Up Your List of Works

Force each title on the list and all associated information to take up one and only one line (you can clearly see the items at a glance).

Order the list chronologically by year, beginning with the present and working backward. Works done long ago with fuzzy dates go under decade dates (like "1980s"). As you continue to make new poems or stories it's easy to update the list, using exact dates. Every time I complete a first draft of a new work, I put it on the list, with its date of original composition (the date the first draft was completed).

Your list includes the title of the piece. It includes the date of original composition. That is, when did you complete the first draft? That's the date you want. Date of "final" completion is not of interest and in any case it floats. As you move backward in time you will no doubt have to guess at some dates. The date you achieve that first draft is autobiographically interesting and once fixed, never has to move. (Visual artists do it a bit differently since they typically do not consider a work a work until it is finished.)

Put after each title the word "published" or the word "circulating," unless it is neither published nor circulating, in which case put nothing after it. Literary writers such as poets, who are not working on commission, typically have several pieces working and some lying dormant, ready to be taken up at a later date.

Finally, and this is important: The one line of information per title does not say where a piece appears if it has been published, it does not say where is circulating *to*, and it does not contain any sort of judgment or assessment or plan (such as "abandon?" or "revise" or "shorten"). This is not a work plan. It is a record.

A piece you may never revise just sits there, like my short story written in 1964. It is part of your body of work. It shows you where you have been. For me, that first story of mine, however amateur, is a remarkable repository of threads I find woven into subsequent writing. Thus may a creator's preliminary works have interest and value. (Besides, some day I may revise that old story.) Here is a literal copy of a segment of my list.

LIST OF WORKS — PROSE LIST
2008
"Studio" (November 2008) CIRCULATING
"Memento Metro" (October 2008) PUBLISHED
"Elegy for Roz" (June 2008) PUBLISHED
"Thirteen Ways of Looking at a Fur-Covered Teacup"
    (June 2008) PUBLISHED
"On Quietness" (March 2008) CIRCULATING
"The Keeper" (story) (January 2008)
2007
"My Brain on my Mind" (June–December 2007) PUBLISHED
"From Chaos to Creative Achievement" (July 2007) PUBLISHED
"Got Manure?" (June 2007)
"My Old Friend" (story) (March 12, 2007)
"Polymer Persons" (February 2007) PUBLISHED
"Purple Prose" (February 2007) CIRCULATING
etcetera

Where are these works, physically? I keep one digitalized copy,
latest version only, on the computer and I keep its printed-out hard
copy in chronologically ordered three-ring binders (one for poetry,
one for creative nonfictions, one for short stories). Previous drafts and
marked-up workshopped copies are put far away in archive boxes or in
the recycle bin. The hard copies of current versions have their date of
original composition written on them.

As you begin this process of listing your works, you will make
interesting discoveries, the first being the actual extent of your work
to date. Another surprise for me was to find works I considered vastly
inferior, requiring (I thought) massive revision, which in reality were
close to complete. A lyrical essay I wrote had been gathering dust for
five years. I worked on it for two hours and sent it out. It's a lovely piece

(I now think). It appeared in a lovely literary journal and was that year nominated for a Pushcart!

Constructing your List of Works will help you become a more aware writer. Each year it will give you a measuring stick of your annual progress — defined not by the external world of prizes and publications but by you, the creator.

Finally, the List of Works stands as an emblem of respect for the work. It is a creator's tool that can help artists, poets, and writers realize their dream of creating a meaningful body of work.

WORKING AND PLAYING WITH THE WORK

There are a number of ways to stay productive and many are fun. Take an evening writing class at an adult education center or writer's center and then do your assignments. (You would be embarrassed not to!) There are very well-published writers who continue to take courses from time to time. Consider the assignments to be more than mere make-work: Plan yours to result in a published piece.

Make a schedule with a buddy to do such-and-such an amount of work by such-and-such a date on which you will meet again at a café. Take a book of short creative nonfictions and write one piece a week using each structure in turn (following carefully the guidelines laid out in Part II, so as not to create an imitative piece but to use the deep structure only). Or do what poet Marvin Bell begs us to do:

> Stay up half the night for a week and write one hundred
> poems. Write badly, rawly, smoothly, accidentally,
> irrationally…join the disparate. Make the unlike and the
> unlike like. When you can't write, read. Use the word
> window in every line. Write about colors. Set out to write a
> poem "like a sweater." It makes no difference. The coherence

is already within you. Afterward, you will have learned
more about writing than an entire semester of classes can
teach you.*

All this works its alchemy because work grows out of work.
Productive writers have more fun. The stakes on each piece are lower,
because you are making more pieces. Another lucky thing: When you
learn to be really productive, you begin coming into more surprises and
more interesting turns. As your craft skill becomes more acute, you
come to see that you can turn any piece — at least any piece written
from the heart — into a fine finished piece. It all becomes so much more
engrossing and entertaining and it is the road to that charmed country
we call success.

---

* Marvin Bell, "Three Propositions," in *Writers on Writing*, edited by Robert Pack and
Jay Parini, 10–11.

29.

Success

My ambition was relatively modest.
I just wanted to be part of literature.
—Frank Conroy

SUCCESS IS SWEET. Your first publication is sweet. Your first poem published, or your first article — sweet. Suddenly the world is nodding in agreement. The world is saying, Yes. You are a writer. You are a poet. You are a novelist. And then the world nods again, and then again (never mind those rejection slips). Your dream is coming true. Perhaps a novel begins to sell. Perhaps you are nominated for one of those big awards. Perhaps some actual money drops on your head from afar. Sweet.

Still, every position presents its challenges. The more famous a writer becomes, the greater number of interruptions he or she sustains. (I know, I know. We all have interruptions. But this is a kind of interruption that is difficult specifically because it coincides with your ambition. Can you come and speak?... May I interview you?...) To become a well-known writer is to become to some extent a public figure. Some writers take happily to the choppy waters of public life, but others struggle with it. One novelist, whose gripping and beautiful novels I've read avidly, received that coveted MacArthur Foundation "genius award." Make no mistake, the award just about saved his artistic life. But I read somewhere that he was immediately so inundated with literary and public-service duties and requests that he wrote nothing at all for two years. Another example: An old friend of mine from college days became a renowned scientist whose exquisite and profound essays became bestsellers. He told me once that, beginning about the time he was emerging from relative obscurity, he lost five years of work before he figured out how to deal with the tsunami of invitations and requests.

Another type of challenge is visited upon the moderately successful writer. It is that of having our second book on the midlist and our third book homeless. (This problem increases as publishers turn into multi-media conglomerates willing to switch from books to bling-bling if that will help their bottom line.) Perhaps, as Donald Maas allows in *Writing the Breakout Novel,* these third books are just not good enough. Then the task is to make them better. But perhaps they are good enough. A writer can start to receive an encouraging series of publications and prizes, and then, suddenly, fall into a trough, the zero trough, the nothing-doing trough, the *nada* trough. The well-known, twenty-seven-book novelist James Lee Burke writes:

> The most difficult test for me as a writer came during the middle of my career, when, after publishing three novels in New York, I went thirteen years without a hardback publication. My novel, *The Lost Get-Back Boogie,* alone received 110 rejections during nine years of submission, supposedly a record in the industry.

It was during this period I had to relearn the lesson
I had learned at 20...you write it a day at a time and let
God be the measure of its worth; you let the score take
care of itself; and most important, you never lose faith in
your vision.[*]

Never lose faith in your vision. But what if we do? Who among us does not fall, from time to time, into the terrible anxiety of ambition? One day Tolstoy wrote in his diary: "I am doing nothing and thinking about the landlady. Do I have the talent to compare to our modern Russian writers? Decidedly not."[**] And here is Kafka in a funk: "I will write again but how many doubts have I meanwhile had about my writing. At bottom I am an incapable, ignorant person..."[***]

We are all incapable, ignorant persons. Still, we must keep on. If confidence fails, which it may, the task is to continue working without confidence. Writing does not require confidence: It requires only a pen and a notebook. Get discouraged but don't quit. Writers who write when they hope and quit writing when they don't hope don't get far. ("I'm going to write this novel, and if it succeeds, then...")

There is the special problem of writers blessed and later saddled with early success: "Will I ever be able to do that again?" ("Undoubtedly not. I am an incapable, ignorant person.") The necessity in this case is to turn inward again, to shut out the too-bright light of the limelight — to appreciate its warmth, to be sure, its praise, its remunerations, and then to return to the blank page. Success is sweet, but it turns us inside out, it puts a smile on our face. To make new work we need to return to the

---

[*] James Lee Burke, "Writers on Writing: Seeking a Vision of Truth, Guided by a Higher Power," *The New York Times*, December 2, 1902, E2.

[**] Leo Tolstoy quoted in *The Writer's Life*, edited by Carol Edgarian and Tom Jenks, 181.

[***] Franz Kafka, *Diaries, 1910–1913*, translated by Joseph Kress and edited by Max Brod, 308.

interiority inside of which we did our first work. We need to listen to the muses, to take the risk of failing, to return to the desk where once we wrote in a notebook hidden from all other eyes. In this way, we need to begin again.

Agents and editors frequently pressure successful authors to repeat the previous book in a slightly different form, to become a manufacturing enterprise, churning out what is essentially another version of that mass-produced commodity that sold so well. I once attended a panel on "How to Get a Literary Agent," which featured literary agents. One agent encouraged her writers to follow up on a previously successful work with a second one along the same lines designed to fit the same market. She said, with some irritation in her voice, "I do this to help your career!" Apparently she had run into resistance.

Certainly, we should do whatever is feasible to help our careers. And we should listen closely to our helpers — peer writers, mentors, teachers, editors, agents. But shouldn't we also use our own values and make our own choices about what to produce in the time allotted to us? About what we think is important? About what we hope to leave behind in a body of work?

Here Scott Russell Sanders — that master-writer — speaks of his own progression as a writer:

> As though I had not already violated enough boundaries by
> writing science fiction, historical fiction, criticism, fables,
> and contemporary short stories, during the 1980s I added
> personal essays, documentary narrative, biographical fiction,
> and children's books to my profusion of forms. And why not
> a profusion? The world is various. Nature itself is endlessly
> inventive, trying out one form after another. How dull, if
> birds had stopped with sparrows and not gone on to ospreys
> and owls. How dull, if plants had not spun on from ferns to
> lilacs and oaks. Why squeeze everything you have to say into

one or two literary boxes for the convenience of booksellers and critics?*

Speed of production is another contested issue. We should all be concerned with completing work. But speed of production ought to be balanced against quality of product. Charles Frazier's novel *Cold Mountain* took him more than ten years to write and his next novel, *Thirteen Moons*, took him eight years — most of a decade. I recently read an interview in which an agent suggested that an author, for the sake of maximum marketability, extrude a book every two years. For a writer, this depends very much on what you want your legacy to be. Some writers are just fast and original and great. But a great many writers who produce a book every two years are writing the same book over and over again. My own choice is to try for work that has a chance of lasting, a chance of becoming part of literature. Whether I succeed or not is not mine to know. But if you've read the brilliant and profound *Cold Mountain* you will understand that no writer could possibly have written it in two years.

Poet and novelist James Dickey wrote: "I think the tragedy of my poetic generation is that people are willing to let stuff go and be published simply because there are people who can and will publish it. The bookstores are flooded with forgettable books that are good but not good enough. They just don't make it around the bend into the area of being good, or memorable, or with luck, even unforgettable."**

I find it useful to preserve the distinction between worldly success — any worldly recognition or publication whether honorary or monetary — and artistic success (my judgment). If I am receiving a flood of rejection slips, if my agent has skipped town or if I can't find an agent, if my

---

* Scott Russell Sanders, "Letter to a Reader," in *My Poor Elephant*, 249.
** Bruce Joel Hillman, "James Dickey" in *On Being a Writer*, edited by Bill Strickland, 183.

phone has mislaid its ring, if my email is 99 percent spam, still, I am composing a poem or an essay or a story that may succeed artistically. The value of this distinction is that I am not leaving it up to the world to tell me whether or not I am an incapable, ignorant person. That is for me to decide.

Still, getting an acceptance letter or an award or a check in the mail is thrilling. Getting a note from someone who has read your book and found it moving is thrilling. Getting the recognition you feel your work deserves is thrilling. But gaining more technical skill, more depth, more range is also thrilling. The joy of realizing a poem or a story — is there anything like it?

It is also gratifying to find yourself part of a vibrant community, reading to audiences, getting published, getting readers, getting more readers. Of course, rejections continue as well. But acceptances come more often now. Your writing is improving…

But perhaps the greatest pleasure of all is to put aside the striving and anxiety of ambition, if only for a while, and to sit down to the blank page, clean and empty and inviting. And then you begin again.

Acknowledgments

I am grateful to my mother, the late Dr. Barbara H. Long, and to my father, Winslow Long, for reading to us children every day — from the bible to *Oliver Twist* to *Pride and Prejudice* (this last a bit mystifying to a 6-year-old). Their focus on reading was for me a sustaining foundation in life as in literature. I'm grateful, too, to my Uncle Rodney Henry for honoring my 14-year-old writing, no matter which way spelled. Miss Edna Bergey, my ninth-grade English teacher at Quakertown High School, dubbed my "Autobiography" the best in the class and required me to stand up and read it to the class. These caring adults (and my young uncle was barely an adult) made it possible for me to realize my greatest dream: to become a writer.

My first poetry teacher was the late Harold Bond of the Cambridge (Massachusetts) Center for Adult Education. At the same indispensable institution I took two entertaining and enlightening courses, The Art of the Sentence and the Art of the Paragraph, taught by engineer Buchanan Ewing. I am grateful to these teachers and to my first fiction teacher, Charles Brashear, of San Diego State University.

In my view the best time to pursue an MFA (Master of Fine Arts) degree is after you've written for a decade or two, after you've published your first book, after you already know a lot, after you know — or sense — how much there is yet to learn. The Creative Writing Program in the English Department at the University of Washington in Seattle sheltered my writing for two years in the late 1980s. It gave me two years of exhilarating talk about literature. It gave me two years in which to write and in which to instruct (as a teaching assistant with a class of her own) a new batch of fresh composers each quarter. It gave me as mentors David Bosworth, Lois Hudson, and the poets Colleen McElroy and Heather McHugh. It gave me Hazard Adams who gave me Yeats. It gave me two fabulous years of writing. Thank you.

Perhaps every writer hits a low point, the less said about which the better. As for my low point, two grants, one from The Authors League Fund and the other from the Carnegie Fund for Authors, provided crucial funds and also what felt like a tap on the shoulder from the community of writers, as if to say, "You are one of us. Stick it out. We need you here." I am very grateful.

I owe my longtime workshop more than thanks. I believe these poets and artists were dispatched to my door by the muse. As we work, reflect, perform, and work some more, I am sustained and inspired to do better. I am grateful to Jack Remick, M. Anne Sweet, Geri Gale, Gordon H. Wood, Irene Drennan (1922–2008), Kevin Coyne, Don Harmon, Joel Chafetz, Jo Nelson (1947–2001), Francia Recalde, and Jim Karnitz.

For many years I've sent poems, stories, and essays hot off the printer to my old friends Saul Slapikoff, Louis Kampf, Howard Zinn, and Roz Zinn. Their own essential work and their support of mine has meant more than a few words can express; that Roz had to leave us in 2008 leaves a great hole in the world. And as we go to press in 2010, Howard is gone. Goodbye, old friends.

The dearest of Dear Readers are first readers. These pages originated as study sheets presented to writers I mentor and teach, writers who over the years have amazed me with their development and who have nurtured my own. First readers of *The Writer's Portable Mentor*, the book, include peer poets, dear friends, and the writers who roll up their sleeves and work like bricklayers in my classes. They include Bethany Reid, Scott Driscoll, Ralph Keyes, and Jay Schlechter. They include Carol Ann Miraben (formerly Shade), Rabbi Elana Zaiman, MaryLee Martin, Corry Venema-Weiss, Patricia Smith, and Neil Mathison. Professor Maya Sonenberg scrutinized the text and gave valuable suggestions. Jennifer Wong and my sister Pamela O. Long have been unflagging supporters. To each of these writers I give fervent thanks.

When I began preparing this book for actual publication, as opposed to photocopying the latest version for a class, I had a moment of trepidation. Here was a book I was passionate about, a book that would provide untold benefits, I knew, to the conscientious writer who took it to heart. How then to help it out into the world? There were many tasks, too many tasks, and did I even know what they all were? I soon realized "it takes a village." My committee of advisors is composed of five superb writers with book savvy and energy to boot. Grateful thanks to Andrea Lewis, Suzan Huney, Susan Knox, Kathie Werner, and Waverly Fitzgerald. Add my fellow poet Geri Gale, copyeditor par excellence. May I find a way down the road to repay you in kind. And thanks to Ms. James Kessler for cheerful, competent assistance in all departments.

During the decade of writing this book, I was also editing that fat Internet volume, HistoryLink.org, the free online encyclopedia of Washington state history. HistoryLink has become a pride to our state. It was my great good luck to hook up with the history-obsessed, creative, argumentative, hardworking, quirkily copacetic team that runs it.

Book design, happily, is not a lost art. This comely book was designed by Nancy Kinnear (interior) and Tracy Wong (cover). Thank you.

My sister Elizabeth Long, in the midst of her exacting and demanding work as a supervising Critical Care Unit nurse, in the midst of raising her children and reading to them constantly, in the midst of climbing mountains with her dear husband, David Messerschmidt, and their aforementioned offspring, in the midst of running marathons, in the midst of pedaling to work and back, in the midst of doing whatever it is one does in triathlons, in the midst of training her dogs and keeping their tails wagging joyously, in the midst of tending her garden, in the midst of reading novels and science and natural history, my little sister, I say, has also found time to bring me a bag of groceries once or twice a month. No writer could wish for more. Although Liz declines to write anything more lengthy than a grocery list, or so she says, I dedicate this book to her.

Credits

Bibliography

Abbey, Edward. *Desert Solitaire.* New York: Ballantine Books, The Random House Publishing Group, Inc., 1971.

Ackerman, Diane. "Mute Dancers: How to Watch a Hummingbird." *The New York Times Magazine,* May 29, 1994, 35.

Adams, Alice. "Roses, Rhododendron." In *The Best American Short Stories of the Century,* edited by John Updike, 520–532. New York: Houghton Mifflin Company, 1999.

Agee, James. *A Death in the Family.* New York: Vintage Books, 1956.

Agee, Joel. "Eros at Sea." In *The Best American Essays 1995,* edited by Jamaica Kincaid, 27–41. Boston: Houghton Mifflin Company, 1995.

Albers, Anni. Quoted in *The Woven and Graphic Art of Anni Albers.* Intro. by Lloyd E. Herman. Washington, D.C.: Smithsonian Institution Press, 1985.

Alexie, Sherman. "What You Pawn, I Will Redeem." In *The Best American Short Stories 2004,* edited by Lorrie Moore, 1–21. Boston: Houghton Mifflin Company, 2004.

Als, Hilton. "A Pryor Love." In *Life Stories: Profiles from The New Yorker,* edited by David Remnick, 382–402. New York: The Modern Library, 2001.

Anderson, Sherwood. "The Flood" (243–256), The Return" (27–56), and "Death in the Woods" (3–27). In *Death in the Woods and Other Stories.* New York: W. W. Norton & Co., 1961.

———. "I Want to Know Why." In *The Egg and Other Stories.* Mineola, NY: Dover Publications, Inc., 2000, 1–8.

Andrews, Tom. "Codeine Diary." In *Random Symmetries: The Collected Poems of Tom Andrews.* Oberlin: Oberlin College Press, 2002, 111–129.

Angel, Ralph. "The Poem, As and Of Address." In *Words Overflown by Stars,* edited by David Jauss, 315–327. Cincinnati: Writer's Digest Books, 2009.

Bachelard, Gaston. *The Poetics of Space,* translated by Maria Jolas. Boston: Beacon Press, 1964.

———. "Reveries Toward Childhood." In *The Poetics of Reverie,* translated by Daniel Russell. Boston: Beacon Press, 1969, 97–141.

Baldwin, James. "Notes of a Native Son." In *The Art of the Personal Essay,* selected and introduced by Phillip Lopate, 587–604. New York: Anchor Books/Doubleday, 1994.

Barthelme, Donald. Quoted in *The Sound on the Page* by Ben Yagoda. New York: HarperCollins Publishers, 2004, 68.

Bass, Rick. "Days of Heaven." In *The Best American Short Stories 1992*, edited by Robert Stone, 15–29. Boston: Houghton Mifflin Company, 1992.

Bayles, David and Ted Orland. *Art & Fear*. Santa Cruz, California, and Eugene, Oregon: The Image Continuum, 1993.

Beard, Charles A. and Mary R. Beard. *The Rise of American Civilization*. Revised and enlarged ed. New York: The Macmillan Company, 1934.

Bearden, Romare. "Diary, September 8, 1947." In *Origins and Progressions*, edited by Cynthia Jo Fogliatti. Detroit: Detroit Institute of the Arts, 1986.

Bell, Marvin. "Three Propositions." In *Writers on Writing*, edited by Robert Pack and Jay Parini, 1–14. Lebanon, NH: University Press of New England, 1991.

Berger, John. "Drawing" (10–14), "Gauguin's Crime" (65–67), "Thicker Than Water (Corot)" (206–209), and "The Hals Mystery" (393–398). In *John Berger: Selected Essays*, edited by Geoff Dyer. New York: Vintage Books, 2001.

Bergman, Robert L. "Blue Notes: Poetry and Psychoanalysis." In *Mindless Psychoanalysis, Selfless Self Psychology and Further Explorations*. Seattle: Alliance Press, 2008, 184–190.

Berriault, Gina. "Don't I Know You?" In *Passion and Craft*, edited by Bonnie Lyons and Bill Oliver, 60–71. Urbana: University of Illinois Press, 1998.

Boland, Eavan. "Lava Cameo" (3–34) and "The Woman Poet: Her Dilemma" (239–254). In *Object Lessons*. New York: W. W. Norton & Company, 1995.

———. "Letter to a Young Woman Poet." *The American Poetry Review*, May / June 1997, 23.

Bollas, Christopher. *Being a Character: Psychoanalysis and Self Experience*. New York: Hill and Wang, 1992.

Bonner, John Tyler. *Life Cycles*. Princeton: Princeton University Press, 1993.

Bouwsma, O. K. "The Mystery of Time." In *Philosophical Essays*. Lincoln: University of Nebraska Press, 1965, 99–127.

Bowles, Paul. *Up Above the World*. Hopewell, NJ: The Ecco Press 1982.

Boyd, William. "Michael Andrews" (337–348) and "Anton Chekov: An A–Z" (245–255). In *Bamboo*. London: Penguin Books, 2006.

Boyle, T. Coraghessan. "Chicxulub." *The New Yorker*, March 1, 2004, 78–83.

Brande, Dorothea. *Becoming a Writer*. New York: Jeremy P. Tarcher / Putnam, 1981.

Brashear, Charles. *Elements of the Short Story*. Santa Rosa, CA: Books, etc., 2005.

Brown, Norman O. *Love's Body.* New York: Vintage Books, 1966.

Burke, James Lee. "Writers on Writing: Seeking a Vision of Truth, Guided by a Higher Power." *The New York Times,* December 2, 2002, E2.

Burroway, Janet. *Writing Fiction: A Guide to Narrative Craft.* 5th ed. New York: Addison Wesley Longman, Inc., 2005.

Butler, Major General Smedley D. "War Is a Racket (1935)." In *Voices of a People's History of the United States,* edited by Howard Zinn and Anthony Arnove, 252–255. New York: Seven Stories Press, 2004.

Butler, Robert Olen. *From Where You Dream.* New York: Grove Press, 2005.

Byatt, A. S. "Art Work." In *The Matisse Stories.* New York: Vintage Books 1996, 29–86.

Carson, Anne. *Eros the Bittersweet.* Normal, IL: Dalkey Archive, 1998.

———. "Very Narrow." In *In Brief,* edited by Judith Kitchen and Mary Paumier Jones, 59–62. New York: W. W. Norton & Co., 1999.

Carter, Karen Rauch. *Move Your Stuff.* New York: Simon & Schuster, 2000.

Chabon, Michael. "Trickster in a Suit of Lights." In *Maps and Legends.* New York: HarperCollins Publishers, 2009, 1–14.

Chandler, Raymond. *The Big Sleep.* In *The Raymond Chandler Omnibus.* New York: Alfred A. Knopf, Inc., 1976, 1–155.

Chetkovich, Kathryn. "Envy." In *The Best American Essays 2004,* edited by Louis Menand, 9–29. Boston: Houghton Mifflin Company, 2004.

Chicago Manual of Style, The. 15th ed. Chicago: University of Chicago Press, 2003.

Cisneros, Sandra. *The House on Mango Street.* New York: Vintage Books, Random House, Inc., 2009.

Clark, Mary Higgins. "Touched by an Angel." In *The Writing Life: Writers on How They Think and Work,* edited by Marie Arana, 35–38. New York: Public Affairs, 2003.

Conroy, Frank. Audio interview by Lacy Crawford, March 2004. *Narrative Magazine,* Winter 2009 (http://www.narrativemagazine.com).

Davenport, Kiana. "Bones of the Inner Ear." In *The Best American Short Stories 2000,* edited by E. L. Doctorow, 78–88. Boston: Houghton Mifflin Company, 2000.

Debs, Eugene. "Statement to the Court, September 18, 1918." In *Voices of the People's History,* edited by Howard Zinn and Anthony Arnove, 297–298.

DeLillo, Don. *White Noise.* New York: The Penguin Group, 1985.

Dickey, James. Quoted in "James Dickey" by Bruce Joel Hillman. In *On Being a Writer,* edited by Bill Strickland, 180–186. Cincinnati: Writer's Digest Books, 1989.

Didion, Joan. "Goodbye to All That." In *The Art of the Personal Essay,* selected and introduced by Phillip Lopate, 681–688.

Dillard, Annie. "Seeing." In *The Art of the Personal Essay,* selected and introduced by Phillip Lopate, 643–706.

Doerr, Anthony. *Four Seasons in Rome.* New York: Scribner, 2007.

Doyle, Brian. "Grace Notes." In *Leaping: Revelations and Epiphanies.* Chicago: Loyola Press, 2003, 25–40.

Durrell, Lawrence. "Lawrence Durrell." In *Writers at Work* edited by George Plimpton, 259–282. New York: Penguin Books, 1959.

Eighner, Lars. "My Daily Dives in the Dumpster." *Harper's Magazine,* December 1991, 19–22.

Eisenberg, Deborah. "Some Other, Better Otto." In *Twilight of the Superheroes.* New York: Farrar, Straus and Giroux, 2006, 43–88.

Elbow, Peter. *Writing with Power.* New York: Oxford University Press 1998.

Erickson, Joan M. *Wisdom and the Senses.* New York: W. W. Norton & Co., 1988.

Ernst, Max. Quoted in *Max Ernst.* A film by Peter Schamoni, 1991.

Faulkner, William. "Dry September." In *Collected Stories William Faulkner.* New York: Vintage Books, 1977, 169–183.

Fenza, D. W. "Who Keeps Killing Poetry?" *The Writer's Chronicle,* December 2006, 16–24.

Ford, Richard. "In the Face." In *The Best American Essays 1997,* edited by Ian Frazier, 51–55.

Fowler, H. W. *A Dictionary of Modern English Usage.* London: Oxford University Press, 1926.

———. *The New Fowler's Modern English Usage.* 3rd ed. edited by R. W. Burchfield. Oxford: Oxford University Press, 1996.

Fowles, John. *The Magus.* Boston: Little, Brown and Company, 2001.

Franklin, Jon. *Writing for Story.* New York: Penguin Books USA, 1994.

Frazier, Charles. *Cold Mountain.* New York: Vintage Books, 1997.

———. *Thirteen Moons.* New York: Random House, 2006.

Gardner, John. *The Art of Fiction.* New York: Alfred A. Knopf, 1983.

Garner, Bryan A. *Garner's Modern American Usage.* New York: Oxford University Press, 2003.

Gass, William H. "Gertrude Stein and the Geography of the Sentence." In *The World Within the Word.* Boston: David R. Godine, 1979, 63–123.

Gates, Henry Louis, Jr. "In the Kitchen." *The New Yorker,* April 18, 1994, 82–86.

Gautreaux, Tim. "Welding with Children" (1–19) and "Misuse of Light" (21–38). In *Welding with Children.* New York: Picador USA, 1999.

Gelb, Michael J. *How to Think Like Leonardo da Vinci.* New York: Dell Publishing, Random House, 1998.

Gilb, Dagoberto. "Victoria." In *The Best American Essays 1999,* edited by Edward Hoagland, 105–110. Boston: Houghton Mifflin Company, 1999.

Ginzburg, Natalia. "He and I." In *The Art of the Personal Essay,* selected and introduced by Phillip Lopate, 423–430.

Goldbarth, Albert. "Farder to Reache." In *In Short,* edited by Judith Kitchen and Mary Paumier Jones, 299–300. New York: W. W. Norton & Co., 1996.

Goldberg, Natalie. *Long Quiet Highway.* New York: Bantam Books, 1993.

———. *Writing Down the Bones.* New York: Shambhala, 1986.

Goldman, Emma. "Patriotism: A Menace to Liberty (1908)." In *Voices of a People's History of the United States,* edited by Howard Zinn and Anthony Arnove, 270–272.

Gordon, Karen Elizabeth. *The Deluxe Transitive Vampire.* New York: Pantheon Books, 1993.

Gordon, Mary. "My Mother's Body." *The American Scholar,* Autumn 2006, 63–78.

Gray, Francine du Plessix. "The Work of Mourning." In *The Best American Essays 2001,* edited by Kathleen Norris, 60–72. Boston: Houghton Mifflin Company, 2001.

Greene, Melissa Fay. "On Writing Nonfiction." In *The Confidence Woman,* edited by Eve Shelnutt, 227–240. Atlanta: Longstreet Press, 1991.

Grosholz, Emily. "On Necklaces." In *The Best American Essays 2008,* edited by Adam Gopnik, 75–89. Boston: Houghton Mifflin Company, 2009.

Gruber, Howard E. Quoted in *Notebooks of the Mind* by Vera John-Steiner. Albuquerque: University of New Mexico Press, 1986.

Guest, Judith. *Ordinary People.* New York: Penguin Books, 1976.

Haines, John. "Three Days" (58–79), "Stories We Listened To" (30–42), "Snow" (3–5), and "Shadows"(149–160). In *The Stars, the Snow, the Fire*. Saint Paul: Graywolf Press, 2000.

Hamilton, Jane. *A Map of the World*. New York: Anchor Books / Doubleday, 1994.

Hammond, Jeffrey. "Close Enough for Jazz." *River Styx* 79, 2009, 13–25.

Harries, Karsten. *The Ethical Function of Architecture*. Cambridge: The MIT Press, 2000.

Hemingway, Ernest. "In Another Country" (267–272) and "Big Two-Hearted River, Part 1" (207–218). In *The Short Stories of Ernest Hemingway*. New York: Charles Scribner's Sons, 1925.

————. *The Sun Also Rises*. New York: Charles Scribner's Sons, 1926.

Hemon, Aleksandar. "Blind Jozef Pronek." In *The Best American Short Stories 2000*, edited by E. L. Doctorow, 166–181.

Hempel, Amy. "The Annex." In *Tumble Home*. New York: Simon & Schuster, 1998, 57–62.

Hendrickson, Robert. *The Literary Life and Other Curiosities*. San Diego: Harcourt Brace, 1994.

Hillman, Bruce Joel. "James Dickey." In *On Being a Writer*, edited by Bill Strickland, 180–186.

Hills, Patricia. *May Stevens*. San Francisco: Pomegranate, 2005.

Hoagland, Edward. "Journal Vermont, 2002–2004." *The American Scholar*, Autumn 2004, 151–155.

Hollander, John. *The Poetry of Everyday Life*. Ann Arbor: University of Michigan Press, 1999.

Humphreys, Helen. *The Lost Garden*. New York: W. W. Norton & Co., 2002.

Hurston, Zora Neale. *Their Eyes Were Watching God*. New York: Harper & Row, Publishers, 1990.

Irving, John. "Getting Started." In *Writers on Writing: A Bread Loaf Anthology*, edited by Robert Pack and Jay Parini, 98–104.

Job. *Holy Bible*, translated by George M. Lamsa from the Aramaic of the Peshitta. New York: Harper & Row, Publishers, 1968.

Johnston, Alva. "The Education of a Prince." In *Life Stories*, edited by David Remnick, 245–274.

Kael, Pauline. "Vulgarians and Ascetics." In *State of the Art*. New York: E. P. Dutton, 1985, 122–127.

Kafka, Franz. *Diaries, 1910–1913*, translated by Joseph Kress and edited by Max Brod. New York: Schocken Books, 1965.

Kerouac, Jack. *On the Road*. New York: Penguin Books USA, 1955.

Keyes, Ralph. *The Courage to Write*. New York: Henry Holt and Company, 1995.

Kitchen, Judith. "Culloden" (27–29) and "North Yorkshire" (81–82). In *Only the Dance*. Columbia: University of South Carolina Press, 1994.

Komunyakaa, Yusef. Interview by Miller and Zoe Anglesey. *The Writer's Chronicle*, October/November 2000, 13–17.

Kramer, Jane. "The Reporter's Kitchen." In *The Best American Essays 2003*, edited by Anne Fadiman, 146–159. Boston: Houghton Mifflin Company, 2003.

Lahiri, Jhumpa. "The Third and Final Continent." In *The Best American Stories 2000*, edited by E. L. Doctorow, 248–265.

Lakoff, George and Mark Johnson. *Metaphors We Live By*. Chicago: University of Chicago Press, 1980.

Leduc, Violette. *La Bâtarde*. New York: Riverhead Books, 1964.

Le Guin, Ursula K. "Some Thoughts on Narrative" (37–45) and "The Fisherwoman's Daughter" (212–237). In *Dancing at the Edge of the World*. New York: Harper & Row, Publishers, 1990.

Lê Thi Diem Thúy. "The Gangster We Are All Looking For." In *The Best American Essays 1997*, edited by Ian Frazier, 190–202. Boston: Houghton Mifflin Company, 1997.

Lightman, Alan. *Einstein's Dream*. New York: Pantheon Books, 1993.

Long, Priscilla. "Snapshots: The Eastern Shore of Maryland." *North Dakota Quarterly*, Winter 1987, 93–99.

———. "Archaeology of Childhood." *The Journal*, Spring/Summer 2001, 97–109.

———. "Genome Tome." *The American Scholar*, Summer 2005, 28–41.

———. "Solitude." *The Gettysburg Review*, Winter 2008, 573–578.

———. "Living for Robert." *The Chaffin Journal*, 2008, 145–156.

———. "My Brain on My Mind." *The American Scholar*, Winter 2010, 20–37.

Lopate, Phillip. "Introduction." In *Art of the Personal Essay*, selected and introduced by Phillip Lopate, xxiii–liv.

Lopez, Barry. "Effleurage: The Stroke of Fire." In *About This Life*. New York: Knopf, 1998, 144–174.

———. "Replacing Memory." In *Modern American Memoirs*, edited by Annie Dillard and Cort Conley, 372–389. New York: HarperCollins Publishers, 1995.

Lott, Bret. "Toward a Definition of Creative Nonfiction" (79–91) and "Against Technique" (93–114). In *Before We Get Started*. New York: Ballantine Books, 2005.

Maas, Donald. *Writing the Breakout Novel*. Cincinnati: Writer's Digest Books, 2001.

MacLeod, Alistair. "The Road to Rankin's Point." In *Island*. New York: Vintage Books, Random House, Inc., 2000, 143–179.

Maddan, Patrick. "On Laughter." *Portland Magazine*, Fall 2006, 16–17.

Mailer, Norman and John Buffalo Mailer. "Generations." In *The Big Empty*. New York: Nation Books, 2006, 3–11.

Mallonee, Barbara. "Semi-colon." In *Short Takes*, edited by Judith Kitchen, 188–191. New York: W. W. Norton & Company, 2005.

Marius, Richard. *A Writer's Companion*. New York: Alfred A. Knopf Inc., 1985.

Martin, Alexander C. *Golden Guide to Weeds*. New York: Golden Press, 1987.

Martone, Michael. "Contributor's Note." In *Short Takes,* edited by Judith Kitchen, 176–180.

McClanahan, Rebecca. "Considering the Lilies." In *In Brief,* edited by Judith Kitchen and Mary Paumier Jones, 180–185.

McElroy, Colleen J. *Over the Lip of the World*. Seattle: University of Washington Press, 1999.

McPhee, John. "Silk Parachute." In *The Best American Essays 1998,* edited by Cynthia Ozick, 176–178. Boston: Houghton Mifflin Company, 1998.

———. "Travels in Georgia." In *Life Stories,* edited by David Remnick, 161–195.

McPherson, James Alan. "Gold Coast." In *The Best American Short Stories of the Century,* edited by John Updike, 477–492.

McQuade, Molly. "Stealing Glimpses." In *Stealing Glimpses*. Louisville: Sarabande Books, 1999, 23–26.

Menand, Louis. "Saved from Drowning." *The New Yorker,* February 23, 2009, 68–76.

Michaels, Anne. *Fugitive Pieces*. New York: Vintage Books, 1998.

Miller, Henry. *To Paint Is to Love Again.* Alhambra, CA: Cambria Books, 1960.

Mitchell, Stephen. "Introduction." In *The Selected Poems of Rainer Maria Rilke,* translated by Stephen Mitchell, xi–xliv. New York: Vintage Books, 1989.

Moore, Dinty W. "Son of Mr. Green Jeans." In *Short Takes,* edited by Judith Kitchen, 283–291.

Mosley, Walter. *Always Outnumbered, Always Outgunned.* New York: Simon & Schuster Inc., 1998.

———. "For Authors, Fragile Ideas Need Loving Every Day." In *Writers on Writing,* compiled by John Darnton, 161–164. New York: Henry Holt and Company, 2001.

———. *This Year You Write Your Novel.* New York: Little, Brown and Company, 2007.

Naslund, Sena Jeter. "Ice Skating at the North Pole." In *Ice Skating at the North Pole.* Bristol, RI: Ampersand Press, 1989, 23–37.

Nin, Anaïs. *Ladders to Fire.* Chicago: The Swallow Press, Inc., 1959.

Oates, Joyce Carol. "Joyce Carol Oates in the Studio." *American Poetry Review,* July / August 2003, 15.

O'Brien, Tim. *The Things They Carried.* New York: Broadway Books/Random House, 1990.

O'Connor, Flannery. "Writing Short Stories." In *Crafting Fiction in Theory and Practice,* edited by Marvin Diogenes and Clyde Moneyhun, 11–19. Mountain View, CA: Mayfield Publishing Company, 2001.

Oliver, Mary. "The Ponds" (37–43), "Owls" (17–22), and "Of Power and Time" (1–7). In *Blue Pastures.* San Diego: Harcourt Brace & Company, 1995.

———. "Building the House." In *The Best American Essays 1998,* edited by Cynthia Ozick, 179–186.

Olsen, Tillie. "I Stand Here Ironing." In *Tell Me a Riddle.* New York: Dell Publishing Company, Inc., 1959, 9–21.

Olson, John. "The Bell of Madness." In *Backscatter.* Boston: Black Widow Press, 2008, 19–21.

Ondaatje, Michael. "7 or 8 Things I Know About Her." In *The Cinnamon Peeler.* New York: Vintage International, 1997, 169–171.

Ozick, Cynthia. "On Being a Novice Playwright." In *The Writing Life,* edited by Marie Arana, 250–257.

Pearlman, Edith. "Her Cousin Jamie." *Salamander,* 12: 1, 37–44.

———. Edith Pearlman website. http://www.edithpearlman.com.

Peters, Elizabeth. *The Mummy Case.* New York: Tom Doherty Associates, 1985.

Porter, Katherine Anne. Quoted in *Grammar as Style,* by Virginia Tufte and Garrett Stewart, vii.

Pritchett, V. S. "Forrest Reid." In *Lasting Impressions.* New York: Random House, 1990, 11–115.

Prose, Francine. "Cauliflower Heads." In *The Peaceable Kingdom.* New York: Henry Holt and Company, 1993, 25–52.

Proulx, Annie. "The Perfect Word: Interview by Michael Upchurch." In *The Glimmer Train Guide to Writing Fiction,* 248–249. Cincinnati: Writer's Digest Books, 2006.

Raban, Jonathan. "Notes from the Road." In *The Writing Life,* edited by Marie Arana, 344–350.

———. Quoted in *The Sound on the Page* by Ben Yagoda, 132.

Ray, Robert J. and Bret Norris. *The Weekend Novelist.* New York: Watson-Guptill Publications, 2005.

Ray, Robert J. and Jack Remick. *The Weekend Novelist Writes a Mystery.* New York: Dell Publishing, 1998.

Red Eagle, Philip H. *Red Earth.* Duluth: Holy Cow! Press, 1997.

Remick, Jack. "The Machine." In *Terminal Weird.* Seattle: Black Heron Press, 1994, 21–31.

Restak, Richard. "20 Questions on our Minds." *The American Scholar.* Spring 2006, 16–17.

Rhys, Jean. *Wide Sargasso Sea.* New York: Popular Library, 1966.

Robinson, Marilynne. *Housekeeping.* New York: Picador, 1980.

Ruiz, Ramón Eduardo. *The Great Rebellion.* New York: W. W. Norton & Company, 1980.

Rukeyser, Muriel. *The Life of Poetry.* Ashfield, MA: Paris Press, 1996.

Sadoff, Ira. "Ben Webster." In *An Ira Sadoff Reader.* Hanover, NH: Middlebury College Press, 1992, 254–258.

Sanders, Scott Russell. "Under the Influence." In *The Art of the Personal Essay,* selected and introduced by Phillip Lopate, 733–744.

———. "Letter to a Reader." In *My Poor Elephant,* edited by Eve Shelnutt, 239–253. Atlanta: Longstreet Press, 1992.

Sarton, May. *After the Stroke.* New York: W. W. Norton & Company, 1988.

———. *Plant Dreaming Deep.* New York: W. W. Norton & Company, 1983.

Selzer, Richard. "The Knife." In *The Art of the Personal Essay,* selected and introduced by Phillip Lopate, 708–714.

Shakur, Assata (Joanne Chesimard). "Women in Prison: How We Are." In *Voices of a People's History of the United States,* edited by Howard Zinn and Anthony Arnove, 471–476.

Shields, David. "Spider's Stratagem." *Iowa Review,* Spring 2006, 78–85.

Silber, Joan. "My Shape" (13–34) and "Gaspara Stampa" (65–96). In *Ideas of Heaven.* New York: W. W. Norton & Company, 2004.

Simonton, D. K. "Creativity from a Historiometric Perspective." In *Handbook of Creativity,* edited by Robert J. Sternberg, 122–124. Cambridge: Cambridge University Press, 1999.

Simpson, Mona. "Lawns." *The Iowa Review,* Fall 1984, 80–98.

Skloot, Floyd. "Gray Area: Thinking with a Damaged Brain." In *The Best American Essays 2000,* edited by Alan Lightman, 147–159. Boston: Houghton Mifflin Company, 2000.

Slater, Lauren. *Lying.* New York: Penguin Books, 2000.

Smith, Annick. "Sink or Swim." In *In Brief,* edited by Judith Kitchen and Mary Paumier Jones, 221–223.

Sonenberg, Maya. "Beyond Mecca." In *Voices from the Blue Hotel.* Portland: Chiasmas Press, 2006, 119–136.

Sontag, Susan. "The Wisdom Project" (49–62), "A Century of Cinema" (117–122), "A Mind in Mourning" (41–48), and "Writing Itself: On Roland Barthes" (63–88). In *Where the Stress Falls.* New York: Farrar, Straus and Giroux, 2001.

———. "Directions: Write, Read, Rewrite. Repeat Steps 2 and 3 as Needed." In *Writers on Writing,* edited by Robert Pack and Jay Parini, 223–229.

Soyinka, Wole. "Why Do I Fast?" In *The Art of the Personal Essay,* selected and introduced by Phillip Lopate, 454–457.

Stevenson, Robert Louis. Quoted in *The Literary Life and Other Curiosities,* by Robert Hendrickson. San Diego: Harcourt Brace, 1994, 3.

Strayed, Cheryl. "Heroin/e." In *The Best American Essays 2000,* edited by Alan Lightman, 169–181.

———. "The Love of My Life." In *The Best American Essays 2003,* edited by Anne Fadiman, 291–307.

Tharp, Twyla. *The Creative Habit.* New York: Simon and Schuster, 2003.

Thompson, E. P. *The Making of the English Working Class.* Westminster, MD: Random House, 1966.

Thúy. *See* Lê

Tolstoy, Leo. Quoted in *The Writer's Life,* edited by Carol Edgarian and Tom Jenks. New York: Vintage, 1997.

Toomer, Jean. *Cane.* New York: W. W. Norton & Company, 1988.

Tufte, Virginia. *Artful Sentences: Syntax as Style.* Cheshire, CN: Graphics Press LLC, 2006.

Tufte, Virginia and Garrett Stewart. *Grammar as Style.* New York: Holt, Rinehart and Winston, Inc., 1971.

Twain, Mark. *Huckleberry Finn.* New York: Harper & Brothers Publishers, 1912.

Updike, John. "Nabakov's Lectures." In *Hugging the Shore.* New York: Alfred A. Knopf, Inc., 1983, 223–246.

——. "The Writer in Winter." In *The Best American Essays, 2009,* edited by Mary Oliver, 172–176. Boston: Houghton Mifflin Harcourt, 2009.

Valian, Virginia. "Learning to Work." In *Working It Out,* edited by Sara Ruddick and Pamela Daniels. New York: Pantheon Books, 1977, available online at http://maxweber.hunter.cuny.edu/psych/faculty/valian/valian.htm.

van Gogh, Vincent. *The Letters of Vincent van Gogh,* edited by Mark Roskill. New York: The Macmillan Publishing Company, 1963.

Vollmann, William T. "Three Meditations on Death." *McSweeney's Quarterly Magazine* 9, Summer/Fall 2002, 7–25.

Vowell, Sarah. "Chelsea Girl." In *Take the Cannoli.* New York: Simon & Schuster, 2000, 81–94.

Walker, Alice. "The Civil Rights Movement: What Good Was It?" (119–129) and "The Unglamorous But Worthwhile Duties..." (130–137), and "Looking for Zora" (93–116). In *In Search of Our Mother's Gardens.* Orlando, FL: Harcourt Inc., 1983.

Wallace, David Foster. "Consider the Lobster." *Gourmet,* August 2004.

Ward, Peter D. *Rivers in Time.* New York: Columbia University Press, 2000.

Weiner, Jonathan. *The Beak of the Finch.* New York: Vintage Books, 1994.

Welty, Eudora. *One Writer's Beginnings.* New York: Warner Books Inc., 1984.

White, E. B. "Bedfellows" (80–89) and "Once More to the Lake" (197–202). In *Essays of E. B. White.* New York: Harper & Row, Publishers, 1977.

Wideman, John Edgar. "In Praise of Silence." In *The Writing Life,* edited by Marie Arana, 260–281.

Wilcox, Annie Tremmel. *A Degree of Mastery.* New York: Penguin Books, 1999.

Williams, David B. *The Street-Smart Naturalist.* Portland, Oregon: Westwinds Press, 2005.

Wolff, Tobias. *This Boy's Life.* New York: Harper & Row, Publishers, 1989.

———. "Bible." In *The Best American Short Stories 2008,* edited by Salman Rushdie, 312–323. Boston: Houghton Mifflin Company, 2008.

Wright, C. D. *Cooling Time.* Port Townsend: Copper Canyon Press, 2005.

———. "Hidebound Opinions, Propositions, and Several Asides from a Manila Envelope Concerning the Stuff of Poets." In *By Herself: Women Reclaim Poetry,* edited by Molly McQuade, 380–397. Saint Paul: Graywolf Press, 2000.

Yagoda, Ben. *The Sound on the Page.* New York: HarperCollins Publishers, 2004.

Young, Tommy Scott. Quoted in "Tommy Scott Young" by Gayle R. Swanson and William B. Thesing. In *Conversations with South Carolina Poets* edited by Swanson and Thesing, 139–158. Winston-Salem: John F. Blair, Publisher, 1986.

Zacharias, Lee. "Buzzards." In *The Best American Essays 2008,* edited by Adam Gopnik, 260–281. Boston: Houghton Mifflin Company, 2008.

Zinn, Howard. "Objections to Objectivity" (29–42) and "Failure to Quit" (157–164). In *Failure to Quit.* Monroe, ME: Common Courage Press, 1993.

Index

CPSIA information can be obtained at www.ICGtesting.com
Printed in the USA
BVOW05s1231111114

374606BV00001B/43/P